LAW, CULTURE AND SOCIETY

For Elijah and Kezia
Our newest generation

Law, Culture and Society
Legal Ideas in the Mirror of Social Theory

ROGER COTTERRELL
Queen Mary and Westfield College,
University of London, UK

ASHGATE

Published by
Ashgate Publishing Limited
Wey Court East
Union Road
Farnham
Surrey, GU9 7PT
England

Ashgate Publishing Company
110 Cherry Street
Suite 3-1
Burlington
VT 05401-3818
USA

Ashgate website: http://www.ashgate.com

British Library Cataloguing in Publication Data
Cotterrell, Roger (Roger B. M.)
   Law, culture and society : legal ideas in the mirror of
   social theory. - (Law, justice and power series)
   1.Sociological jurisprudence 2.Law and the social sciences
   I.Title
   340.1'15

Library of Congress Cataloging-in-Publication Data
Cotterrell, Roger (Roger B. M.)
   Law, culture and society: legal ideas in the mirror of social theory / by Roger
Cotterrell.
       p. cm. -- (Law, justice, and power)
   Includes bibliographical references and index.
       ISBN 0-7546-2505-2 (hardback) -- ISBN 0-7546-2511-7 (pbk.)
1. Sociological jurisprudence. 2. Law--Philosophy. 3. Comparative law--Sociological aspects. I. Title. II. Series.

   K370.C68 2006
   340'.115--dc22

                                                            2006003910

ISBN-10: 0 7546 2505 2 (hardback)
ISBN-13: 978 0 7546 2505 6 (hardback)

ISBN-10: 0 7546 2511 7 (pbk.)
ISBN-13: 978 0 7546 2511 7 (pbk.)

MIX
Paper from
responsible sources
FSC
www.fsc.org   FSC® C013985

Printed in the United Kingdom by Henry Ling Limited, at the Dorset Press, Dorchester, DT1 1HD

Contents

Introduction

Approaching Law

Points of Contact

This book argues that an adequate understanding of legal ideas – for lawyers, no less than for other citizens – is impossible without adopting a sociological perspective, a perspective informed by social theory. Social theory seeks to explain the nature of the social in general terms. It considers the general character of social relations, social institutions and social change. The book's main aim is to show what such an approach to legal study entails and how it can illuminate basic problems, familiar to legal scholars, in interpreting and analysing contemporary law and studying its effects.

The focus of the book is on legal doctrine – rules, procedures, principles, normative concepts and values in law and the specialized modes of reasoning applied to these. What makes doctrine 'legal' is its institutionalization: the fact that it is created, interpreted or enforced in certain socially established ways, through the use of recognized procedures and agencies. So, law is taken here to be institutionalized doctrine (see further Cotterrell 1995: Chapter 2). My concern is with the sociology of legal ideas, but not only with legal ideas that are familiar to lawyers. From a sociological viewpoint, there may be more to law than the legal doctrine that lawyers recognize and work with. Law as institutionalized doctrine can be found outside the 'official' legal system of the state. Law, in some sense, may flourish in social sites and settings where lawyers or police never venture. Equally, it could be a mistake – looking at matters sociologically – to think that the state legal system is necessarily a unified entity. The law created, interpreted and enforced by the state is itself sometimes subject to fierce internal conflict or competition, with different agencies of the state adopting different legal positions, or with potential contradictions unrecognized or unresolved. The coexistence, and sometimes conflict, of legal regimes and sources of legal authority in the same society is a central idea of 'pluralist' views of law, and a legal pluralist view – explained and defended in Chapter 2 – is part of the sociological perspective relied on in this book.

Law and social theory (which can be taken here to include all broad theoretically-oriented sociological studies)[1] sometimes seem like oil and water – impossible to mix; or like chalk and cheese – indigestible if combined. But as modes of analysis they have some important characteristics in common.

---

1   The close but changing relations of sociology as an academic field and social theory are discussed in Chapter 1.

Law is a mode of practical analysis of social life. Lawyers seek to systematize law's interpretations of the social. Like social theory, law generalizes and conceptualizes social relations, actions, circumstances and institutions in abstract terms so that they can be considered systematically. By this means legal doctrine recognizes similarities between actions and situations and defines differences between them. Lawyers see justice as a matter of treating like cases alike and unlike cases differently. The art of law is to judge reliably which are like cases and which are unlike. To treat unlike cases as similar or to deal differently with identical situations is unjust. To do justice is to categorize and to act consistently on the basis of the categorizations made.

Social theory has no direct link with the promotion of justice. The responsibility of the social theorist is to understand – not control, shape or judge – the social. But social theorists are often driven by images of what they think a good or better society could be. As Chapter 1 explains, they have often aimed to understand the nature and destiny of the 'modern' forms of social life that arose with Western urbanization, industrialization and secularization. And it seems hard to separate this quest for understanding from implicit or explicit judgments about the virtues or defects of modern society, or its contemporary postmodern transformations. Students of the classics of social theory are familiar with Max Weber's anguished ambivalence about modernity's 'iron cage' of efficiency-driven routine, Emile Durkheim's intense commitment to moral individualism and social solidarity, Ferdinand Tönnies' measured nostalgia for elements of a lost pre-modern world of close-knit communities, and Karl Marx's angry condemnation of what he saw as the inherent inhumanity of modern capitalism. Images of justice and its elusiveness have often been real for social theorists, as for lawyers.

There are also important parallels in method, as between legal analysis and social theory. Both require rigour in the definitions and conceptualization they use, and both must define and conceptualize very elusive aspects of human behaviour. Both must, to some extent, systematize experience and be empirical in orientation, basing their analyses on observation of occurrences in the social world. In different ways they have to make sense of the strategies and the accidents of history. They have to interpret interests, intention, causation and chance (Turner and Factor 1994). Both also require a kind of foresight about the social; an imagination about social possibilities, about the range of variation of social phenomena. Without such an imagination in legal analysis, wise rule-making to govern the future is impossible.

As will be seen in subsequent chapters, legal analysis focuses most readily on what it takes to be rational – especially instrumentally driven – action. And it has particular difficulties in dealing with matters of affect (that is, the emotion that lies behind or gives rise to action). Social theory has often seemed to have a similar emphasis. The sociology of emotions is a relatively undeveloped field. Yet both law and social theory need to recognize and address the non-rational or perhaps *differently* rational aspects of social life. This is why rational choice (economic) models of action have not been generally accepted as adequate foundations for either legal analysis or social theory (although interesting and striking exceptions exist, especially in the US).[2] Law and social theory both have to find ways to understand the ambiguous, complex meanings of social action, and to recognize that social relations can be of radically different types. So they must abstract from the infinite variety of social circumstances, producing generalized analyses and interpretations than can make sense of the bewildering complexity of the social.

Small wonder, then, that law and social science have sometimes been seen as *in competition*, offering rival ways of interpreting the social world.[3] Social scientists have often declared law unimportant as an object of study for them, insofar as they have claimed to be able to explain legal phenomena without recourse to lawyers' categories of juristic understanding. Correspondingly, lawyers have often rejected social science as irrelevant to the kind of explanations and understandings they seek. Sociologists (on this juristic view) have interpreted the social world; the lawyer's job is to regulate it and make its wheels turn, developing legal ideas about the social as required to achieve necessary results. These rivalries are discussed in Chapter 1.

Nowadays, however, the fact that there are strong links (in terms of areas of interest, practical aims and even methods of practice) between legal studies and social research is relatively widely accepted. And interest in social theory among legal scholars has grown as social theory has come to be seen no longer as 'owned' solely by the academic discipline of sociology, but as a more general resource for all scholars who need to be able to make sense of social life in systematic, empirically informed ways.

Legal Participants and their Viewpoints

Chapter 3 addresses directly the question of the relation of juristic and sociological perspectives on law. When the essay on which it is based first appeared in print it attracted a detailed, typically thoughtful reply from David Nelken (1998), and a brief discussion here, based on some themes in his critique, may clarify ideas that underlie many arguments in this book.

I argue in Chapter 3 (against Nelken and others) that law has no uniform way of looking at the world, no 'truth' of its own, that can be set directly against sociological understandings. Certainly, legal analyses often seem distinctive and (from some perspectives) sometimes eccentric or ignorant. But it is not 'law' that has these understandings, as if law had some outlook or point of view of its own, as a unified discourse or system of communication. Legal ideas are the varied understandings of lawyers, judges and other participants in legal processes (for example – to take a random selection – administrators, business executives, criminals, legislators, prisoners, trade unionists, campaigners, members of ethnic minorities, taxpayers and

---

2   Economic analysis of law is a flourishing field in some American law schools. In social theory, rational action theory (related to rational choice theory in economics) has been a focus of recent discussion in both Britain and the US.

3   Cf. Nicholas Timasheff's (1939: 45) much-quoted statement (referring primarily to the writings of Auguste Comte) that sociology 'was born in the state of hostility to law'.

asylum seekers). Lawyers, too, are diverse, with various kinds of practice, experience and aims, and different legal understandings, seeing different 'truths' in and through law. Law may appear differently from the vantage point of different courts, and certainly of different kinds of state agencies. So, legal understandings are *people*'s understandings; a diversity of people to be studied sociologically – that is, through systematic, empirical study of their social actions and networks of social relations.

Non-lawyers sometimes see a special distinctiveness of law which practising lawyers themselves (often concerned on their clients' behalf with ending or avoiding disputes or setting up deals, arrangements and structures) do not. At least in the Anglo-American common law world, there has been increasing recognition of the 'porosity' of law as a form of knowledge or reasoning. It has few distinctive methods of argument, analysis or decision-making, but its formal procedures are supposed to (and in a perfect legal system would) make the common-sense consideration and resolution of practical problems as workable as possible, in situations where those problems may be very complex, where there are strong conflicts of view, or where much is at stake (financially or in terms of personal well-being). State law seems strong and distinctive as a discourse because political authority guarantees and controls it, but perhaps not really because of anything inherent in law as a system of communication. Hence, as Eugen Ehrlich (1936) insisted (in his seminal work published just before the First World War), law (in some form) lives in all human associations. Putting the matter differently, wherever community exists, so does law. Law is a dimension of social relations of community. It is not set apart, uniquely confronting society, but is an aspect of social life; a field of social experience focused on problems of governmental organization and regulation.

Thus, intellectually, law and social theory might be brought into relation with each other more easily than is sometimes supposed, but this does not mean that there are few practical obstacles to doing so. There are strong *political* interests in maintaining law's apparent self-sufficiency and pre-eminence as a normative discourse or knowledge-field. By contrast, sociology and social theory have no such basic importance to the state and the political order. Sociology is buffeted by adverse reactions to its natural tendency to dig out social evidence inconvenient to various sections of society, or it is undermined by its low status among the established academic fields because of its critical tendencies and the controversial nature of its subject matter. Academic sociology is surely fated to be law's poor relation in terms of practical power and status. Yet sociology as a resource (unconfined by the departmental or disciplinary boundaries of the academy) remains available to help to shore up some of law's intellectual weaknesses when processes of legitimation for the legal order or for legal studies falter for some reason (Cotterrell 1995: Chapter 3). And as regulatory demands on law increase, the incentives for law and social research of many kinds to form alliances may well continue to grow.

Chapter 3 argues that if the sociological study of legal ideas has an allegiance it is to law itself, not to the academic discipline of sociology. This argument has been sharply criticized for seeming to make the sociological study of law subordinate to lawyers' concerns – even making it a kind of sociological jurisprudence (Nelken 1998:

410). But this would be true only if allegiance to law meant allegiance to *lawyers* or to the *state legal system*. There is no retreat to sociological jurisprudence (that is, to social science employed merely as reformist, technical or rhetorical support for state legal regulation) if law is always conceptualized in a wide, pluralistic sociological perspective, in the mirror of social theory. Law viewed in this way is not just what lawyers do, or the legal ideas that lawyers professionally manage, though it certainly includes lawyers' law.

Law understood sociologically in a broad sense is *the regulation of communities* through institutionalized doctrine. Some social relations and networks of community are within lawyers' everyday experience and of much concern to them professionally, but others are not. Hence, allegiance to law is not allegiance to the lawyer's professional world. If anything, it is allegiance to an idea of peaceful, stable regulation of social life, and to aspirations for justice in the life of communities.

The object in confronting law with social theory, studying it in sociological perspective, is not, then, to try 'to understand law better than it understands itself' (cf. Nelken 1998: 409), because law, itself, can understand nothing (it is not a person), and law's innumerable professional and non-professional participants understand law's meanings in many different ways. The aim of a sociological perspective should be to broaden participant understandings of law, and of the social interpreted in law, so as to enable people to know better the society they live in, and (amongst other things) to regulate it in a better informed way. Sociology and social theory do not dictate what should be regulated and how, but they can clarify the contexts in which decisions about regulation must be made.

David Nelken (1998: 417–18, 425–6) doubts that a broader perspective is necessarily better than a narrower participant perspective fitted to the task in hand. Certainly, at least in the common law world, lawyers' typical methods involve narrowing issues to make them manageable, and avoiding broad generalization; focusing on the present case, here and now, and not on an infinity of possibilities. But a sharp, exclusive focus on particular problems is not made impossible or even more difficult by adopting a broader social perspective. Viewing matters in broadening perspective entails, however, that any limiting of issues is *deliberate*, a considered choice made as a way of managing a well-recognized social complexity. It should not be a default position reflecting and justifying social ignorance. A broadening of perspectives does not invalidate narrower participant perspectives, but should contextualize and clarify them. A sociologically informed lawyer is not necessarily a less able lawyer, just as a citizen who reads social theory ought not to be disabled thereby from engaging in everyday social relations! On the contrary, surely both may hope to gain new insight into the meaning of their everyday practices through · a broadened perspective.

Another related point deserves mention here. This book argues, often implicitly, against disciplinarity; that is, against a strong concern with the integrity or distinctiveness of intellectual disciplines. Thus, sociology of law (especially sociological understanding of legal ideas) is not, in my view, a sub-discipline of the academic discipline of sociology. To see it that way would be (as Chapter 3 argues) to belittle the wide aspirations of the modern founders of sociological inquiries about law. Law is too important socially to be treated as a sub-field 'imprisoned' in a parent discipline (academic sociology) that has very little interest in it today. Many researchers (including me) who came to sociology of law to escape the narrow disciplinary outlook of academic law, which they experienced as undergraduates, are unlikely to want to seek refuge behind other disciplinary walls. Intellectual advance in social studies now often occurs by *ignoring* disciplinary prerogatives, boundaries and distinctions. The need is not, however, to 'weaken' the ties of sociolegal studies to academic sociology (cf. Nelken 1998: 412, suggesting I advocate this). It is to ensure that those inevitable ties in no way hamper imaginative inquiries across *all* available sources of social insight.

As Nelken (1998: 412) notes, however, 'it is not so easy to become undisciplined'. For myself, there is nothing to be gained by disowning academic traditions (of law and sociology) that have provided an intellectual formation; and it is also important to respect different methodological practices that allow research to be organized and evaluated. But these considerations should not limit research aspirations in any way. The literature of sociolegal research now gives researchers a wealth of theories, hypotheses, methods and exemplars to build on. The canon is multidisciplinary and includes much work that defies any useful disciplinary categorization. It invites, through its very existence, legal scholars to read their way on to the broad, imaginative vistas of social theory, and social theorists to explore the sometimes richly precise social observation promised by the lawyers' method of detail.

Clearly not all lawyers are interested in sociological perspectives (in the wide transdisciplinary sense of 'sociological' that this book adopts in Chapter 3), but I think that the best, the most imaginative and practical-minded, often are. They wish to use legal doctrine to achieve social effects (if only as regards the immediate social relations that involve their clients). Thus, they need to understand law sociologically in a broad sense. Correspondingly, sociologists and social theorists achieve little in studying law if they fail to enter into the minds of legal participants (including lawyers) – thinking with and through law as institutionalized doctrine. In this context, juristic and professional sociologists' points of view are part of a vast continuum of participation in, and observation of, law.

A Framework of Community

While the first three chapters of Part 1 explore various dimensions of a sociologically oriented legal theory, and the relations of law and social theory more generally, Chapter 4 introduces the central conceptual framework used, in the rest of the book, in studying more concrete issues about legal doctrine and its social consequences and contexts. For convenience, I call this framework a law-and-community approach to legal studies. An earlier collection of my adapted essays was entitled *Law's Community* (1995) and some of its chapters explore the usefulness of ideas of community for legal inquiries. They provide some groundwork for the present volume. But it was only in the year after *Law's Community* appeared that I developed what I now think is a defensible concept of community for the specific purposes of legal studies. The concept, and an outline of the framework of inquiry that it suggests, was first set out in spring 1996 in a paper which now appears in revised form as Chapter 4. So, as regards its analysis of legal ideas in terms of community, the present book starts from the exact point at which *Law's Community* left off.[4]

A main problem with the concept of community is that it is often much too vague to be empirically useful in sociological inquiry or applicable in doctrinal legal analysis. It is a woolly, fuzzy idea that contrasts unfavourably with both the attempted precision of modern juristic categories and the rigorous concepts needed in developing worthwhile social theory. A second major problem of 'community' is that it is weighed down with valuations. Whatever it may be, community is usually considered 'good' and its absence a matter for regret. The 'loss of community' literature in sociology professionally repackages aspects of a diffuse popular lament for an imagined, disappeared world: village life; strong kinship ties; reliable neighbourliness; God-fearing, industrious settlements; cherished traditions; safe streets, and so on. A theoretically valuable concept of community must free itself from the myths and romanticism that cling to these associations. It has to be a notion flexible enough in its social imagery to be applicable to the complex, diverse, mobile and individualistic populations of advanced twenty-first-century societies.

Chapter 4 presents an approach to community as a legally relevant concept that attempts to meet this specification. The main motivation for invoking community is a sense that old concepts of 'law and society' or 'law in society' no longer adequately represent law as a social phenomenon. Society – understood typically as the politically organized society of the nation state – has become a less obviously useful concept in recent decades, with the growth of transnational networks of cultural and economic relations of many kinds, and with the development of multiculturalism. Community, appropriately conceived, can represent vital kinds of social relations that take the form of networks or groups not necessarily bounded by a 'society'; fluctuating, forming and reforming, crossing national or political boundaries, having overlapping memberships, conflicting, cooperating or merely coexisting.

A key to developing a concept of community with this flexibility is the use of Max Weber's sociological method of ideal (or pure) types. Thus, the emphasis is on pure, basic, abstract types of community that, in actual social life, are usually found only in elaborate networks and combinations. This approach makes it possible to do two important things: (1) to keep clearly in mind the complexity and variability of contemporary social relations, rarely static for long, and the multiplicity of group memberships and of people's social interactions; and (2) to distinguish with a degree of analytical rigour a strictly limited number of irreducible, contrasting types of

---

4   The emphasis in *Law's Community* on mutual interpersonal trust as the basis of community, and on community seen as 'basic orientations of social interaction' rather than 'a sociological object' (Cotterrell 1995: 328–31), is fundamental also in the present book.

social bonds and to explore the special problems of regulation that apply to each of these.

A law-and-community approach, as proposed here, is, thus, an attempt to examine problems, conditions and consequences of legal regulation by developing the idea that each pure type of community may have its own distinctive regulatory aspects. In studying how law can regulate networks of social relations that develop as combinations of types of community in actual social life, it may be possible to clarify a very complex sociolegal picture by clearly separating out for analytical purposes the various legal aspects of community.

This approach can be presented less abstractly by applying it in a range of specific contexts of legal inquiry. This is what most of the chapters in Part 2 seek to do. They apply the law-and-community approach to consider, for example, how far it is possible to predict the success or otherwise of legal transplants – the carrying of legal ideas from one legal system to another – (Chapter 7), and what possibilities and constraints attach to time-honoured (but now increasingly favoured) comparative law projects of unifying or harmonizing law across national boundaries (Chapter 9). The law-and-community approach can also be used as a way of reformulating and perhaps throwing a different light on current ideas about the nature, aims and responsibilities of comparative legal studies (Chapters 8 and 9). Thus, applications of the idea of community make it possible to reconsider the kinds of authority comparative lawyers can rely on in recommending legal reforms based on foreign legal models. It is possible to discuss in new ways the place of values, beliefs, traditions and shared historical experiences as underpinnings of law, as well as the conditions under which law promotes or constrains globalization, and how far it can express, promote or protect various aspects of culture.

Culture and Comparison

This suggests a very ambitious agenda. The studies collected in Part 2 are merely exploratory essays in these fields of inquiry. What most directly links them as regards subject matter is a focus on law's relations with culture and on comparative legal studies. Culture and especially legal culture have become important foci for the emerging field of comparative sociology of law, in which David Nelken has been a pioneer. The paper on which Chapter 5 is based was originally written at his invitation. To my regret, I found that the brief given, to examine the concept of legal culture in recent sociology of law, led me to very negative conclusions. For reasons explained in Chapter 5, I think the concepts of culture and legal culture are of limited *explanatory* value for sociolegal studies. As many anthropologists and sociologists have noted, culture is an amorphous term, covering an indeterminate range of phenomena: it is a kind of aggregate, useful to refer in general terms to a broad swathe of experiences or impressions of a place or time. But it does not indicate precise variables. Chapter 5 is solely concerned with the use of concepts of culture and legal culture in the literature of sociology of law, but lawyers, especially comparative legal scholars, have also begun to use these ideas frequently and Chapter 6 addresses the various juristic aspects of culture.

Chapter 5 was written (as a conference paper) before the law-and-community approach used elsewhere in this book began to emerge. It is one of the few almost entirely negative and critical studies I have written. After the completion of the original paper, I wanted to find a much more positive, constructive approach that would unambiguously recognize the growing importance of culture as a focus for legal studies but would avoid the disabling problems (which Chapter 5 emphasizes) of vagueness and imprecision in discussions of the idea of culture. Chapter 6 sketches a more positive approach of this kind. As with Chapter 5, the paper on which Chapter 6 is based was written in response to a specific invitation, with an assigned title. The late Aleksander Peczenik's invitation to me to give a plenary lecture on 'Law in Culture' at the IVR Congress in Lund in 2003 offered an opportunity to rethink the idea of culture using a law-and-community approach. The chapter disaggregates 'culture' into elements of tradition, beliefs and values, affect and instrumentality that are the basis of different types of community. It remains to be seen whether such a breaking down of culture into community-focused components with relatively distinct legal attributes proves useful in dealing with matters of legal culture. But directions for further research are indicated, the complexity and contradictions of law's relations with culture are demonstrated via the typology of community, and some crucial reasons for this situation are explained.

Chapter 8 (like all other chapters except Chapter 5) relies on the law-and-community framework but it is focused less directly on this than is most of the rest of Part 2. The main concern of Chapter 8 is to make direct connections between the development of comparative legal studies, on the one hand, and sociology of law, on the other. The chapter claims (as many comparative lawyers have done) that there need be no incompatibility between the aims of comparative legal studies and legal sociology. In fact, the whole of Part 2 is concerned in one way or another with the nature, outlook or projects of comparative law as a research field; several chapters are based on papers addressed primarily to audiences of comparative law specialists.

Comparative law seems to me at present to be a relatively open research field, in which collaboration with legal sociologists and social theorists is being encouraged by some leading comparative law scholars. The experience I have found – as a legal theorist and legal sociologist – of being welcomed into certain debates about comparative legal studies in recent years is reminiscent of the openness I found in British sociology as an organized research enterprise, when I first became involved with it in the second half of the 1970s.

It might be said that this kind of openness (the opposite of rigid disciplinarity) is symptomatic of a research field that is institutionally vulnerable, with its collective self-confidence shaken. That was true of sociology in some respects in the late 1970s, as it has been at other times, and similar worries about the situation of comparative law as a research field are often expressed in the literature (Ewald 1995a: 1961–5). However, my overwhelming impression of sociology (especially social theory), when I first encountered it, was that it was a rich, exciting, scholarly, imaginative and promising field (it still seems that way, despite too much mediocre research production). In a somewhat similar way, comparative law now appears as a field of great intellectual significance and very exciting possibilities. It is centrally placed to study the trajectories of proliferating transnational law and transnational legal aspirations, as well as the increasing significance of the relations of law and culture. Chapter 8, besides emphasizing some remarkable early links between comparative law and sociology of law, urges much more extensive communication between comparative legal scholars and legal sociologists. They share responsibility for work at the cutting edge of contemporary legal inquiry.

Acknowledgements

This book reflects my work since the mid-1990s on the sociological study of legal ideas. The texts of previously published essays have been adapted as necessary to form the basis of chapters but the original arguments of those essays have not been changed. A few references to sources (for example, superseded editions of books) have been updated, and passages have been abbreviated and altered to avoid repetition. Limited editing has been done in some places for purely stylistic reasons, but generally I have left the original texts to speak for themselves. Cross-references between chapters mainly correspond to references in the original publications, but the form of the cross-references has often been changed for consistency and continuity. New linking introductions now preface chapters, and section or sub-section headings have been added in Chapters 6, 7 and 8 and altered in Chapters 4 and 9.

I have accumulated many debts in working on the ideas in this book. David Nelken first invited me to write about legal culture and, by doing so, started me on inquiries that have been important for this book. Beyond that, I have treasured his warm friendship and close intellectual comradeship in sociology of law (even when we disagree!) for more than two decades. I am grateful for consistent support over the years from Michael Freeman, Sir Neil MacCormick, the late Per Stjernquist, Phil Thomas and William Twining, and from many colleagues at Queen Mary and Westfield College. Others who have helped, through their interest, enthusiasm and ideas, during the past decade when I have been working on the substance of these chapters include Reza Banakar, Zenon Bankowski, Peter Fitzpatrick, Lawrence Friedman, Volkmar Gessner, Andrew Harding, Ralph Henham, Nicola Lacey, Pierre Legrand, Werner Menski, Alan Norrie, Esin Örücü, the late Aleksander Peczenik, W.S.F. (Bill) Pickering, Jiří Přibáň, Austin Sarat, Philip Selznick, Gunther Teubner, Wibren Van Der Burg, Paul Van Seters and Willem Witteveen. The most important debt by far is to Ann Cotterrell, who has improved the material in this book through her careful criticism, and who provides support and encouragement for all my work.

The permission of copyright holders to republish material in adapted form is acknowledged with thanks: Blackwell Publishing (Chapters 1, 3 and 6); Oxford University Press (Chapter 2); Canadian Law and Society Association (Chapter 4);

David Nelken and (original publisher) Dartmouth Publishing Company (Chapter 5); Oñati International Institute for the Sociology of Law and (original publisher) Hart Publishing (Chapter 7); Cambridge University Press (Chapter 8); Institute of Advanced Legal Studies, London, and (original publisher) Kluwer Academic Publishers (Chapter 9). The following previously published essays have been adapted for this book: 'Law in Social Theory, and Social Theory in the Study of Law' in A. Sarat (ed.), *Blackwell Companion to Law and Society* (New York: Blackwell, 2004) pp. 5–29 (Chapter 1); 'Law and Community: A New Relationship?' in M.D.A. Freeman (ed.), *Legal Theory at the End of the Millennium: Current Legal Problems*, vol. 51 (Oxford: Oxford University Press, 1998) pp. 367–91 (Chapter 2); 'Why Must Legal Ideas Be Interpreted Sociologically?' (1998) **25** *Journal of Law and Society* 171–92 (Chapter 3); 'A Legal Concept of Community' (1997) **12** *Canadian Journal of Law and Society* 75–91 (Chapter 4); 'The Concept of Legal Culture' in D. Nelken (ed.), *Comparing Legal Cultures* (Aldershot: Dartmouth, 1997) pp. 13–31 (Chapter 5); 'Law in Culture' (2004) **17** *Ratio Juris* 1–14 (Chapter 6); 'Is There a Logic of Legal Transplants?' in D. Nelken and J. Feest (eds), *Adapting Legal Cultures* (Oxford: Hart, 2001) pp. 71–92 (Chapter 7); 'Comparatists and Sociology' in P. Legrand and R. Munday (eds), *Comparative Legal Studies: Traditions and Transitions* (Cambridge: Cambridge University Press, 2003) pp. 131–53 (Chapter 8); 'Seeking Similarity, Appreciating Difference: Comparative Law and Communities' in E. Örücü and A. Harding (eds), *Comparative Law in the Twenty-First Century* (The Hague: Kluwer, 2002) pp. 35–54 (Chapter 9). The material in the Introduction and Conclusion is previously unpublished.

PART 1
Perspectives
(Legal and Social Theory)

Chapter 1

Law and Social Theory

The relationship between legal studies and social theory has been ambivalent and often difficult. Why is this so? What is the value of social theory in legal studies today and why is law an important social phenomenon for social theory to consider? This chapter addresses these questions and considers recent challenges to the projects of social science and social theory. It also introduces the special problems posed for theoretical studies of law by globalization and the growth of transnational law.

What can social theory contribute to legal studies? And what place does law have as a concern of social theory? Three or four decades ago, when 'law-and-society' (sociolegal) studies were first becoming a lively, popular focus for research, defining the relations of law and social theory meant mainly locating law's place in the theoretical traditions of the academic discipline of sociology, and asking what those traditions might offer the study of law. Now, however, social theory is not the preserve of any particular academic discipline. It has to be defined in terms of its objectives rather than particular traditions that have shaped it.

Law in Classic Social Theory

Social theory is systematic, historically informed and empirically oriented theory seeking to explain the nature of 'the social'. And the social can be taken to mean the general range of recurring forms, or patterned features, of interactions and relationships between people. The social is the ongoing life of human beings lived alongside and in relation to others; the compendium of institutions, networks, patterns and structures of collective life resulting from human coexistence. So, it is the collective life of human groups and populations, but also the life of individuals insofar as this is shaped by their relation to those populations or groups. The social is a realm of solidarity, identity and cooperation, but also of power, conflict, alienation and isolation; of stable expectations, systems, custom, trust and confidence, but also of unpredictable action, unforeseen change, violence, disruption and discontinuity.

Described in these expansive terms, the social seems bewilderingly general as an object or field of study. Debates about its nature and significance are fundamental today in assessing the significance of social theory itself. And the essence of the social has been seen in social theory in radically different ways. For example, in Max Weber's (1968) classic sociological writings it appears as a limited number of distinct types of social action combined in innumerable ways to give rise to what we recognize as 'capitalism', 'bureaucracy', 'domination' and all the other seemingly solid structures of the social world. Sometimes the social has been seen in terms of an evolution of human relations – for example in Marcel Mauss' (1990) famous analysis of the significance of gift relationships. Its essence has also been found in different types of cohesion of human populations (Durkheim 1984) or sociality or bonding between the members of social groups (Gurvitch 1947). Sometimes it has been understood as categories or institutional forms in terms of which individuals interrelate – for example, in Georg Simmel's (1971) analyses of 'the stranger', 'the metropolis', 'fashion', 'conflict', 'exchange' and other phenomena.

The object that has served – implicitly or explicitly – as the primary focus for most social theory is *society*, conceived as a unified totality in some sense, so that the study of how that totality exists could be distinct from, though related to, the study of politics, law, the economy or other more specific kinds of social action or experience. Society in this sense is 'the sum of the bonds and relations between individuals and events – economic, moral, political – within a more or less bounded territory governed by its own laws' (Rose 1996: 328). Even where social theory has not treated society directly as its object, its characterizations of the social assume that social phenomena cohere in a significant way: that social life forms a fabric of some kind; that it has continuity and scale and that particular exemplifications of the social relate to larger patterns, even if their exact limits or boundaries may be variable or hard to specify. The social includes class, race and gender relations, and specifically economic relations, for example, but social theory assumes it must treat all of these as components or aspects of more general patterns or features of human interaction, and that its consistent focus must be on that generality. The social is always assumed to be in some sense intelligible as a unity.

In the classic social theory of the late nineteenth and early twentieth century, 'society' was mainly typified by the politically organized and territorially bounded society of the modern Western nation state. Given this position, it is not surprising that a strong sensitivity to law is found in the most ambitious and influential contributions to this theory – the work of Emile Durkheim, Weber and Karl Marx. The reach of society could be seen as paralleling the jurisdictional reach of nation state legal systems. As social theory examined the general social relations and structures comprising society, it encountered modern law as a society-wide system of definition and regulation of these relations and structures. In a sense, law and social theory competed in characterizing modern society, but law could be treated in social theory as exemplifying certain structures and patterns fundamental to this society.

So, for Durkheim, the substance of modern law (particularly contract, commercial, property and criminal law) and its processes expressed the particular characteristics of modern social solidarity, by which he meant the manner in which modern society was integrated and given a sense of unity despite its increasing complexity, changeability and diversity. A study of the development of law across the centuries could show how the structures of solidarity allowing modern society to cohere had gradually formed (Durkheim 1984). His conclusion was that the only value system that could integrate modern societies – and so must be the moral foundation of all modern law – would be one requiring universal respect for the autonomy and human dignity of every individual citizen (Durkheim 1975a; Cotterrell 1999: 103–47).

In a completely different way and using different methods, Weber also securely linked the study of law with the study of the social in its modern forms. Modern law exemplified a kind of rationality mirroring and running parallel with the rationalization of other aspects of life in the West. While formal legal rationality was a distinctive mode of thought and practice, it could be seen as part of a far wider rationalization of the modern world. The study of legal rationality's development and its interrelations with other varieties of rationality (especially in economic action, administration and politics) could, in Weber's view, provide major insights into the nature of the social in the unique forms it had taken in the West (Weber 1968: Part 2, Chapter 8).

Marx, seeking to analyse the nature and destiny of capitalism, saw law as in one sense superstructural, a product rather than an engine of capitalism's trajectory as a mode of production and as the overall structure of the social in the modern West. But he emphasized law's role in defining social relations, repressing class unrest and helping to constitute the ways of thinking – above all in terms of property and contract – that serve as fundamental ideological supports of capitalist social relations (Cain and Hunt 1979). Thus, like Durkheim and Weber, Marx saw a need to take account of the development of law to identify the way it produced particular ideas, ways of reasoning or forms of practice at certain stages in history.

So, each of these writers saw law as essential in transforming the social – establishing foundations of modern society, however differently they might characterize this modernity in their work.

These brief comments may be enough to illustrate two points: that the concept of *modernity* has often, in practice, been inseparable from that of society in the vision of social theory and that law was often treated in classic social theory as, in some way, a crucial marker, component or agent of the coming into being of the modern world. More recent social theorists have often treated the emergence of a certain kind of legal system as crucial in this sense. Talcott Parsons, for example, saw the emergence of a 'general legal system' – cutting across all traditional special statuses and providing a universal system of rights and obligations – as 'the most important single hallmark of modern society' (Parsons 1964: 353). But we shall see later that the concepts of modernity and society, so central to social theory, are at the heart of debates surrounding it as an enterprise today.

Leaving aside these debates for the moment, what has social theory in its classic or traditional forms been able to offer legal studies? If social theory is abstract and broad in scope, law as a practice, and often as a field of study, has been said, by contrast, to be wedded to the 'method of detail' (Twining 1974), focused on particularity and immediate problem-solving. Social theory in general has claimed that philosophical analyses, reflections on historical experience and systematic empirical observations of social conditions can be combined to explain the nature of society. Social theorists' considerations of law are coloured by this amalgam of philosophical, historical and observational orientations. As a by-product of its general concerns, social theory has often assessed law's capacities, limits, conditions of existence and sources of authority and power.

Its attraction for some legal scholars has been that its perspectives on law have been much wider than those the legal specialist alone could usually be expected to command. So, social theory has been called on in sociolegal studies to escape the limits of law's method of detail as well as to counter narrow social scientific empiricism. The promise has always been to *broaden* social perspectives on law. The corresponding risk has always been that the broad perspective loses the richness and specificity of particular experiences or practices of 'the legal'. The method of detail may need supplementing but has its value nonetheless.

Despite these claims for social theory's usefulness to legal studies and the prominent presence of law in the classics of social theory, the link between legal studies and social theory has usually been tenuous. That various changes in both law and social theory are bringing about a greater mutual dependence will be a main argument later in this chapter. Nevertheless, until quite recently, the relationship could be characterized as predominantly one of disinterest or token acknowledgment.

Despite the example set by the classic writers, social theorists have often doubted whether law is important enough or sufficiently identifiable as a distinct social phenomenon to deserve special consideration in any theory of the social. Could most of what needs to be analysed be treated in terms of concepts such as administrative action, state coercion, social norms, social control, ideology, reciprocity, conformity and deviance, bureaucratic norms or custom? Law, as such, might not need theorizing: that could be left to jurists for their own purposes. The term 'law' would remain for the social theorist only a common-sense label that might usefully designate clusters of phenomena to be explained theoretically without essential reference to it. In any event, law's identity and significance vary considerably between different societies. And general conceptions or definitions of law are dominated by juristic perceptions which most social theorists have not sought to upset.

For example, social theorists have rarely adopted the radical reformulations of the concept of law associated with what is now called social scientific legal pluralism (Griffiths 1986; Merry 1988). Legal pluralism in this sense explicitly denies that juristic conceptions of law are universally adequate and adopts some wider conception of law that can embrace, for various analytical purposes, phenomena that the lawyer would not recognize as legal – for example, private or 'unofficial' norm systems of various kinds. Among major social theorists only Georges Gurvitch stands out as having radically rejected juristic conceptions of law in favour of an intricate, fully elaborated theory of legal pluralism integrated into his broader social theory. Significantly Gurvitch reached this position on the basis of his early sociolegal and philosophical inquiries (Gurvitch 1935; 1947), rather than as a by-product of his later general sociological theory.

Indeed, in contrast to social theorists, it is those social scientists who see law as central to their research careers, and tend to refer to themselves as 'law-and-society' or sociolegal scholars, who have most often embraced legal pluralist perspectives. But many sociolegal scholars have been content to follow social theory's general lead, paying homage to the broad insights about law to be found in classic social theory but otherwise mainly using 'law' as a pragmatic umbrella term for clusters of social phenomena analysed in terms of concepts familiar in their parent social science disciplines.

Just as social theory has tended to avoid law while considering its social manifestations, so lawyers and legal scholars have mainly avoided social theory. And certainly, from a juristic standpoint, the usefulness of a theory of the social may not seem obvious: the social might be viewed as what law itself creates as its own jurisdiction, the structure of the social being simply the regulatory structure that law provides. In this sense the social is the taken-for-granted locus and environment of legal practice. And, undoubtedly, from a juristic viewpoint, law seems endlessly resourceful in defining and adjusting its reach and the nature of the relations it regulates: the social is what law treats as such.

Law and Contemporary Social Change

What is happening to change this typical relationship of disinterest? Relevant changes in the situation of law and legal studies, on the one hand, and of social theory, on the other, have often been associated with the idea of the passing of modernity and its replacement with the postmodern. 'Post' implies that the new can only be understood as related to and, in some sense, a supplement or reaction to what preceded it, but also that modernity's features can now be identified with finality, so that what follows is distinct from them.

According to Jean-François Lyotard's celebrated dictum, the most profound exemplification of postmodernity is a loss of faith in 'grand narratives' (Lyotard 1984: 37) in a fluid, rapidly changing, intensely self-questioning and uncertain (Western) world: the coming of 'a new age of radical rootlessness and doubt' (Douzinas and Warrington 1991: 9). This applies not only to comprehensive systems of thought such as Marxism and the great religions, but to general theories of 'society' as a stable, integrated totality, to political ideologies of all kinds and to the very idea of 'science' as the progressive unveiling of truth. All are said to flounder on the rocks of patent social contingency and indeterminacy.

The result is a new privileging of 'local knowledge' (Geertz 1983) and a perception of the failure or pointlessness of all attempts to generalize broadly about social change or social phenomena. The tendency in such circumstances might be to abandon social theory altogether. A new focus on the local and the specific, on the instability of social structures and institutions, and the exhilarating or frightening rootlessness of individual lives casts doubt on the usefulness of treating society as an object sufficiently solid to theorize (Rose 1996; Bauman 1992: 190). The dialectic of order/change and structure/agency in traditional sociological analyses of society does not seem to capture the sense of radical fluidity that postmodern thought associates with contemporary human coexistence in the most highly developed nations of the world.

The idea that it is no longer useful to theorize society has sometimes led into more general but very opaque claims about 'the death of the social' (Baudrillard 1983: Chapter 2). The doomsday scenario here is that social theory loses its integrity, having lost its object. It is replaced with a host of competing discourses – especially literary, feminist, psychoanalytic, economic and cultural theory – that focus on human relations no longer considered in terms of any explicit overall conception of the social.

More concrete ideas bearing directly on the destiny of law can also be mentioned. The social is sometimes claimed to be disappearing as a specific primary field of government intervention, and enterprises organized around it (such as social work, social welfare, sociology and socialism) are losing prestige (Simon 1999: 144–7). A further claim is that the social as a field distinct from the political is atrophying. From one viewpoint, the social has become merely a population mass, silent and inert, no longer the active source of political energies but merely a passive recipient of governmental actions (Baudrillard 1983: 19–25). A consequence would seem to be that legal interventions can hardly look for effective legitimation or direction from this source.

From another viewpoint, an individualization of lifestyles puts in issue the stability of many social institutions (for example, traditional family, employment and gender relations) but creates unprecedented opportunities for a radical remaking of the social through the spontaneous choices of individuals in relation to their own lives (for example, Beck and Beck-Gernsheim 2002). Thus, politics is potentially transformed, its focus shifted towards the local and the personal but also, very importantly, towards the global (as in many environmental, security and health concerns widely shared across national boundaries). Meanwhile, politics in nation states becomes increasingly moribund in the traditional public sphere. Indeed, in a revitalized politics, lines between public and private, and national and global, might eventually become meaningless (Beck 1992: Chapter 8; 2000: Chapter 2). The primary implication for legal studies would seem to be that the horizon and appropriate methods of regulation are changing in very fundamental ways.

The importance of this recent theorizing is certainly not to undermine the social as a category. Indeed, many theorists – including some, such as Jean Baudrillard, who have dramatically declared the social's demise – continue to refer to 'society' without apparent embarrassment (Smart 1993: 55–6). For legal studies, the importance of these writings is to show that the nature of the social cannot be assumed as unproblematic. Law may define the social as it regulates it, but it does so under conditions that the social itself provides. Law presupposes a conception of the social that defines not only its technical jurisdiction, but also the arena in which its interventions require rational integration, and the general source of its legitimation and cultural meanings. It follows that, as the identity, coherence and shape of the social are questioned, assumptions about the nature and efficacy of law are also put in issue.

In contemporary social theory, Michel Foucault's work provides one of the most important vehicles for reconsidering the nature and scope of law in terms of fundamental long-term changes in the character of the social. It raises the question of whether law has failed to keep step with these changes and become marginalized as a result, increasingly giving way to other kinds of regulation and control. Foucault's works describe processes by which new kinds of knowledge and power have arisen, reinforcing each other to create what he calls disciplinary society (Foucault 1977: 216). The prison, the asylum, the school, the medical clinic and other particular institutional sites have been primary foci for the gradual emergence of constellations of knowledge/power in which technical norms, expertise, training and surveillance combine to regulate populations and define the place of individuals as autonomous, responsible subjects.

In lectures towards the end of his career, Foucault elaborated the general implications for law of his earlier studies. He sharply contrasts the majesty of law with the 'art of government' focused on administering social life (Foucault 1991: 92). Law is, in his view, the expression of sovereign power: what is most important about it is that it demands obedience and requires that all affronts to the sovereignty it embodies be punished. The essence of law is, therefore, coercion. Foucault contrasts, with law's 'occasional or discontinuous interventions in society', something he sees as very different: 'a type of power that is disciplinary and continuously regulative and which pervasively, intimately and integrally inhabits society' (Fitzpatrick 1992: 151). This is an autonomous, expert form of governing, focused specifically on regulating economy and population and relying on 'multiform tactics' and a range of techniques, expertise and information united only by a need for 'wisdom and diligence' (Foucault 1991: 95, 96).

Foucault calls this pervasive regulatory activity 'governmentality' rather than government, to emphasize that it goes beyond and uses a far wider range of techniques than government in the usual political sense, and its sites of operation are not restricted to what is usually thought of as the public sphere but relate to all aspects of life. Nevertheless, the rise of governmentality marks a stage in the development of the state, from the 'state of justice' and law, through the 'administrative state' of regulation and discipline organized territorially, to the 'governmental state' which aims at guaranteeing security and is 'essentially defined no longer [exclusively] in terms of its territoriality ... its surface area, but in terms of the mass of its population with its volume and density ...' (Foucault 1991: 104).

Significantly, law's destiny is left vague. Perhaps ultimately it is for jurists and sociolegal scholars to sort this out. The state's stages of development are cumulative so that eventually legal, administrative and governmental state forms coexist. Some writers see Foucault as claiming that law is progressively replaced by technical and disciplinary norms, and charge him with propounding a narrow view of law, apparently ignoring its current scope and character (Hunt 1993: Chapter 12). Others argue that Foucault well recognizes law's nature and scope in contemporary society (Ewald 1990) and sees only its old regulatory supremacy as undermined. His claim, undoubtedly, is that law has been reduced from its grandly sovereign status to a position alongside many other regulatory techniques, no more than a 'tactic' of government to be used or not used, as appropriate (Foucault 1991: 95).

From another point of view, the key debate around Foucault and law is about law's *potential*. In the newly recognized complexity and indeterminacy of society, does action through and on law provide an important means of navigating the social and the many decentred locations of power which Foucault's work emphasizes (as suggested, for example, by Munro 2001), or is it increasingly a distraction as a focus for solving or campaigning on important social issues (Smart 1989), being tied to forms of state action and political projects that are increasingly remote from many regions of the social?

The ambiguous implications of Foucault's work show that social theory's changing images of the social destabilize established ideas of law, pointing in different directions towards new conceptualizations. A broad, loosened conception of law might see it metamorphosing into diverse regulatory strategies, forms and tactics attempting to mirror the fluidity, contingency and indeterminacy of the social (Rose and Valverde 1998). Law might seem an indefinite aspect of a range of tactics of governance operating in contexts – for example, schools, religious practices, rural traditions, campaigns to protect local industries (Cooper 1998) – often distanced from the direct operation of state agencies.

In this context, new unifying principles arise, focused, for example, on the control of risk, so that risk emerges as a major category for making sense of the normative implications of contingency (Beck 1992). Perceptions or calculations of risk can then be seen to operate as signals to alert or set in motion regulatory processes and provide their focus (see, for example, Ericson and Haggerty 1997). Equally, they can be rallying points for political and legal action (Franklin 1998).

By contrast, conceptions of law that in some way emphasize its autonomy or distinct identity rather than its tactical flexibility might see it as in crisis, overburdened with regulatory tasks for which it is unsuitable (Teubner (ed.) 1987). Or they might emphasize as somewhat remarkable the fact that, in such conditions of complexity, the legal system copes; that it pours out rules and decisions despite the ever-increasing diversity of social life and the rapidity of social change.

Autopoiesis theory, developed as a form of social theory by the sociologist Niklas Luhmann (1995), can be seen in this context as a particularly inventive way of conceptualizing how law copes with changes in the nature of the social without losing its special identity in the process, and becoming – as Foucault seems to suggest – just part of a continuum of regulatory tactics. Autopoiesis theory seeks to explain how law retains a distinctive character and stability in complex societies, at the same time as it addresses an ever-increasing range of problems thrown up by the fluidity and complexity of the social. The theory also suggests why legal interventions often produce unforeseen and unintended social consequences and why law often seems persistently unresponsive to demands emerging from the social.

In Luhmann's formulation, law is cognitively open but normatively closed, insofar as it has become an autopoietic (self-observing, self-producing and self-reproducing) system of communication (Luhmann 1992a). This means that, like other social systems of communication (such as the economy, the polity and science), law is necessarily open to information from its environment but, no less necessarily, it reads this information only in its own discursive terms. Law processes information solely for the purposes of applying its unique normative coding of legal/illegal in terms of which all its decisions must be made. Similarly, other systems interpret legal rules and decisions in terms of their own system codings, for example the criteria of efficient/inefficient in the case of the economy.

As social theory, autopoiesis theory clearly pictures law in the way it so often appears to jurists – as a self-founding discourse unfazed by circularity in its reasoning and invocations of authority. It shows how law can operate in this way and explains sociologically why it does. The theory claims that the increasing complexity of the social gives rise, in an evolutionary process, to the gradual differentiation of society into a number of specialized systems of communication, of which law is one. The legal system is thus not defined in terms of rules and institutions – as, for example, in Talcott Parsons' (1977: 174–6) earlier theory of social differentiation as a response to complexity – but by its distinctive discourse of legality and illegality.

Hence, law can pervade the spaces of the social. As discourse it can exist anywhere and everywhere and the thematization of issues as legal (Luhmann 1981) can occur in contexts not restricted to the formal legal institutions of the nation state. Thus, autopoiesis theory can accommodate the idea of an emerging 'global law without a state' (Teubner (ed.) 1997), or of law's presence in the private realms that social theorists have identified as contemporary sites of a new politics and of the transformation of the social.

Nevertheless, the theory suffers, as many critics have pointed out, from an almost impenetrable abstraction. Attempts to use it in empirical sociolegal research have had limited success although it has provided a striking way of emphasizing, for example, legal discourse's perceived deafness or incomprehension when sometimes faced in court with the discourses of social welfare in cases involving children (King and Piper 1995). Despite being among the most sophisticated and rigorous recent contributions to social theory and having had its legal implications extensively elaborated (for example, Teubner 1993; Přibáň and Nelken (eds) 2001), autopoiesis theory stands some way apart from many of the themes this chapter has stressed. It has not extensively examined the changing character of the social in concrete terms in relation to law, and it has not indicated how contemporary legal change can be interpreted in the light of social theory. It leaves relatively unexplored the details of the discursive character that it attributes to developed law. And the theory explains little about how autopoietic law will actually respond to what the social may throw up as regulatory problems. Its concern seems only to affirm that law will seek to address these matters always from its own point of view with its own discursive resources.

Foundations of Legal Authority

Autopoiesis theory attempts to bypass one question that has long been a major focus for social theory: What is the source and foundation of law's authority, the legitimacy that enables it to demand respect and command obedience? For Luhmann, the issue of law's legitimacy has been replaced by that of function: the question is simply about efficiency – whether law can effectively fulfil its social task of producing decisions according to its own criteria of legality/illegality. But one might still want to ask how functional success is to be judged and recognized. In fact, much recent social theoretical writing wrestles with questions about law's 'grounds', its ultimate bases of authority or legitimacy.

Durkheim's classic social theory assumed that law and morality are inseparable and that morality is law's 'soul'. Since he understood morality as the normative structure of society, his social theory makes the strong claim that law finds all its meaning, authority and effectiveness ultimately in this moral structure. Without such a grounding it becomes mere force or empty words (Cotterrell 1999). In a sense, Weber's social theory turned these Durkheimian claims upside down. Modern law, having lost its 'metaphysical dignity' with the discrediting of natural law theories, is revealed, in his view, as no more than 'the product or the technical means of a compromise of interests' (Weber 1968: 874–5). Law needs no moral authority. Instead, its rules and procedures, in their abstract formality, can themselves become a means of *giving* authority, as in the political authority of the rule of law as a legitimation of government. Weber's work is thus one of the clearest sources of the familiar idea of legitimacy through legality or procedure (Cotterrell 1995: Chapter 7).

Interestingly, the broad problems, if not the substance, of both Durkheim's and Weber's opposing positions are strongly present in recent writing on law in social theory and in invocations of social theory in legal studies. Postmodern ideas about the collapse of grand narratives might suggest that the authority or validity of all large-scale structures of knowledge has been put in question. But it could be argued that some kind of Weberian legitimacy through legality remains the only possibility of stable authority in the postmodern social environment. Contemporary law – explicitly constructed, particular and local in scope, and ever-changing – might seem the quintessentially postmodern form of knowledge or doctrine: not in any sense a grand narrative, but the perfect pragmatic embodiment of contingency, impermanence, artificiality, transience and disposability; its doctrine continually adapted, amended, cancelled, supplemented or reinterpreted to address new problems.

Hence, postmodern writing on law has often emphasized law's simultaneous moral emptiness and social power in a world that has lost faith in other discourses (Goodrich 1990). And autopoiesis theory's unconcerned recognition that the very essence of legal discourse is circular reasoning has some affinities with claims informed by postmodern perspectives (Cotterrell 2003: Chapter 9): for example, that law's self-founded authority acts powerfully to disguise the incoherences of concepts such as 'society' and 'nation', even though legal thinking itself presupposes these concepts (Fitzpatrick 2001).

Not unrelated to these lines of thought is a stress, in much recent sociolegal writing, on law's constitutive power (for example, Brigham 1996) – its ability actually to create the social (not just for immediate regulatory purposes but also in the wider consciousness of all who participate in social life) by shaping over time such general ideas as property, ownership, responsibility, contract, rights, fault and guilt, as well as notions of interests, identity and community. To be theoretically coherent, the idea of law as constitutive in this sense – with antecedents stretching back to Marx's emphasis on law's ideological power – must ultimately either presuppose some notion of law as self-founding or recognize that law and the social are *mutually* constituting, that law gains its meaning and ultimate authority from the social at the same time as it shapes the social through its regulatory force. In other words, law is an aspect or field of social experience, not some mysteriously external force acting on it.

This last conclusion might reopen Durkheimian questions about the social bases of law's authority and imply that the social is more coherent, stable and susceptible to theorization than many writings on postmodernity assume. This is what Jürgen Habermas' influential social theory claims. He presents an image of society as made up partly of systems (for example, economic, political and legal systems), such as Luhmann describes, and partly of what Habermas calls the 'lifeworld'. The lifeworld is the environment of everyday social experience in which customs, cultures, moral ideas and popular understandings are formed and reproduced. The lifeworld provides experiential 'background knowledge' (Habermas 1996: 23) with the aid of which people interpret each other's conduct and communicative actions. It is also the source of solidarity and legitimations necessary to the maintenance of the various systems that make up society. Yet it is continually colonized, invaded and transformed by these systems. So, for Habermas, the social exists in the interplay of system and lifeworld.

In contrast to all postmodern portrayals of contingency, indeterminacy and moral vacuity as characteristics of contemporary life, Habermas pursues the Enlightenment project of the discovery of reason in law, society and nature. He sees law not as self-grounding but as deriving its authority from reason – what he calls a communicative rationality, dependent for its adequate development on certain ideal conditions under which agreement between persons pursuing opposed or divergent interests becomes possible. Law, for Habermas, is the only medium that can link the lifeworld and the various systems of complex modern societies. Law, as a system itself, depends on the lifeworld for its authority and significance. The Durkheimian aspect of Habermas' thought is thus his insistence that law must be rooted in and express lifeworld sources of social solidarity. He sees law as having the main responsibility to coordinate contemporary societies, participating in both the instrumental rationality that pervades social systems and the consensus-oriented communicative rationality that the maintenance of lifeworld solidarity requires.

In his major work on legal theory (Habermas 1996), he insists that law and morality are distinct, though both derive from the same ultimate founding principle of communicative rationality. The conditions for this rationality to flourish include certain specified basic rights which can only be secured through legal processes. These processes, in turn, presuppose and must be designed to support democratic structures. Law and democracy are thus inseparably interwoven.

Habermas' ideas on law have been much discussed in sociolegal literature perhaps mainly because they clearly affirm law's relation to reason and the possibility of law's rational justification in the face of postmodern doubts. But these ideas have significantly shifted location over time. From components of an empirically oriented social theory focused notably on conditions of legitimate government in capitalist societies (Habermas 1975), they have turned into a more speculative legal philosophy. Interestingly, Habermas (1987: 249) has criticized Foucault's view of power as 'utterly unsociological' but the same might be said of some of his own very abstract, general discussions of communicative rationality.

Perhaps the most thought-provoking feature of Habermas' recent work is the fact that law has come to assume a very central position in his picture of society. Law might seem in some images of postmodernity to be the epitome of contemporary valid knowledge, but in Habermas' entirely different outlook it appears, potentially at least, to epitomize essential social processes of consensus formation; its interpretive procedures hold out possibilities for developing communicative rationality. Law's procedures are the devices by which rationally-oriented communicative action becomes practically possible on a society-wide basis. From a certain standpoint, then, the significance of law for social theory is affirmed in the most unambiguous terms. Law is the foundation of central structures of social life; a set of processes and procedures on which society's very integrity depends.

Law Beyond Nation States

I suggested earlier that law had often been able to avoid entanglement with social theory because it could take the nature of the social for granted. Law constitutes in regulatory terms what it treats as the social but it has to *presuppose* an overall conception of the social in which its regulatory actions can make sense. For a long time, Western legal thought presupposed the political society of the modern nation state as its overall conception of the social.

The growth of transnational regulation and regulatory aspirations (in human rights, commerce and finance, intellectual property, environmental protection, information technology and many other areas) creates new incentives for legal studies to draw on the resources of social theory. This is because it potentially disturbs long-standing presuppositions about law's stable relation to the political society of the nation state. Social theory's efforts to understand the social as extending beyond the bounds of society in this sense, or as shaped by powerful transnational forces, are presently organized mainly around the portmanteau concept of globalization. But law does not figure prominently in theories of globalization, perhaps because it is usually seen as following rather than actively shaping the transnational extension of the social. Globalization is often described in terms of particular forms of this extension such as the harmonization of markets, the transformation of culture (understood, for example, as traditions, basic values or beliefs), or the effects of new communication technologies. Law's role, even where seen as vital in these developments, is usually thought of as purely technical. Relatively few writers (cf. Teubner (ed.) 1997; Santos 2002) see the need for theories of 'global law' or legal transnationalization. Law in its traditional forms is widely assumed to be endlessly adaptable, capable of relating to the social wherever legal practice encounters it.

I think that some of the most important future relations of legal studies and social theory will, however, focus on the need to understand the changing character of law as it participates in developments currently associated with globalization. How far is social theory (which so often assumed the political society of the nation state as the social) helpful as law increasingly relates to a social realm demarcated in other terms?

As has been seen, debates inspired by Foucault's work address the nature of contemporary regulation (with its intricate, if somewhat indeterminate, links to the law created by sovereign power) and the complexity of networks of power in the social. These debates have great relevance for attempts to understand the nature and social contexts of transnational regulation. It will surely be necessary to ask whether, at some point, transnational regulatory forms can presuppose, to use Foucault's terms, the 'cutting off of the king's head' (Foucault 1979: 88–9) – in other words, the freeing of regulatory strategies from the coercive demands of national sovereign power. It will be necessary to consider how far transnational social spaces can be created in which dispersed but pervasive power can be used not merely to discipline individuals, but also to create possibilities for their autonomy – the dual aspects of this power that are analysed in Foucault's work. In related ways, Ulrich Beck's writings (for example, Beck 1992; 2000) identify, in terms of individualization and risk, new regulatory problems but also new foci of liberating political action that can, as he stresses, relate as much to transnational as national arenas.

An engagement between legal studies and social theory beyond the nation state focus does not depend entirely on posing new sociolegal questions. It can also be a matter of presenting old ones in new contexts. Some of the most important old questions are about the way law secures authority through responsiveness to the experience or understandings of the population it regulates. Durkheim, always concerned with these issues, offered an important theory of democracy that has been largely unrecognized in sociolegal studies. He understood democracy, as an ideal practice, to be less a matter of popular representation than of sensitive, informed deliberation by means of which understandings, issues and values rooted in widespread everyday social experience can be recognized and translated into effective regulation (Cotterrell 1999: Chapters 10 and 11).

Durkheim's concerns about the moral groundings of law have not become irrelevant. But they are much more difficult to address when the social can no longer easily be thought of simply as a unified national political society. It has become hard to assume or specify a basis of moral cohesion in such a society, given what social theory has taught about the diversity, fluidity and contingency of the social. And the wider terrain of the social over which transnational regulation now operates might seem even more obviously culturally diverse, variable, fragmented and indefinite in scope.

Communitarian writings have explored what moral bonds are possible and necessary in complex modern societies but, despite efforts to ground their analyses in the traditions of social theory (Selznick 1992), they tend to be vague about the extent of existing moral consensus in these societies (Bauman 1993: 44–5) and risk lapsing into nostalgia for old forms of social solidarity or moralistic exhortations to recover values. Some alternative approaches have sought a pre-social 'ethics of alterity' as a basis of moral evaluation of the social (Bauman 1989: Chapter 7; 1993: 47–53) and, by extension, a means of morally evaluating contemporary law (for example, Cornell 1992).

A different way forward might be to accept the concept of community as a potentially useful replacement for or supplement to that of (national) society, and to accept the need for solidarity in communities as the moral justification for regulating them. But community would need to be seen as existing in varied forms: in instrumental relationships such as those that provide the basis of commerce; in affective relationships of friendship, love or care; in relations based on shared beliefs or ultimate values; and in traditional relations based on shared environments or historical experiences. On such a view, the social is structured by the fluid, intricate interweaving of different types of community, whether this interweaving constitutes the society of the nation state, or particular groups or patterns of human interaction in this society, or networks of interaction, interests or concerns extending across nation state borders. On this view, law is the regulation and expression of communities.[1]

Old questions about law's bases of authority or legitimacy remain very important as the social seems increasingly 'globalized', unless a view such as Luhmann's is adopted, suggesting that law's successful functioning is all that matters. Even if function is everything, it is still necessary to ask what ultimate conditions can ensure that law's regulatory functions are fulfilled. Habermas (1996: 33) writes that coercive law 'can preserve its socially integrating force only insofar as the addressees of legal norms can understand themselves, taken as a whole, as the rational *authors* of those norms' (emphasis in original). Whatever view is taken of his ideas about communicative rationality, this restatement of an old problem has new urgency as law extends its reach beyond national frontiers, and national law-making is more generally seen as driven by transnational forces.

If democracy, as Habermas claims, can in some conditions provide a sense of popular authorship of law in the political societies of nation states, where is such a sense to be found in the social realms addressed by transnational regulation or by national law subject to transnational pressures? How is Durkheim's democratic deliberation about the social to be achieved transnationally to create regulation that promotes solidarity? Marxist writings have properly emphasized – sometimes in debate with Foucault (Poulantzas 1978: 76–92) – law's sources in organized power and the nature of its coercive and persuasive force (Jessop 1980). But questions about its *moral authority* remain. As the nature of the social changes, sociolegal research is challenged to consider these questions anew, perhaps long before they become dilemmas disrupting law's everyday practice of the method of detail.

---

1   The approach outlined in this paragraph is developed in detail in Chapter 4, below.

Chapter 2

Legal Philosophy and Legal Pluralism

How do legal philosophy and legal sociology relate to each other? What does a sociological perspective add to legal philosophy? This chapter argues that its most significant contribution is to cast new light on questions about the nature and sources of law's authority. It forces us to examine the character of 'the social'; that is, the social settings of law that give it meaning, define its practical jurisdiction and ground its legitimacy. A sociological approach questions lawyers' typical assumptions about the social. It requires that law be seen pluralistically: not just as the unified, systematized law of the nation state, but as produced and interpreted in many competing sites and processes in and beyond the state and often relying on conflicting, unclear or controversial authority claims.

The Question of the Social

How can sociology help to reformulate central issues in theoretical studies of the nature of law? Sociological studies of law contribute to legal theory in ways that ultimately cannot be disentangled from philosophical contributions. Legal philosophy and legal sociology are co-workers in a common enterprise of legal explanation. As Jürgen Habermas (1996: Chapter 2) insists, a philosophy of justice and a sociology of law must complement each other. He might also have added analytical jurisprudence into this intellectual teamwork.

What distinguishes sociological contributions to legal theory from others? Every significant conception of law treats it as in some sense a social phenomenon, acting in and relating to social life. All significant legal theory studies law systematically and, in some sense, empirically. What distinguishes sociological approaches, however, is that they insist that this cannot be done without studying, no less systematically and empirically, the nature of the social. Here, 'the social' means the patterns of human connections and interactions in relation to which law exists and which in some way it expresses and regulates. Law is part of social life. So, a theory of law relates to a theory of the nature of society – in other words, social theory.

Eugen Ehrlich, the best known of the jurists who developed modern sociology of law early in the twentieth century, declared famously that, if a single claim must sum up all of legal sociology, it is that the centre of gravity of legal development lies not in legislation or judicial decisions but in society itself (Ehrlich 1936: xv). A sociological focus is, therefore, not just a focus on law in society, but on how society's nature is expressed in and through law. It means little to say that law is a social phenomenon unless the social is conceptualized. Sociological study of law makes the problem of the social central to the problem of the nature of law.

My object in this chapter is to suggest that the question of the social is complex for legal theory, and central to it, but that it has often been avoided, or considered impressionistically, rather than systematically and empirically. I shall claim that this question relates to others about law's systematic character, authority and sources. So, it raises issues for legal philosophy, no less than for legal sociology. Sociologically oriented analyses of law seek to turn the phrase 'law in society' into sharp questions: What society? And therefore: What law?

More needs to be said, by way of introduction, about the nature of sociological perspectives on law. Some legal sociologists and some legal philosophers have claimed that a sociological view of law is an 'external' view, an outside or non-participant perspective in some sense.[1] But I now think that the formulation is misleading and counterproductive. A sociological perspective in legal theory should recognize that the 'inside-outside' dichotomy in law is a particular construction of certain (powerful and widespread) kinds of legal thought that purport to close law off as a more or less self-contained world of thought and practice distinct from a non-legal environment (Cotterrell 1995: Chapter 5). Thus, the social theorist Niklas Luhmann (1988) describes law as a communication system which envisages and identifies its own environment. It creates its own 'inside' and 'outside'. Law can present the terms – for example, certain criteria of argumentation, interpretation, reasoning and validity – on which its discourse operates. In other words, it purports to control the tickets of entry into its own discursive or normative world.

Legal sociologists observe these operations of law and study the practices that reinforce, result from and depend on them. But – as I argue more fully in Chapter 3, below – legal sociology must ultimately deny or transgress internal–external or observer–participant distinctions. To understand law, the legal sociologist has to understand it as a participant, or as a participant does; or rather, as many different kinds of participants do – lawyers or citizens, for example, living in the world of law (Weber 1968: Chapter 1).[2] Equally, participation blends with observation; there are innumerable, continually shifting forms of involvement and distancing that make up the diversity of legal experience and understanding.

Indeed, legal sociology problematizes what is involved in living in the world of law – because it samples, inhabits, imagines, explores, compares, questions and confronts different participant perspectives. It asks who is treated as an insider (and by whom?), who accepts or rejects the identity of insider (why?; what does this identity entail?). And what exactly is it that one is thought to be inside? If legal officials or lawyers (in the many different fields of professional practice) are insiders, are they all insiders in the same sense or to the same degree? How far is the citizen who values living under the rule of law an insider? Or non-citizens resident in law's

---

1   Black 1989: 20; Carbonnier 1994: 17; Hunt 1987: 12; Cotterrell 1995: 25; Dworkin 1986: 13; cf. Twining 1997: 220; and see, generally, Tamanaha 1997: Chapter 6.

2   For a particularly strong claim of this nature, see Travers 1993.

jurisdiction, or those who cannot or do not as a practical matter exercise the rights of citizens? How many different ways are there of being an insider in a legal system,[3] or in a community of people interpreting – making sense of – law? What kinds of interpretive communities exist? Under what conditions do they exist? (See, for example, Brigham 1996.) To ask these questions is to participate in understanding law and to observe it as a social phenomenon; to observe through participation, and to participate by observing.

As Luhmann notes, internal–external or observer–participant distinctions are a problem for sociologists' practice. If sociologists are observers of society, they must also observe themselves observing society (Luhmann 1997: 29; cf. Habermas 1996: 47). The situation seems absurd, unless like Luhmann one is prepared to accept it as an 'unresolvable indetermination'. Otherwise, rigid observer–participant distinctions seem untenable. What exist are different perspectives, some broader than others, implying different forms and degrees of involvement with an aspect of social life, such as law. These perspectives, arising from different kinds of encounters with law, can be broadened by confrontations, conversations and comparisons between them. Legal sociology is the enterprise of trying to broaden legal perspectives while understanding the narrower perspectives of particular professional or other encounterers of law.

It does not seem possible, then, to distinguish sociological from other views of law on an internal–external basis. But sociological emphasis on the nature of the social urges that legal perspectives must be made sensitive to the social settings in which they exist; hence that they should incorporate reflection on their own conditions of existence in society. Habermas, in his recent work on law, has seen the teamwork he proposes between legal sociology and a philosophy of justice as required by a permanent tension in law between what he calls facticity and validity (1996: 90). Law's facticity is its character as a functioning system, ultimately coercively guaranteed. To understand this facticity is to understand social or political power working through law. Law's validity, however, for Habermas is a matter of its normative character, its nature as a coherent system of meaning, as prescriptive ideas and values. Validity lies ultimately in law's capacity to make claims supported by reason, in a discourse that aims at and depends on agreement between citizens (1996: 14, 29–30). Accepting law in these terms is not just a matter of adapting to conditions of power, but of seeing moral meaning in law.

Habermas' (1996: 29–31) use of the term 'validity' to indicate, amongst other things, the guarantee of law's legitimacy seems initially surprising. Social scientists, and some jurists, often refer to law's *legitimacy* as its moral or reasoned acceptance or acceptability by citizens at large (for example, Weber 1968: 36–8; Hyde 1983; McEwan and Maiman 1986). But lawyers usually refer to law's *validity* – the validity of a legal rule or set of rules – to indicate recognition of law according to familiar lawyers' tests that determine the law in force at any given time (Hart 1994: 99; Raz 1979: 150–1, 153; cf. Habermas 1996: 29). Legal validity in this sense puts

---

3   Cf. Tamanaha 1997: 182, on the variety of participant attitudes towards rules.

to one side large questions of law's legitimacy, and replaces them with professional protocols for identifying the law in force, protocols assumed to be universally accepted (Kelsen 1945: 30). In a sociological analysis, however, lawyers' and legal officials' views of what is authoritative as law represent only one kind of perspective – though perhaps a very important one – in considering the organization of power through law. From other perspectives, legal authority is part of the larger matter of law's acceptability, reasonableness (Raz 1979: Chapter 1) or moral meaningfulness to those it regulates, or claims to regulate (Habermas 1996: 72).[4]

Questions about legal authority might be a focus for cooperation between legal philosophy and legal sociology. Habermas sees particular changes of outlook as needed for this cooperation. He argues that legal philosophy must recognize fundamental changes in the social environment of beliefs and values – the lifeworld – in which contemporary law's claims to authority must ultimately be grounded. Today, 'lifeworld certainties ... are pluralised and ever more differentiated' (1996: 26). Yet it is still necessary to find 'public criteria of the rationality of mutual understanding' (1996: 524). Meanwhile, law's reach grows as it integrates larger 'functionally necessary spheres of strategic interaction ... in modern economic societies' (1996: 26). Hence governmental tasks become ever more complex (1996: 434, 436). The difficulty is that in modern secular societies law's facticity (its existence as a sanctioned governmental force) and its validity (its foundation in 'rationally motivated beliefs') appear to 'have parted company as incompatible' (1996: 26).

For Habermas, any legal philosophy that ignores the complex nature of the social, as social science studies it, will be increasingly irrelevant in addressing the problems of contemporary law. But sociological approaches to law that 'screen out all normative aspects' (1996: 6), treating law 'externally' as an object, will be no less irrelevant, since they do not address questions of law's moral meaning to those who live subject to it and need its authority. What is needed is 'an analysis equally tailored to the normative reconstruction and the empirical disenchantment of the legal system' (1996: 66); one might say to law as ideal and reality.

This broad diagnosis of the conditions legal philosophy and legal sociology must address seems correct. But other claims Habermas makes are more problematic. He asserts that sociology 'seems to devalue law in general as a central category of social theory'. It describes law in language that 'neither seeks nor gains an entry into the intuitive knowledge of [legal] participants' (1996: 48). The main object of attack here is Luhmann's systems theory. But Habermas misrepresents legal sociology in general. Almost all the classical writers who established sociology of law concerned themselves in one way or another with understanding legal thought, legal values and legal reasoning.

---

4   For an instructive example, from a large literature of empirical studies of citizens' attribution of authority to law, see Tyler et al. 1997. See also Tyler 1990.

This is so even for Emile Durkheim, who presents himself as a positivist observer of law,[5] or Max Weber, whose legal sociology is oriented to causal explanation of social action (Kronman 1983: Chapter 2; Turner and Factor 1994: Chapter 6). Ehrlich, and other classical writers such as Leon Petrazycki and Georges Gurvitch, focused their work on the experience of individuals in establishing meaning in their legal relations with others – specifically on the question of what it means to be a participant in law as a field of social experience (Ehrlich 1936; Gurvitch 1935; Petrazycki 1955).[6] In these scholars' work, law is not devalued but seen as a central category of social theory. Perhaps Habermas too readily assumes that legal sociology's concern is to emphasize law's facticity as governmental direction and not also to consider its validity – the conditions of its existence as a structure of reason and principle. His view of legal sociology is rooted in the assumption, earlier criticized, that it 'externally' observes legal behaviour, but does not 'internally' explore legal experience (Habermas 1996: 50–1).

Comparable problems arise with his characterization of legal philosophy. He treats John Rawls' (1999) work as exemplifying philosophies of justice that confront legal sociology. These postulate interpretive practices and procedures by which meaning can be given to an idea of justice expressed in institutions. Habermas criticizes philosophy in this form for failing to take account of the empirical nature of the social, presupposed or postulated in social justice theories (1996: 57). But here he neglects analytical jurisprudence's contributions to legal theory, referring to them only later in discussion. Hence, legal philosophy as a tradition is presented initially, in sharp contrast to legal sociology, as a kind of disembodied exploration of reason in 'the rational project of a just society' and criticized for ignoring 'the disenchantment of law in social science' (1996: 57). Reference to analytical traditions of legal philosophy – as in the work of John Austin, Hans Kelsen and H.L.A. Hart – would, however, emphasize that, just as legal sociology has concerned itself with both facticity and normativity, so has legal philosophy. Analytical jurisprudence has wrestled with questions of system, hierarchy, authority and unity in law and their relation to law's efficacy and coercive power (for example, Raz 1979: Chapter 5; Raz 1980). It has done so in a way parallel to, though obviously differently oriented from, sociological studies of law's functional and coercive organization.

In fact, dichotomies related to Habermas' concepts are familiar in both legal philosophy and legal sociology. Thus, for Lon Fuller (1946), law is both fiat and reason; for Franz Neumann (1986) it is *voluntas* and *ratio* – that is, governmental power or imposed authority, on the one hand, and negotiated understandings based on shared reason and evolved principle, on the other. Analytical jurisprudence has sought to integrate theoretically these aspects of law, just as legal sociology has

---

5   Cf. Durkheim: 'A legal rule is what it is and there are no two ways of perceiving it' (1982: 82).

6   Petrazycki (1955: 14–15) writes: 'A man suffering from absolute legal idiotism – that is to say, complete inability to have legal experiences – could not possibly know what law is or understand the human conduct evoked thereby.'

done. The broad difference between philosophical and sociological approaches to this task is again found in legal sociology's focus on the social. Legal philosophy has often sought explanation in a kind of internal logic of lawyers' legal practice, presupposing or postulating the internal–external distinction referred to earlier; legal sociology has sought to understand both the *voluntas* and *ratio* of law as aspects of the organization of social life (including professional legal and administrative practice) more generally.

Legal Theory and the Nation State

To illustrate this last claim I shall refer to the theme of legal pluralism in modern legal sociology which has existed since its beginnings but has recently developed important new implications. This theme represents only one strand of theoretical concerns in legal sociology but it raises, perhaps in the most radical way, questions about the nature of the social and hence about the nature of law itself as portrayed in legal theory. Significantly, research related to this theme began at the precise moment when Western law had come to mean, almost universally, law of the nation state; that is, law of what Austin called independent political societies (Austin 1832: Lecture 6). Legal sociology attacked the assumption that the nature of the social was unproblematic in legal theory. In particular, it sought to counter the idea that law's jurisdiction and authority were necessarily coextensive with those of the state.

Ehrlich's work is seminal in this research tradition. His theoretical inventiveness, sharp criticism of legal practice and firm commitment to law perhaps make him the Bentham of legal sociology. Writing in the final years of the Austro-Hungarian Empire, as a loyal jurist of a crumbling, anachronistic state, he struggled to alert lawyers to what he saw as threats to law (Ziegert 1979: 227, 231). These arose from a failure to see that what Neumann later called law's *ratio* – its rationality as a system of principle – needs stronger foundations than those provided in the normal fora of interpretation of state law by legal officials whose ultimate authority is guaranteed only by the state's coercive power. For Ehrlich, lawyers as legal interpreters must derive their authority also from knowledge of and sympathy with community experience (Ehrlich 1936: Chapter 15, 476ff.; Ziegert 1979: 245); one might say from a wisdom that state authority alone cannot give. He wanted to make his lawyer-readers see that state law might be relevant only as irritation, not as meaningful regulation, to ethnic and cultural groups holding different beliefs or ideas (for example, about inheritance, binding agreements, property, marriage, or parental rights and obligations) from those presupposed in state law. The theoretical problem is how far law's authority – and, indeed, its meaning – is rooted in commitments arising through particular patterns of association in which individuals live. Law that does not resonate in the experience or consciousness of those it purports to regulate is not law *in society*, hardly law at all.

The result is not a legal vacuum for, Ehrlich insists, everyone lives by law of some kind. Rather, people find law – that is, meaningful social rules enforced by collective sanctions – as these rules are developed and maintained in the groups and social associations in which they live (1936: Chapters 3 and 4). The law of the nation state retreats; its practical jurisdiction is reduced; hence its authority is transformed, changed in character, even perhaps as its bulk increases and its technical sophistication grows. The issue is not one of terminology (which norms should be called law) but of legitimacy (1936: 370–1) or, following Habermas' occasional loosening of terminology, validity.

For lawyers, law's validity might seem unproblematic, controlled by state institutions applying public secondary rules in Hart's (1994: Chapter 6) sense. But this assumes a single form of legal participation; a single criterion of insiders and outsiders; an authority that unifies interpretation. According to Hart (1994: 86–7), it is possible to take an internal view of legal rules as guides to conduct or an external, purely predictive, view of them. An uncommitted interpreter of the rules might occupy an intermediate position (MacCormick 1981: 37–40; Raz 1979: 153–7; and see Tamanaha 1997: 178–83). Ehrlich radically extends such a concept of law, completely relativizing the internal–external distinction. For him, there is no single community of legal interpreters. Rather there are many. Individuals belong simultaneously to several legal communities, or move between them. And such communities form, dissolve and reshape themselves. Thus, the striking result might be reached that, from the standpoint of some legal interpretive communities, lawyers or officials of the kinds Hart mentions (for example, legislators, judges, police, tax inspectors) may be legal 'outsiders' (see Hart 1994: 20, 21, 58, 60–1). They may be fated to hold a merely 'external' view of law – that is, of the authoritative rules that actually govern social interaction.

For Ehrlich, legal internal–external distinctions do not necessarily mark sharp divisions in social life. He sees legal regimes in any society as intersecting, interpenetrating, overlapping. Thus, for him, if state law is to strengthen its authority with social roots it must, in its own practice, engage with (selectively adopt or accommodate to) the experienced normative order or 'living law' of social groups and associations (Ehrlich 1936: Chapter 21). State law's approach must be simultaneously a participation in the living law of communities and social groups and an appropriation of it.

Ehrlich's idea that many groups or associations in a society generate or recognize their own law, alongside that of the state, has been thought shocking or absurd by many jurists since it was first expounded. But it is essential to remember that Ehrlich himself wrote as a jurist, centrally concerned with the role of lawyers and judges in a system of state law (Ziegert 1979: 231). His pluralist view of law must be understood in this context. He asks us to remember that law's authority is not just politically but also morally derived (that is, derived from the moral experience and everyday understandings of those it regulates), and that the relationship between the political and the moral aspects of legal authority is complex, potentially unstable or at least uncertain, and a matter of permanent concern for lawyers. Law can lose authority by being broken, ignored, ridiculed, misunderstood, or merely interpreted in incoherent or inconsistent ways. Issues of authority thus relate closely to interpretative practices.

Interpretation of law takes place in particular sites and settings which provide the taken for granted assumptions to which its organizing principles are referred. Law's meaning may be a matter for negotiation in fora far removed from the courtroom. Who interprets it and where are key issues for the sociological study of law.[7]

Ehrlich did not discuss questions of fragmentation, indeterminacy or conflict of legal authority in the state legal system itself. But they are a necessary complement to his stress on a plurality of sources of legal authority in society. Different agencies of state regulation may interrelate with (and, in a sense, negotiate their practical regulatory authority with) different sectors of society (cf. Teubner 1992: 1448). Thus, the social may differ in nature for different parts of state law.[8] In fact, conflicts or indeterminate lines of authority or control between agencies of the state are familiar phenomena.[9] Sometimes, perhaps often, potential conflicts remain unresolved or even unrecognized: cases are not appealed; state agencies avoid interfering with each other; jurisdictional disputes are not settled; administrative or judicial decisions remain unenforced; inconsistent practices remain undisclosed; doctrinal conflicts or inconsistencies are unresolved. The sociological critique of theories that postulate a unity of legal authority is that, however desirable or even necessary this unity may be, to postulate it theoretically diverts attention from asking how authority is actually negotiated and maintained.

A wide variety of pluralistic conceptions of law is found in the literature of legal sociology and legal anthropology (for example, Griffiths 1986; Galanter 1981; Merry 1988; Fitzpatrick 1984; McLennan 1995: 46–50). The common element in them is their refusal to associate law only with the state as a unified entity. Instead, law is associated with 'plural forms of ordering ... participating in the same social field' (Merry 1988: 873). Law is not a single system but a complex of overlapping systems or regimes of regulation. In a simple pluralist view, the law of the nation state, applied by state courts, and enforced by state police and other agencies, is one (perhaps specially important) kind of law among many.

However, as suggested above, even state law itself might appear from a certain perspective not as a single system but as a complex coalition of jurisdictions and sources of legal authority. Hence the state, no less than the social, appears legally plural, not unitary (Tamanaha 1997: 146–7). Ultimately, a theory of legal pluralism might lead to a position in which any sharp line between state and society, or between the public and the private, becomes problematic (see, for example, Henry 1983). It

---

7 These matters are emphasized, for example, in a large recent literature on 'popular legal consciousness'. See Hunt 1996 for an overview and many references to relevant writings.

8 Cf. Franz Neumann's (1949: lviii) suggestion that the 'constitutional principle of separate powers is ... implemented by the sociological principle of balancing social forces'; in other words, a balanced, stable dispersion of legal authority in the state depends on social diversity itself being maintained in a stable form.

9 For diverse illustrations see, for example, Baldwin 1995: Chapter 6 (and references therein); Barrett and Fudge (eds) 1981; Richardson et al. 1983; Griffith 1993; Rosenberg 1991; Shapiro 1981; Boyum and Mather (eds) 1983.

may be difficult to decide whether certain agencies, tribunals or other institutions are part of the apparatus of the state; from some perspectives they might be, from others not (Abel 1982a; Harrington 1985; Donzelot 1980; Mathiesen 1980: Chapter 6; cf. Spink 1997). A perspective on the social emphasizes the varied jurisdictions of law, and hence law's complex identity.

Pluralist approaches have been fiercely attacked on the ground that they confuse the idea of law (Tamanaha 1993: 193). How is law distinguished in a pluralist view from other normative systems? What makes a social rule system legal? Surely, legal pluralism confers the label 'law' too promiscuously on rule systems or normative orders? (cf. Teubner 1992: 1449–50.) But there is no great problem here if a pluralist conception is understood as a part of the legal sociologist's effort to broaden perspectives on law. A legal sociologist's theoretical specification of law might be different from that presupposed by a lawyer in practice, but it will relate to (indeed, in some way incorporate) the latter, because it must (if it is to reflect legal experience) take account of lawyers' perspectives on law.[10] Thus a pluralist approach in legal theory is likely to recognize what lawyers typically recognize as law, but may see this law as one species of a larger genus, or treat lawyers' conceptions of law as reflecting particular perspectives determined by particular objectives. It may even recognize a plurality among lawyers' conceptions of law, reflecting a variety of professional experiences and perspectives.

Some jurists, such as Fuller (1969: 232) and Karl Llewellyn (1940), have found no difficulty and much value in adopting a pluralistic view of law. They have wished to benefit from a sociological broadening of lawyers' perspectives. Conversely, some legal sociologists and anthropologists apply pluralist criteria of law that are closely comparable with Hart's criteria of 'the legal' as marked by the adoption of secondary rules (Bohannan 1967; Galanter 1981: 19).[11] According to Hart's *Concept of Law* (1994: Chapters 5 and 6), for a legal system to exist there must be general obedience to primary rules, but also a set of secondary rules used by officials to determine what is to count as a valid legal rule and to govern interpretion and change of rules. Nothing in Hart's book seems to indicate that 'officials' for this purpose must be state officials: certainly the judges of an international tribunal and perhaps the priests of a religious group, the elders of a cultural or ethnic group, the committee of an association, or the directors of a corporation could qualify. Each of these kinds of group or association could thus have a kind of law of its own according to its members' concept of law.

Hart's theory, does not, therefore, explicitly identify law with the law of the nation state.[12] The difficulty in reconciling a pluralistic conception of law with his theory is rather that, like all positivist approaches, Hart's cannot easily accept the

---

10 Except, of course, in societies where such perspectives are irrelevant because professional guardians of law do not exist.

11 On Hart's work in relation to sociology of law generally, see Colvin 1978.

12 Raz (1979: 98) describes Hart as having 'overlooked' the question of the relationship between law and state.

idea of law as a complex of overlapping, interpenetrating or intersecting normative systems or regimes, amongst which relations of authority are unstable, unclear, contested or in course of negotiation. Legal pluralism stresses diversity or even conflict of sources of legal authority. Understandably, from the lawyer's standpoint this emphasis is likely to suggest incoherence. A clear hierarchy of legal authority with some ultimate test of what is to count as law in a system is needed to solve practical problems of validity (Hart 1968; Raz 1979: 116–20).[13] Conversely, from a pluralist point of view, the lawyer's insistence on a unifying systemic source of validity may mask the real processes by which authority is constituted in law – processes which involve competition, struggle or negotiation over legal authority between a variety of rule-makers, interpreters and agencies of enforcement. From this viewpoint, law's authority is not a datum but a problem to be solved, presenting itself continually in new forms.

Pluralism in Legal Thought

If, as argued earlier, lawyers' and sociologists' perspectives on law interrelate, the lawyer's task of making sense of law might be aided by a pluralist view. Indeed, Ehrlich, whose career was spent teaching law students, continually made this claim. Harry Arthurs' (1985) detailed study of relations between state law and certain kinds of 'unofficial' law in England in the nineteenth century is a notable affirmation of it by an administrative lawyer. Arthurs' purpose is to find out why and with what consequences various regimes of communal dispute resolution or administration (such as local courts and tribunals of commerce) were incorporated into or abolished by the state legal system in England during the nineteenth century. By this means he seeks to solve problems about the shape and outlook of modern administrative law. His inquiry forces him to discard the internal–external viewpoint typical of legal thought and to look at the social from a variety of perspectives as a source of law. Thus law is presented in his account as an intersection of different ideas, practices and regimes of regulation and as a negotiated pattern of relations between these.

Often, indeed, what Arthurs shows is a struggle between jurisdictions (for example, of local and state court systems) or agencies (for example, state courts and arbitration systems of commercial communities). In such situations the instability of relations and expectations is only removed by the victory of one normative system over another, a division of labour, an accommodation, or a stand-off in which the state claims jurisdiction but in practice is powerless to assert it effectively (as in relation to a wide variety of forms of commercial arbitration). Law appears in this perspective not as a unified system subject to a hierarchy of legal authority determining validity, but as many normative systems and structures, each claiming legitimacy in different ways, and coexisting in a complex, shifting relationship, sometimes of cooperation

---

13 Yet, as Neil MacCormick (1993) has shown, Hart's concept of a rule of recognition can be interpreted to recognize a shifting relationship between UK law and European Union law.

but often of rivalry and mutual suspicion. There is no single relationship between law and society, but rather a diversity of relationships between law and communities, in which it becomes meaningful to see different communities (however defined) struggling to defend and promote their own law or legal expectations and conceptions. Yet these communities are also in flux: interrelating, reforming and changing.

Arthurs' project is a rare use by a lawyer of pluralist perspectives on modern English law. But there have been much earlier attempts to bring pluralist perspectives into mainstream English legal thought. At the beginning of the twentieth century F.W. Maitland's presentation in English of the work of the German legal historian Otto Gierke (1900) offered a historical vision of law founding its authority in community structures, rather than centralized sovereign power. English political pluralism, a movement of thought prominent until the late 1920s, fiercely attacked John Austin's theory of sovereignty and asserted that churches and associations of many different kinds must be recognized as having a legal identity not conferred by Crown or state but inherent in their independent life as communities (Nicholls 1994; Hirst (ed.) 1989). The legal context of these debates – especially the character of trade unions and the autonomy of churches in matters of doctrine and internal organization – is now historical. Political pluralism, as its name suggests, primarily addressed political rather than legal theory. Though Austin's theory was a frequent target of pluralists such as Harold Laski and John Figgis, legal and other forms of sovereignty were often confused in their discussion.

Political pluralism found moral and political significance, however, in two particular issues of legal theory. The first was the question of whether corporate personality was conferred at the will of Crown or state or independently derived from the nature of certain kinds of group existence that created entitlement to legal recognition; the second was the nature of group rights and duties (Webb (ed.) 1958). Figgis declared that the state is a community of communities, controlling and limiting by law the activities of associations 'within the bounds of justice' and adopting criteria of recognition of them, 'proper proofs that ... [corporate life] is being formed and supplied with duly constituted organs of its unity' (Figgis 1914: 80, 103, 251). State law, he claimed, must prevent bodies of persons acting secretly outside government control to the prejudice of others; and it must regulate property and contract (1914: 103–4). What was implied was the need for a new legal theory of the state as *communitas communitatum* to replace the Austinian conception of sovereign and subject. For other writers, such as Laski (1921), a main need was decentralization of governmental power, though he gave few hints as to a legal framework for this.

English pluralism had little long-term impact on legal thought because it often provided only formalistic criticisms of established legal theory (as with the corporate personality issue) and unspecific prescriptions for new legal thinking. However, central problems it raised have not disappeared but merely assumed new forms. In place of Figgis' concern for the rights of churches and associations is a contemporary concern to reflect new demands of multiculturalism effectively in legal and political thought (for example, Kymlicka 1995; Kymlicka (ed.) 1995).[14] Some of these demands are for a pluralism that enjoins respect for different ways of life expressed partly through distinct rights and duties. Questions about the nature of group rights (and duties) and of rights in groups (and duties towards them) remain closely associated with these matters. Again, in place of Laski's demands for administrative decentralization are issues about devolution, regionalism, federalism and subsidiarity in a range of contexts. And in place of efforts to explain corporate personality as arising from autonomous sources outside state authority are questions about the plural nature of sources of contemporary law – in regard to parliamentary sovereignty, European law and international law. Often the theoretical issues remain as inchoate as they were in the writings of the English pluralists. Yet problems about legal system and unity and, above all, about sources of legal authority, not only in the centralized structures of the nation state but also in communities or associations within or beyond it, are evident.

Insofar as the English political pluralists engaged with established legal thought it can be said that they were trying to change its view of the social.[15] Austinian legal thought implied a view of the social as consisting of a sovereign power and individual legal subjects, united only in their allegiance to sovereign power – an image of *imperium* (Cotterrell 1995: 223, 225–7). Such a view recognized collectivities – but only as legal subjects of the sovereign, with the sovereign treating them by concession or fiction as persons (Hallis 1930: Chapter 1). Recognition of corporate personality in state law is not, in itself, a recognition of the diversity and plurality of group experience. Rather than treating groups as communities of social interaction (Hartney 1995: 214–15), it treats them as individual (corporate) actors in the state's own regulated society.

An alternative legal image of the regulated population, however, would indeed be that of an active community, united by shared beliefs or commitments and making its own law collectively (Cotterrell 1995: 223–5, 228–9, 230–2). A legal image of the national society as such a community is represented to some extent in classical common law thought, expressed by seventeenth-century writers such as Matthew Hale and Edward Coke (Postema 1986: 19, 23, 66–76). One can see some such image of community as the source of law reflected in pluralist writings. For example, Maitland's promotion of Gierke's work was, in part, the recovery of old Germanic ideas of law which portrayed it as something produced in communal life. And Gierke's ideas offered parallels with a romanticized, de-politicized view of the communal nature of English common law. It is significant, in this context, that Ehrlich was a profound admirer of what he took to be English common law

---

14 For a range of specific legal issues in Britain see Poulter 1986; 1987; 1989; 1991; 1997; Bradney 1993; Freeman 1995; Cooper 1996; Pearl 1997.

15 On images of the social that are routinely assumed in legal thought, see also Cotterrell 1995: Chapter 11.

methods,[16] emphasizing the role of the common law judge as spokesperson for and expounder of the community's legal principles.[17] But these legal images of community are not empirical portrayals of the complexity of the social. They do not derive from sociological study of the nature and varieties of group life.

Community and Contemporary Law

Themes of community appear differently in current legal discussion. But, in a host of ways, they are important in it. Sociologically oriented analyses emphasize the variety of groups and their diverse legal expectations, and the sometimes difficult conditions of their coexistence in what Figgis long ago called the 'hurly burly of competing opinions and strange moralities' (1914: 120). 'All over the world,' writes Iris Marion Young (1995: 174), 'group-based claims to special rights, to cultural justice and the importance of recognising publicly different group experiences and perspectives have exploded, often with violence.' In such circumstances, law's responsibility, it seems, is to prevent explosions and to defuse the threat of violence by creating security in diversity. If the US is experiencing an 'ethnic revival' (Kymlicka 1995: 61ff.), Europe is, from one viewpoint, 'a community of cultures' (Hugh Seton-Watson quoted in Davies 1996: 14). In fact, the diversity of group demands on law is universal. 'National and ethnic pluralism has been the rule, not the exception' throughout history (Walzer 1995: 139–40).

Law's image of *imperium* – focused on the modern nation state and its law, and on individual subjects of law – has not altered the fact that distinct groups constitute an important part of the social for the purposes of legal regulation (Stoljar 1973; Honoré 1987: Chapters 1 and 2). Joseph Raz asserts the need for a value pluralism that is more than toleration and non-discrimination. It involves recognition of the equal standing of all stable and viable cultural communities existing in a society, and the importance of 'unimpeded membership in a respected and prosperous cultural group' for individual well-being (Raz: 1994: 178). The theme is also familiar in communitarian political philosophy.[18]

Andrew Bainham, partly developing Raz's ideas, has argued that the law of the nation state must be sensitive to cultural diversity while recognizing the oppressive nature of some cultural values and the need to facilitate individuals' ability to escape from membership of an unwanted culture (Bainham 1995: 239). He notes that in

---

16 See generally Ehrlich 1936: Chapter 12. He notes the 'obvious ... superiority of the English method of finding law' but also the excessive centralization and the rigidities of the English precedent system; thus, the juristic science of continental European common law should be, he suggests, the starting point for legal sociology's future development (1936: 295, 480). See also Ziegert 1979: 232.

17 Ehrlich 1936: 292 (noting 'the glorious freedom of action which the English judge enjoys').

18 See also John Finnis' (1980: Chapter 6) important discussion of the concept of community.

various ways, current English family and child law does recognize cultural diversity (1995: 240) and he suggests that difficult balances need to be struck in state law between accepting this diversity in matters of the care and upbringing of children and ensuring minimum standards of upbringing for all children. Thus, state law must negotiate a position between, on the one hand, accepting the validity of regulation inspired by the diversity of group life and, on the other, protecting the rights of individuals irrespective of any memberships they may have in groups other than the political society of the nation state. The issues are far-reaching: for Bainham, the nuclear family centred on marriage should not be seen legally as an ideal in relation to which every other kind of family represents a kind of deviance (1995: 244). In a host of ways, questions of legal recognition of the diversity of group life and expectations present themselves.

Issues such as the above, which merely restate some of Ehrlich's concerns in new contexts, reflect one aspect of contemporary legal concern with the nature of the social. The early tradition of legal sociology and its modern successors have sought to confront assumptions of the systemic unity, dominance and authority of the law of the nation state (cf. Raz 1979: 116–20) with challenges to this reflecting legal expectations of diverse groups or organizations within nation state boundaries. Now, challenges come at least as strongly from transnational and international legal demands and practices. What is the social – the complex of social ties and interactions – to which international human rights law, or international trade law or international financial law relates? And how is Europe to be conceived as the social field in which contemporary European law is developing? What are the sources of its unifying legal traditions? (See, for example, Van Hoecke and Ost 1997.) In these contexts, questions of membership, association and participation in a legal order take on new forms, if a community is thought of as in some sense making, or inspiring, its own law (Ward 1996). Conversely, if the image of the social remains that of *imperium*, questions present themselves as to how law's hierarchy of authority is to be understood, including the relationship between national and transnational legal authorities and law-creating agencies and their jurisdictions.

It is unsurprising, therefore, that efforts have been made to harness the concept of legal pluralism in the analysis of emerging structures of a new European legal order (Arnaud 1995). Equally, some of the most important work in contemporary legal sociology is research on transnational forms of legal practice – especially in commercial matters – and their sometimes ambiguous, conflictual and complex relations with established national legal jurisdictions (see especially Dezalay and Garth 1996). Transnational communities of interest, in commercial and other contexts, rely on state law, but also shape and avoid it, or set legal traditions against each other, in new contexts that merely extend the kinds of struggles over authority and jurisdiction that, for example, Arthurs' study of English legal pluralism showed. Perhaps the most important contemporary projects for legal theory – which should engage the efforts of legal philosophers no less than legal sociologists – are to develop theories of both *legal transnationalism* in its various, often contradictory, contemporary forms and *legal localization* – the demand for forms of regulation that are morally meaningful to the regulated because rooted in local conditions of existence.

As regards the latter, it is important today not to understand the term 'local' solely or even mainly in geographical terms. Boaventura De Sousa Santos (2002: 177) has written of the foci of contemporary aspirations for law as being divided between *rights to roots* and *rights to options*. Thus, some important demands are for law that gives 'roots' – moral security, or a sense of belonging in contexts that are personally significant. These are, less and less, contexts rooted in specific geographical localities. They are diverse and abstract: contexts of meaning rooted in communities best conceptualized as webs of understanding about the nature of social relations. Community, as Anthony Cohen has argued, provides people with a means of orienting themselves. It gives them their sense of identity (Cohen 1985; and see Hunt 1996: 183). Hence community can be a matter of shared beliefs or values, but also of common projects or aims, or common traditions, history or language, or of shared or convergent emotional attachments. For individuals it is all or any of these in intricate, shifting combinations. As I argue more fully in Chapter 4, below, the nature of law's authority and responsibility as a support of community – a framework and expression for it – should be understood in relation to these different kinds of community.

The concept of community, if it is to be meaningful in contemporary conditions, is thus complex. It has nothing in common with the old pre-modern imagery of *Gemeinschaft* (Tönnies 1955), suggesting static, enclosed and exclusive communities. Relations of community today are relations with a multitude of diverse, shifting, open and flexible forms of association and commitment; not with closed or repressive communities or those that deny the fundamental values of individual respect and dignity that transnational human rights law increasingly seeks to assert or reflect.[19] Perhaps, most obviously, this is because, as Santos argues, the demand for rights to roots goes along with the demand for rights to options – that is, demands of individuals for guaranteed freedoms to operate as legal actors without arbitrarily fixed and non-negotiable boundaries of duty, entitlement, allegiance, exclusion or participation, whether established by repressive communities within the nation state, or by state law itself.

Sociological perspectives on legal theory are specially important insofar as they highlight the complexity of the social as law's jurisdictional environment and as the

---

19 Interestingly, Ehrlich (1936: 81–2) claims that such universal rights are a kind of emergent living law, reflecting a slowly developing idea of 'the whole human race' as a community or 'a vast legal association'. But it might be more realistic to say that they reflect (at least potentially) the need for a uniform minimum guarantee to individuals of their security and their participation in (including freedom to exit from and freedom from being forcibly included in) associational life. Such a guarantee is an indispensable complement to recognition of and general respect for a wide range of communal diversity and group autonomy in regulatory matters. Equally important for stable regulation is the requirement that this recognition and respect be reciprocal; benefiting from it carries a corresponding duty of active recognition and respect for other ways of group life.

source of its ultimate authority and meaning for those it regulates. These perspectives present legal theory with a dilemma: how to reconcile in legal thought the demands of the universal and the particular, the global and the local, the consequences of a wide range of both transnational and intranational forces shaping law. Behind this dilemma is a deeper one: how to redefine the relationship between the political and moral bases of law's authority in an era when a nation state of individual subjects of a legal sovereign appears less and less the typical, or adequate, locus of the social for law. The most pressing task for cooperation between legal philosophy and legal sociology is to develop theory appropriate to these conditions.

Chapter 3

Why Must Legal Ideas be Interpreted Sociologically?

Can we go beyond arguments (as in the previous chapter) for cooperation between legal philosophy and legal sociology? Can sociolegal inquiries reshape lawyers' interpretation of law? Can sociology explain legal ideas or clarify questions about legal doctrine? The argument that law has its own 'truth' – its own way of seeing the world – has been used to deny that sociological perspectives have any special claim to provide understanding of law as doctrine. This chapter asks what a sociological understanding of legal ideas involves. It argues that such an understanding is not only useful but *necessary* for legal studies. Legal scholarship requires sociological understanding of law. The two are inseparable.

A Myth about Sociology of Law

A modern myth about sociological study of law survived until recently, encouraged from within legal philosophy and by some legal sociologists themselves. According to this myth an inevitable division of labour governed legal inquiry. Lawyers and jurists analysed law as doctrine – norms, rules, principles, concepts and the modes of their interpretation and validation. Sociologists, however, were concerned with a fundamentally different study: that of behaviour, its causes and consequences. On this view, the legal sociologist's task was solely to examine behaviour in legal contexts.[1] Sociology could contribute little to the understanding of legal ideas, abstracted from their effects on specific actions. Thus, sociology of law conducted inquiries peripheral or even *external* to law as lawyers understood it. Legal sociologists often avoided lawyers' disputes or theories about the nature of doctrine as such.[2] They studied mainly practices of dispute processing, administrative regulation or law enforcement, or social forces operating on legislation, especially as a result of the actions of particular law-making or policy-advocating groups.

---

1   See, for example, Black 1976, treating legal sociology as the study of governmental social control. Correspondingly, Hans Kelsen (1992: 13) wrote of sociology's role as that of inquiring 'into the causes and effects of those natural events that ... are represented as legal acts'. In his final work (1991: 301), he asserted that such a legal sociology 'does not describe the law, but rather law-creating behaviour and law-observing or law-violating behaviour'.

2   Vilhelm Aubert's work provides a significant exception: see, for example, Aubert 1963; Campbell 1974.

The briefest glance at the work of the classic founders of sociology of law makes clear that this division of labour was in no way inevitable. While Weber saw sociology's object as the study of social action, he treated the nature of legal ideas and the variety of types of legal reasoning as central to his sociological concern with law (Weber 1968: Part 2 Chapter 8). Durkheim intended that the enterprise of understanding law as doctrine should itself become a field of sociology, so that lawyers' questions would eventually be reformulated through sociological insight (Durkheim 1982: 260; 1975b: 244). Ehrlich (1936) thought that the lawyer's understanding of law would be simultaneously subverted and set on surer foundations through sociological inquiry into popular understandings of legal ideas. Petrazycki (1955) considered that law should be studied as various forms of consciousness and understanding. Equally, many contributions to legal philosophy, including modern realist jurisprudence in Scandinavia, the US and elsewhere, showed that jurists had serious concerns with behaviour in legal contexts in their efforts to grasp the nature of legal ideas.

To remove a focus on legal doctrine from sociological inquiry would prevent legal sociology from integrating, rather than merely juxtaposing, its studies with other kinds of legal analysis. Without this focus, sociological observation of behaviour might influence policy expressed in legal doctrine. But this would amount not to a sociology of law but to a diversity of sociological information presented to legal policy-makers.[3] The old claim that social science should be 'on tap rather than on top' in legal inquiries reflected the idea that sociology and other social sciences were debarred from offering insight into the *meaning* of law (as doctrine, interpretation, reasoning and argument). Hence, insofar as proponents of legal sociology accepted the myth of an inevitable division of labour, they were tempted to argue defensively that lawyers' debates on doctrine were trivial or mystificatory, and that real knowledge about law as a social phenomenon was gained only by observing patterns of judicial, administrative or policing activity, lawyers' work and organization, or citizens' disputing behaviour. Correspondingly, opponents of legal sociology hastened to dismiss it as unable to speak about *law* at all, fated to remain for ever 'external' and thus irrelevant to legal understanding.

The assumption that there could be no serious rapprochement between legal and sociological views of law often depended on each side in the dispute characterizing the other in excessively positivistic terms (Nelken 1994: 107). Jurists often ignored scholarship expressing well established sociological positions: for example, that action is to be understood in terms of its subjective meaning for those engaged in it; that social life is structured by symbols, or constituted as forms of collective

---

3   Nothing in this chapter should be taken as denying the worth of sociological studies of behaviour in legal contexts. In my view, these kinds of studies have produced insights of the greatest significance and should continue to occupy a central place in social inquiries about law. The argument here is, however, that the sociological interpretation of legal ideas should have a central place in legal studies generally, and that it is important for sociolegal scholarship and for legal scholarship in general that this place should be claimed.

understanding; that social order is explicable in terms of social rules continuously created and recreated in human interaction; or that society may be understood as a system of communication (see, for example, Luhmann 1989). Similarly, social science sometimes treated lawyers' legal understanding as entirely positivistic. Law for the lawyer was often seen by sociologists as a kind of datum (rules or regulations). Social processes central to lawyers' experience – interpretation, argument, negotiation, presentation, influence, decision-making and rule-formulating – were often underemphasized in characterizing the lawyer's outlook on the nature of law as doctrine.

Is Sociology's 'Truth' Powerless?

Criticisms of legal sociology's capacity to understand legal ideas have become more sophisticated, though they have not changed their fundamental character. It is now widely accepted that sociological inquiry is valuable and necessary to illuminate the social or historical processes that shape legal doctrine. Hans Kelsen, for example, moved from a position largely dismissive of sociology's relevance in the study of legal ideas (Kelsen 1992: 13–14, originally published 1934) to recognize an important role for legal sociology in explaining the causes and consequences of ideological phenomena reflected in law, and especially the idea of justice (Kelsen 1941: 270; 1945: 174). Evidently, legal ideas can be understood as the outcome of historical, cultural, political or professional conditions which sociological studies are able to describe and explain.

The most powerful current critique of legal sociology – the one I want to examine and respond to here – does not deny that sociological inquiry can, in its own ways, explain aspects of legal doctrine. It argues rather that sociology has *no privileged way of approaching legal ideas* – no specially powerful insight which can prevail over others. Because of this it has no way of plausibly claiming that its interpretations are better than those that lawyers themselves can give. It therefore becomes an open question why a sociological view should be adopted in preference to any other. In other words, the claim is no longer that law cannot be understood in sociological terms. It is: Why should we want to do so? What is to be gained by doing so, especially for lawyers, or other participants (for example, litigants or lay citizens) in legal processes?

These questions are sharpened with additional claims. It is sometimes suggested that sociology is a very weak and inadequate explanatory discourse. For example, it is claimed to have 'an intriguing inability to constitute its field of study' (Fitzpatrick 1995: 107). So, the concept of the social remains 'remarkably unexamined' in sociolegal studies and, it is said, no longer provides a focus for them (Fitzpatrick 1995: 106). On the other hand, law is now seen by those sceptical of sociology's interpretive capacities as having an intellectual power and resilience which protects it from social science's earlier 'imperial confidence' that it could know law better than law knew itself (Nelken 1996: 108–9).

In a rich discussion of relationships between law and scientific (including social science) disciplines, David Nelken (1994) has claimed that the efforts of these disciplines to tell 'the truth about law' are now confronted with law's own truth. What he means is that law has its own ways of interpreting the world. Law as a discourse determines, in the terms of that discourse, what is to count as truth – correct understanding or appropriate and reliable knowledge – for specifically legal purposes. It resists scientific efforts to interpret it away (for example, in economic cost–benefit terms, psychological terms of causes and consequences of mental states, or sociological terms of conditioning social forces). None of these interpretations, it is claimed, grasps law's own criteria of significance.

When law borrows from scientific disciplines or practices it appears to do so as it sees fit, taking what it deems useful, on its own conditions for its own purposes (Nelken 1994: 101–2). Concepts borrowed are often transformed, turned into 'hybrid artifacts', tailored to legal use (Teubner 1989: 747). And law goes on the offensive. It provides its own explanations of the social world. It interprets social life in its own terms.[4] Law is said to provide truth for itself, for its purposes, which cannot be swept away by sociology, and with which sociology's interpretations are fated merely to coexist. Because of this, sociology cannot reshape legal understanding. It provides at best a resource of ideas from which law may borrow if it finds reasons to do so. In a different sense from before, social science is again 'on tap', but not 'on top'.

From the standpoint of sociology the problem is not merely that its insights can be made to seem irrelevant to legal understanding. It is not just the unpleasantness of rejection that dominates this scenario, but also the frustration of attempting the impossible. The argument goes as follows. As sociology tries to understand law, law disappears, like a mirage, the closer the approach to it. This is because as sociology interprets law, law is reduced to sociological terms. It becomes something different from what it (legally) is; or rather, from what, in legal thought, law sees itself as being. How can legal ideas be understood sociologically without, in the process, being turned into sociological ideas? (Nelken 1996: 112).[5] The 'legal point of view', as Robert Samek (1974) called it in a neglected discussion of related themes, disappears, subsumed into a sociological viewpoint and lost. It cannot be grasped sociologically because it is *not* sociological. It is a specifically *legal* point of view.

Legal sociology's potential is also challenged from another standpoint. For more than a decade, concern among progressive legal scholars has been less and less with how law is produced by society (the traditional outlook of legal sociology)

---

4   Jan Broekman (1989: 323) makes the claim forcefully: '... those elements of social reality which are under the grip of legal thinking are *structurally altered*. Transformations have occurred. This simply means that the one reality is not the other. Legal provisions form a unique whole of its own kind which is a special category of human experience. One cannot understand a contract or a delict unless one recognises one's being as *de iure*'.

5   For example, legal explanations of criminal conduct are in terms of responsibility. When the matter is considered sociologically in terms of causation of patterns of criminal activity through social or economic conditions, legal questions of responsibility may sometimes be partly or even wholly displaced.

and increasingly with the way 'society' is produced by law (Nelken 1986: 325). Not only can law stand alone from sociology with its own basis of understanding, taking or leaving social scientific insights as it sees fit, but it is said to be able also to create the central objects of inquiry – the very ontological basis – of sociology itself. According to some influential scholars, law has no need, and no possibility, of doing more than creating its own normative understanding of its social environment (Luhmann 1988). But in a more radical view law is also seen as responsible, partly at least, for creating the social categories with which sociology itself must work.

For example, the problematic idea of 'society' is said to be actually established by law's methods of determining social inclusion and exclusion. Peter Fitzpatrick (1995: 106) argues that law makes society possible, 'thus reversing the foundational claims of the sociology of law'. His assertion refers mainly to law's role in providing an identity and boundaries for the entity thought of as political society. But, more generally, law can be considered to express or structure the experiences that make up the essential texture of social life. Far from law being coloured by the social context that sociology brought into legal study, context is 'assumed and reproduced in law as a bearer of traditions, or of ideological constructions, or forms of discourse' (Nelken 1986: 325). Thus, law, to a significant extent, actually constitutes social reality.

For these reasons a sharp line between the legal and the social can no longer be drawn and a 'more holistic understanding' is required (Nelken 1986: 325, 338). Legal ideas are a kind of social knowledge in themselves. The often neglected point that legal speculation once provided prototypes for early forms of social theory (Kelley 1990; Murphy 1991; Turner and Factor 1994) acquires a new significance.

Certainly, some legal sociologists continue to ask for evidence of law's ideological effects and to nurse doubts about law's capacity to influence social consciousness (Friedman 1997: 37–9).[6] The demands and doubts are unsurprising given that the postulated direction of influence *from* legal ideas as shaping forces in social life fits uneasily with legal sociology's traditional assumption that society shapes law, and that effects of law on society are always specific matters for empirical study. But newer approaches to the relationship between the legal and the social refuse to see law and society as somehow separate or even competing spheres of influence. They more often treat as self-evident that law constitutes social life to a significant degree by influencing the meanings of basic categories (such as property, ownership, contract, trust, responsibility, guilt and personality) that colour or define social relations. Hence, when the nature of sociolegal studies is considered it is said to be no longer clear (and perhaps never was) whether the enterprise is legal, social or a

---

6   Friedman (1997: 37) criticizes my discussion in what now appears as Chapter 5, below, for specifying the content of 'legal ideology in general', in other words, for essentializing legal ideology as something with a determinate, constant character in all times and places. But I have tried only to indicate some particular ideological elements in contemporary Western law: see generally Cotterrell 1995. There is no constant content of 'legal ideology in general'. Legal ideology may vary greatly from one environment to another. Neither does it necessarily form any kind of unity in relation to a particular legal system or society.

mixture of the two (Fitzpatrick 1995: 105). The field remains undefined: conceptual clarity seems sacrificed to a need to avoid deep controversies about the foundations of social scientific inquiries about law (cf. Nelken 1996: 108).

What then should be made of the effort to understand legal ideas (legal doctrine and the reasoning and forms of interpretation that surround it) sociologically? My argument is that the main problems that are said to undermine this effort are in fact, despite their apparent seriousness, solvable or ultimately false. They do not stand in its way. But they do very properly demand that the nature, aims and methods of sociological inquiry be clarified. Nevertheless, the claim to be made here is not merely that the effort to understand legal ideas sociologically is appropriate. My claim is that the *only* way to grasp these ideas imaginatively as ideas about the organization of the social world is through some form of sociological interpretation.

In the rest of this chapter I shall address the issues raised above by analysing the two main apparent sources of difficulty to which these issues relate. The first of these is the nature of law's own 'truth' – its capacity to interpret the world in its own way. What is this truth which, it is suggested, law produces or inhabits? What is to be made of the claim that law knows itself better than sociology can know it? Can we, indeed, speak of law 'knowing' or 'thinking' anything? (Cf. Teubner 1989.) The second source of difficulty is the need to clarify what is meant by the effort to gain sociological understanding. What kind of understanding is envisaged here? What is sociology's 'truth', or in Nelken's phrase, what kind of 'truth about law' can sociology offer? Does this, for example, imply a need to subsume law as a discipline under the hegemony of another academic discipline, such as sociology?

I argue that no such implication is required. Indeed, it would entirely miss the point. Disciplinary boundaries should be viewed pragmatically, with healthy suspicion. They should not be prisons of understanding. The term 'sociological' is necessary to keep firmly in mind certain definite foci in interpreting law, but these foci and their authoritative definition are not the property of any particular academic discipline. Participants in law – not just lawyers but all those who seek to use legal ideas for their own purposes, to promote or control the interests of others, or more generally for public purposes of direction or control – understand legal ideas in practical terms. The aim in what follows is to show that the most practical view of legal ideas is one informed by sociological insight. Legal ideas are properly understood sociologically.

Does Law have its Own Way of Seeing the World?

In an American context Jack Balkin (1996) has tried to explain law's resilience when faced with the interpretive claims of other disciplines. He argues, echoing earlier writers (such as Posner 1987), that law is inherently weak as an academic field. It is highly susceptible to invasion by other disciplines. Although sociology is one such invader, the disciplines that, in the US, have recently been most successful in invading law have been economics, history, philosophy, political theory and literary theory (Balkin 1996: 965). Balkin claims that law is so easily invaded because it 'is less an academic discipline than a professional discipline. It is a skills-oriented profession, and legal education is a form of professional education' (1996: 964). Law does not have a 'methodology of its own' (1996: 966). It borrows methodologies from any discipline that can supply them. On the other hand, because law is researched and taught in settings that are never far from the professional demands of legal practice, it cannot be entirely absorbed by any other discipline. Its professional focus compensates for the lack of a purely intellectual one.

Thus, even economic analysis of law, by far the most successful recent intellectual invader of the American law school, cannot completely colonize law because its disciplinary direction ultimately diverges from law's professional orientation. There simply is no place in the vocationally organized environment of academic law for the reproduction of the sophisticated research skills and statistical methods that the research culture of advanced economics requires. So, the law school takes what it needs from economics, or any other discipline, simplifying and packaging the insights or methods on offer and presenting them for law's own purposes. Law is continuously invaded but, Balkin asserts, cannot be conquered.

This is an essentially sociological account of law's disciplinary resilience, in terms of the organization of legal education, professional training and the recruitment and socialization of law professors. Consequently, the account is susceptible to sociological rebuttal. Balkin does not explain any reasons inherent in the nature of legal ideas or understanding as to why law cannot be conquered by social science. The factors are merely organizational. The law school environment and the legal profession provide this resistance. He offers no argument as to why these organizational factors must continue to operate. Indeed, law is portrayed as so weak as a discourse that it invites continuous change in the way it is taught, learned and understood. Balkin gives no reason why American law schools should not ultimately turn into graduate schools in applied economics – and it can be recalled that Harold Lasswell and Myres McDougal once seriously advocated turning them into advanced schools of policy science (Lasswell and McDougal 1943). If law has no special characteristics as a discourse, method or body of knowledge, it is unclear why law schools *must* continue to take their current form. Balkin's argument does not explain law's resilience.

In making the claim that law is 'not, strictly speaking, an academic subject' (1996: 966), Balkin means it lacks a methodology of its own. But, in fact, law in contemporary Western societies does embody quite specific methods of intellectual practice: for example, methods of presenting a case in court, drafting a brief, marshalling evidence, citing and reasoning with precedents. A stronger claim for law's weakness would be that it lacks any of the usual intellectual marks of disciplinarity: controlling master theories, distinctive methods of intellectual debate, established paradigms of research practice, familiar epistemological and ontological positions or controversies (Cotterrell 1995: Chapter 3). But it might be said that law has *some* important indicators of its own intellectual outlook or orientation. For its purposes they provide coherence for its practices. These indicators give it a way of interpreting the world, at least the world as it exists in relation to law's purposes.

The strongest current arguments for law's capacity to declare sociological understanding of legal ideas irrelevant are arguments emphasizing these kinds of indicators. In one way or another, these indicators make possible what Nelken terms 'law's truth'. When attempts are made to specify the indicators, however, they seem remarkably limited. They may amount to no more than a consistent focus in any context on marking a distinction between the 'legal' and the 'illegal', right and wrong in terms of specifically legal definitions (Luhmann 1992b). Otherwise, law might be said to be distinctively concerned with institutional rather than brute facts, and with considerations of authority, integrity, fairness, justice, acceptability and practicability. It has to use 'arbitrary cut-off points' in argument, and often chooses not to look behind its presumptions. It seeks to provide certainty and to relate to common sense. It may adopt or reject scientific (including social scientific) knowledge or reasoning in order to pursue these objectives. It gathers and presents facts in ways tailored to adjudicative needs (see generally Nelken 1994: 99–100). It uses practical reasoning and argumentation that may be more or less specific to its governmental, dispute processing or social control tasks. But any enumeration of characteristics of law's truth will miss the point for 'what truth means for law is the result of its own processes' (Nelken 1994: 103). 'Ultimately,' as Arthur Leff puts it, 'law is not something we know but something that we do' (quoted in Nelken 1994: 99). It is not grasped by description from 'outside' but by working and thinking within it.

But does this argument really go much further than Balkin's more directly stated point that law's social conditions of practice determine the forms of knowledge appropriate to it? The difference seems to be that it is not just the law school, the profession and constraints on the professoriat that are said to reproduce law's ways of interpreting the world. It is apparently law in a more abstract sense that does this. Changing any of the specific social settings of law that Balkin emphasizes would not alter the fact that the legal point of view is distinctive.

Thus law tends to become, in arguments about 'law's truth', an abstract site of understanding removed from particular kinds of social locations. For some writers, such as Niklas Luhmann, law's truth is that of a communication system not tied to any specific empirical settings. These scholars treat law as a discourse but typically do not stress the potential *diversity* of legal discourses of particular lawyers in particular courts, particular claimants or defendants in relation to specific claims, or particular political actors pursuing their special interests or projects or promoting their particular values. Law in some abstract sense is presented as having a unified, cohesive mode of understanding, a distinctive viewpoint, or a specific style of interpretation or reasoning.

From a sociological standpoint, however, it is an empirical question how far and in what forms this cohesion, distinctiveness or specificity may exist. Lawyers operating between different legal systems can experience different truths of law, and sometimes have difficulty in establishing a shared discourse. Even within the same system, outlooks on almost all matters legal may sometimes differ radically as between different participants in legal processes. As Balkin suggests, there may be much disagreement on matters of method no less than on the interpretation of particular matters of doctrine. And it contributes little to envisage all these actual or potential disagreements as part of an ongoing conversation on the justice or integrity of law. Such a conversation may exist only because the structure of political power forces those who wish to have access to or protection from that power to adjust their claims and arguments. It may force them to press these claims and arguments in ways that distort the particular legal 'truth' which they would otherwise wish to express.

Law's basic 'truth' may be merely the provisional, pragmatic consensus of those legal actors who are perceived at any given time to be supported by the highest forms of authority within the legal system of the state. Another way of putting the matter would be that there is no 'law's truth', no single legal point of view, but only the different – sometimes allied, sometimes conflicting – viewpoints expressing the experience, knowledge and practices of different legal actors and participants. What links all of these as 'legal' in some official sense is their varied relationships with matters of government and social control and with institutionalized doctrine bearing on these matters.

Undoubtedly, law is presented professionally as a more or less unified, specialized discourse. But, as Balkin notes, it is an intellectually vulnerable, open discourse, liable to invasion by many kinds of ideas, including sociological ones. Ultimately, it is given discursive coherence and unity only because its intellectual insecurity, its permanent cognitive openness, is stabilized by political fiat.[7] The political power of the state, which guarantees the decisions of certain official legal interpreters, puts an end to argument, determines which interpretive concepts prevail, asserts favoured normative judgments as superior to all competing ones, and guarantees normative closure by the threat of official coercion.[8] The *voluntas*, or coercive authority, of law, centralized by political structures and organized through legal hierarchies, stabilizes and controls potentially unlimited, often competing and conflicting, elaborations of *ratio* – reason and doctrinal principle – in a host of diverse sites and settings of legal argument and interpretation.

Seen in sociological perspective this is the nature of law's truth as a unified, distinctive discourse: a contingent feature of particular social environments. Sociological interpretation both reveals law's character and is, like many other forms of knowledge, available to enrich law's debates, colour its interpretations and strengthen or subvert the strategies of control to which legal discourse is directed.

---

7   Cf. Hobbes' (1971: 55) formulation: 'It is not wisdom, but authority that makes a law'.

8   Thus, as Robert Cover (1983: 40) puts it, the problem that requires a court to make an authoritative legal ruling is not that the law is unclear but that there is *too much law*. Courts (and especially ultimate courts of appeal in a legal system) exist 'to suppress law, to choose between two or more laws, to impose upon law a hierarchy'.

Sociological insight is simultaneously inside and outside legal ideas, constituting them and interpreting them, sometimes speaking through them and sometimes speaking about them, sometimes aiding, sometimes undermining them. Thus a sociological understanding of legal ideas does not reduce them to something other than law. It expresses their social meaning *as law* in its rich complexity.

At the same time, as noted earlier, law defines social relations and influences the shape of the very phenomena sociology studies. Thus, legal and other social ideas interpenetrate each other. A line between law and society is, as has been seen, no longer capable of being sharply drawn. Law constitutes important aspects of social life by shaping or reinforcing modes of understanding of social reality. It would be remarkable if the power of law as officially guaranteed ideas and practices could have no such effects. One might indeed wonder what law as an expression of power is for, if not for this. But a sociological perspective makes it possible to observe and understand this effect of legal discourses and situate it in relation to the social effects of other kinds of ideas and practices. Law constitutes society insofar as it is, itself, an aspect of society, a framework and an expression of understandings that enable society to exist. A sociological perspective on legal ideas is necessary to recognize and analyse the intellectual and moral power of law in this respect. To interpret legal ideas without recognizing, through sociological insight, this dimension of them would be to understand them inadequately. It would be to treat them as less significant and less complex than they are shown to be in a broader sociological perspective.

What is a Sociological Perspective?

Is it, however, really necessary to invoke the word 'sociological' here? Why privilege sociology? Nelken (1994: 125; 1996: 115) argues that sociology is sometimes presented as supreme only by downgrading law's disciplinary status. He doubts that sociology can ultimately transcend its own methods of argument and style. The legal sociologist may stand too close to sociology to understand law. And, in any case, why should a sociological, rather than, for example, an economic or psychological viewpoint be favoured? (See Nelken 1994: 125.) Why should sociology impose *its* understandings? On the other hand, if it does not do so, its analyses of law can be criticized as being parasitic on law's own definitions of the legal (Pennisi 1997: 107).

But most of these problems surely disappear once it is recognized that use of the word 'sociological' does not imply adherence to the distinct methods, theories or outlook of the academic discipline called sociology. A sociological perspective is indispensable in orienting oneself, whether for practical (participatory) or theoretical purposes, to contemporary law as a social phenomenon. But the term 'sociological' must be taken in a methodologically broad and, at the same time, theoretically limited sense. This rejects any implication of attachment to a specific social scientific or other discipline. Sociological understanding of legal ideas is *transdisciplinary* understanding (Cotterrell 1995: Chapter 3). But it is properly termed sociological because it consistently and permanently addresses the need to reinterpret law systematically and empirically as a social phenomenon. This terminology also suggests, however, that a legal outlook can itself be sociological, involving a systematic, empirical view of the social world, though it need not be so. As noted earlier, sociological understanding is simultaneously inside and outside legal ideas.

Thus, the essence of a sociological interpretation of legal ideas lies in three postulates. First, law is an entirely *social* phenomenon. Law as a field of experience is to be understood as an aspect of social relationships in general, as wholly concerned with the coexistence of individuals in social groups. Secondly, the social phenomena of law must be understood *empirically* (through detailed examination of variation and continuity in actual historical patterns of social coexistence, rather than in relation to idealized or abstractly imagined social conditions). And thirdly, they must be understood *systematically*, rather than anecdotally or impressionistically: the aim is to broaden understanding from the specific to the general. It is to be able to assess the significance of particularities in a wider perspective, to situate the richness of the unique in a broader theoretical context and so to guide its interpretation.

A sociological perspective could be defined and clarified in relation to other perspectives relevant to law. Literary fiction, for example, provides much insight into social relations in novels or short stories. But it does not usually claim to offer systematic interpretation of social phenomena. Its great power is in the rich presentation of particularity in a way that evokes general interest. The telling of stories, the evocation of mood, character and circumstances can present human individuality as simultaneously a matter of unique and universal experiences (cf. Durkheim 1975c: 323–4). Fiction can offer to the reader a means of reflecting on the nature of the social world. It does this when it inspires the conviction that its ideas extend social experience – the experience or observation of the reader, either direct or vicarious.

Fiction contributes to sociological ideas when it creates in the reader the sense that its stories, characterizations and evocations, or certain elements in them, can be used to interpret or inform aspects of social experience. The reader may empathize with characters or imagine situations as if they were presented as factual reports of experience. Empathy and imagination supply empirical reference for fiction, and give it its power to supply insight into 'the human condition' in some sense. Thus, fiction presupposes for its success some plausible reportage of human experience. Hence the line between fiction and non-fiction is itself problematic. But a story or a characterization – whether fictional or non-fictional – does not, in itself, provide the means for generalizing from the particular. Hence, it typically remains an unsystematic, untheorized account of individual or social circumstances. It offers, at its best, a richly detailed presentation of particularities of human experience, made profound by its capacity to attract empathy and engagement.

One might characterize typical orientations of many intellectual disciplines specifically in relation to the systematic, empirical and social aims and orientation of sociological inquiry. By contrast with the latter, theology's dominant concerns, for example, are not entirely social. A focus on relationships between human beings may be derived from a primary focus of the relation of humans to spiritual things – 'the central mystery of faith and unbelief' (Neill and Wright 1988: 448). The approach is only partly empirical in the senses referred to earlier, but usually generalized and often systematic and theoretically oriented (Neill and Wright 1988: 439–49). Much the same contrast with sociological inquiry might be sketched very broadly as regards philosophy as a discipline. Perhaps the most basic focus here is on self-knowledge (Cassirer 1944: 1), systematic reflection on general human experience in all its forms, not all of this experience necessarily being encompassed in social relations and not all being capable of illumination through empirical study.

Art's aesthetic creations do not offer systematic insight into the nature of the social world. 'For the artist, there are no laws of nature or history that must always be respected' (Durkheim 1961: 270), but the insights inspired may nevertheless be powerful when the observer of art or the participant in artistic experience finds points of real or imagined empirical reference on which the power of artistic creativity is sensed as focusing. Again, history is usually determinedly empirical and richly related to the understanding of social life, but may limit its effort to be explicitly systematic or generalized in its portrayal of the social, in order to achieve a multifaceted insight into particular people, actions, developments or events similar to that offered by the rich evocations and descriptions of great fiction.

As a final example, economics combines a concern with the empirical and a determinedly systematic and theoretical outlook with its own distinctive focus on the social. But, for all the contemporary claims of some economists to be able to analyse every aspect of social life in rational choice terms, economic analysis concerns itself with only certain aspects of social relations, or tends to reduce their complexity to a single model or strictly limited range of models (cf. Rosenberg 1979). From many legal participant perspectives and certainly from sociological perspectives these models appear inadequate to encompass the *entirety* of legal aspects of social life.

Approaches to legal inquiry that are set up as in some way opposed to sociological perspectives are, to the extent that they are presented in this competitive way, restricted forms of understanding of law as a social phenomenon. This is so when they actually exclude sociological insight in certain ways. Otherwise these other approaches are best seen as allied with and (insofar as they seek to offer social insight) appropriately organized by means of a (perhaps implicit) sociological perspective. They should be treated, in this context, as specialized co-workers with sociological inquiry.

Equally, sociological inquiry needs to be open and receptive to a variety of forms of legal inquiry that are not generally thought of as sociological. It must recognize their special power and merit and draw from and interact with them. Sometimes, indeed often, these forms of inquiry produce sociological insights while declaring justifiably that their ideas and approaches are directed to quite different purposes, and founded on quite different bases, from those that they associate with sociological studies.

A sociological perspective is thus not exclusive of or separate from the perspectives offered by the various disciplines mentioned above. Indeed, it may be contributed to by all of them, and by others. And it does not need to derive or seek its justification from the traditions of academic sociology, which nevertheless provide much important material to inform it. It is justified by the fact that for practical purposes law is appropriately understood as a social phenomenon, a phenomenon of *collective human life*, an expression and regulation of communal relationships, a means of codifying, being systematically aware of, working out, planning and coordinating the relationships of individuals coexisting in social groups. One important aspect of this is that, in some respects (but not all), law is thought of and experienced as an external, constraining force on the individual, a social fact in Durkheim's (1982) sense, something set apart from individual life and acting on it as a social force.

Again, for practical purposes of thinking and working with law, understanding it as an aspect of society and using that understanding to control conditions of social life as well as possible, it is essential that understanding of law should be *systematic and general*, theorized and organized. At the very least, this is necessary to manage both legal doctrinal and social complexity. Theorizing legal ideas is not a separate enterprise from theorizing the nature of social life. It is an aspect of a single but unending endeavour. Because systematic understanding of law is necessary, systematic understanding of social phenomena generally is needed. A sociological perspective must, by its nature, seek an integrated, continually broadening view of what it studies.

Finally, such a perspective needs to be *empirically grounded* – based on observation of the diversity and detail of historical experience. Speculation about the nature of or the meaning of legal ideas that does not relate its inquiries to historical experience in this way is impractical and may lack point since it ignores the specificity of the contexts in which the meanings of legal doctrine are shaped. So, while the need for systematic understanding exerts pressure towards generalization and the broadening of perspectives, the requirement for an empirical basis of understanding exerts pressure to reject broad speculation that ignores or generalizes beyond what the detail of particular experience and observation can support as plausible.

Is the claim that law should be understood in a perspective emphasizing the social, the systematic and the empirical a philosophical or an empirical claim? Ultimately it is a claim that thinking about law in this way offers the most general possibilities for encompassing the widest range of participant perspectives on law. Thus, it is an empirical claim since it makes assertions about the nature of legal experience. At the same time it can be considered a philosophical claim because it asserts that legal experience is usefully interpreted in a certain light: in relation to certain constant concerns, elaborated in many different ways in different times and places.

For example, it is possible to think of law in an asocial manner, as a kind of pure calculus unrelated to any idea of social relations. But it is hard to do so. And for most legal participants – that is, people who have experience of law or involvement with it in some way – it may be difficult to see great value in doing so.

Again, it is possible to renounce any connection between law and systematic knowledge. Weber (1968: 976–8) wrote of 'kadi justice' as a form of legal interpretation or decision-making that rejects any aspiration to subsume particular instances within general categories. Yet most legal experience of which we have historical and contemporary knowledge seems to value the aspiration towards system in law – whether as rational codification, wise consistency in the administering of justice, the citizen's or subject's ability to predict legal outcomes, aspirations towards simplicity or clarity in legal doctrine, an effort towards standardization or unification of law, or the control of arbitrariness. The aspiration has not always been for rational systematization, and rationality takes different forms. Sometimes the aspiration goes no further than a demand for some stability or certainty of outcome or some possibility of generalization. But in most legal experience this aspiration towards system is present in some form and is recognized in the development of law and its practice.

So, too, with a concern for the empirical. Like the concerns with the social and the systematic, this can be considered a fundamental component of most legal experience in all times and places for which knowledge is available. Law is often created in substantial ignorance of the empirical conditions of its application. It might be supposed that this has been a problem for all legal systems and societies beyond a certain size and level of social complexity. Yet most legal experience involves the application of legal ideas to specific instances, particular cases. Law is generally understood as significant in experience only if applied and related to specific contexts. This is the other side of law as system: law as the 'wilderness of single instances'. The effort to draw legal ideas from practices of resolving problems in particular empirical settings or to adapt and refine these ideas in applying them to such problems has been at the heart of most participant experience of law. It is possible to think of law in isolation from specific empirical references and the effort at systematization continually pulls law away from the particularities of context. But most legal experience does not avoid some concern for the empirical as a central aspect of law.

The task of interpreting law, which might also be thought of as a fundamental aspect of legal experience, can be seen in this light as part of the never-ending activity of balancing the empirical and the systematic, and doing so by drawing on continually changing conceptions of law's nature as a social phenomenon, an aspect of social life to be related to other aspects. Legal interpretation in this sense is the aspect of legal participation that is specifically concerned with reconciling or balancing concerns with the social, the systematic and the empirical in law.

How Should Legal Ideas be Interpreted?

The term 'sociology of law' remains useful as a label for identifying a vitally important body of research on legal processes and as an important focus of self-identification for scholars committed to extending this research. But it is a somewhat unsatisfactory and misleading term when used to refer to the sociological study of legal ideas. It often suggests a sub-discipline or a specialism, a branch of sociology or a distinct compartment of legal studies. In considering the interpretation of legal ideas it would be better to speak of sociological perspectives or insights, or sociological understanding or interpretation.

Sociological interpretation of legal ideas is not a particular, specialized way of approaching law, merely coexisting with other kinds of understanding. Sociology of law in this particular context is a transdisciplinary enterprise and aspiration to broaden understanding of law as a social phenomenon. It certainly insists on its criteria of the social, the systematic and the empirical, reflecting the conviction that these criteria are inscribed in some sense and in some degree in participant understandings of the nature of law itself as a social phenomenon. It seeks to go beyond many such understandings. But sociology of law is otherwise *inclusive* rather than exclusive. Sociological insight is found in many disciplinary fields of knowledge and practice.

If sociological inquiries about law have an intellectual or moral allegiance, then this is to law itself – that is, to its enrichment through a radical broadening of the perspectives of participants in legal processes, practices and forms of knowledge.[9] Sociological inquiry is critical because it insists that the legal perspectives of many of these participants (whether lawyers or non-lawyers) are *insufficiently* systematic and theoretically informed or sensitive to empirical variation, and have *too narrow* an awareness of law's social character. But it is also constructive because it cannot merely condemn existing legal ideas. It must also ask at all times how law might be *reinterpreted*, and so reimagined and reshaped, when understood in a broader sociological perspective.

It should be clear that the discussion above of sociological understanding of legal ideas takes for granted the need to reject the familiar dichotomy between internal and external views of law, or between insider and outsider perspectives. This dichotomy is familiar within legal philosophy. Its assertion is a device that accompanies the false assertion of the uniqueness of 'law's truth'. The internal–external distinction is, for the most part, merely a feature internal to lawyers' thinking. It reflects especially a professional self-image in terms of a special kind of reasoning and understanding (Cotterrell 1995: Chapter 5). When legal thinking is understood sociologically the distinction disappears between internal (legal participant) views of law and external

---

9   Cf. Hubert Rottleuthner's (1989: 79, 82) assertion, in an address to lawyers, that 'sociological research can ... help us to look beyond our daily routine ... As sociologists of law we go beyond the individual field of experience ... we transcend the individual perspective ... we establish correlations systematically instead of relying on unproved everyday theories. And by using a different frame of reference we point out new aspects to which inadequate attention has been given in your legal practice ... we offer a cognitive background for your daily work'. These claims seem justified apart from the suggestion that sociological knowledge contrasts with unproved theories. I think it cannot provide 'proof' but rather potential enlightenment – a deeper understanding – by reinterpreting everyday understandings in a broader, more systematic, more consciously empirical perspective. And, of course, it offers this not just for lawyers but for legal participants generally.

(for example, social scientific observers') views. It is replaced by a conception of partial, relatively narrow or specialized participant perspectives on (and in) law, confronting and being confronted by, penetrating, illuminating and being penetrated and illuminated by, broader, more inclusive perspectives on (and in) law as a social phenomenon.[10]

It might be asked what happens to justice and legal values in sociological understanding. Can a sociological understanding of legal ideas address questions of justice? The answer is, clearly, yes. Sociological insight should, as has been seen, both inform and interpret legal ideas. The question of whether sociology is inside or outside law becomes redundant. As I argued in Chapter 2 above, it is both inside and outside, and so the inside–outside demarcation becomes meaningless in this context. The line between law and society, and thus between legal and sociological interpretation, becomes indistinct. Law constitutes society in certain respects, social understanding informs law in certain ways. But insofar as sociological interpretation of legal ideas relates them to the entire context of social relationships in general it focuses attention on the patterning of those relationships which is the specific concern of justice.

Justice is a perception of social relations in balance. It is one aspect of a sense of social cohesion or integration (cf. Durkheim 1984: 77). The radical broadening of perspective which sociological interpretation seeks makes it possible to enrich understandings of the social conditions of justice. The consistent focus of sociological inquiry on the social, the systematic and the empirical provides the essential dimensions of this enriched understanding. Sociological inquiry cannot abolish disagreement as to what justice demands in any particular situation. But it can reveal the meaning of justice claims in a broader perspective by systematically analysing the empirical conditions that provide postulates underlying these claims.

If sociological interpretation of legal ideas is to be characterized in these ways, can we say anything concrete and specific about its *methods*? As noted earlier, settled methodology is the unifying feature which, according to Jack Balkin, law so crucially lacks. Can such a settled methodology be attributed to sociological inquiry?

The answer must recognize a crucial claim made earlier. This is that, if sociological inquiry about legal ideas is to be treated as having any specific intellectual allegiance it is to law as a social phenomenon, not to an academic discipline of sociology or to any other social science discipline. Hence the sociological understanding of legal ideas reflects methodologically law's own fragmentary and varied methodological characteristics as understood by those who participate in or are affected by legal practices. This is inevitable because of the interdependence of legal and sociological

---

10 In this context Philip Lewis' (1988) concept of 'representations' – forms of understanding ('description and accounts') present in legal thinking with regard to social institutions, practices and relations – seems useful. It highlights types of social knowledge that become a part of legal thought, so that, to this extent, legal and social understanding blend into each other as inseparable.

understanding referred to earlier. Sociological interpretation extends legal analysis. It broadens the perspectives of legal participants.

It does not necessarily replace those perspectives or contradict them by the use of a specific methodology foreign to the diverse methods already used by legal participants. If it did so *generally* this would be to replace law with sociology, to fall into the trap which, as noted earlier, has been said by some commentators to ensnare all sociological attempts to grasp law's truth. So, the methodology of sociological understanding of legal ideas is the deliberate *extension* in carefully specified directions of the diverse ways in which legal participants themselves think about the social world in legal terms. It seeks radically to extend the already partially systematic and empirical characteristics of this legal thinking, and thereby sets out to transform legal ideas by reinterpreting them.

An illustration may help to clarify this argument. The English law of trusts has developed a strange impasse in one narrow and somewhat arcane area of legal doctrine. While property can be held on trust by trustees to benefit individuals or groups of individuals in a wide variety of ways, English law, unlike some other common law jurisdictions, has declared that property may not be held on trust for abstract non-charitable purposes – for example, to promote press freedom, or sport outside an educational context.[11]

When it is asked why English law takes this particular stance on private purpose trusts and how the law in this area should be developed in the light of the precedents, answers are not particularly straightforward. The cases refer to particular private purpose trusts as illustrations, and offer various reasons for a tradition of judicial hostility to them. The matter is dealt with by the courts partly by looking at what has been decided in the past, partly by detailing technical problems that would be faced by law if private purpose trusts were to be declared generally valid (for example, problems of enforcement), and partly by offering policy arguments about the social or economic rights and wrongs of allowing particular kinds of trusts to be set up.

Legal thinking in this area is empirical up to a point, looking at what has been decided and the specific judicially stated circumstances in which particular decisions were taken. It considers how law in this area has been and can be enforced. It tries also to be systematic, seeking general principles which can unite the judicial approaches taken (but it ultimately admits failure, declaring that cases in which some private purpose trusts have been upheld are anomalous). It is also aware of the nature of the law in this field as an expression of social relations. Thus, it considers policy: for example, the social and economic pros and cons of restrictions on alienation of property and of particular kinds of testamentary freedom. But legal analyses do not seem to remove the deep-rooted controversies surrounding the law in this area. Commentators take a variety of positions on the issues, some supporting the general legal hostility to private purpose trusts, others declaring it unjustified. And

---

11 See, for example, Re Astor's *Settlement Trusts* [1952] Ch 534; *Re Nottage* [1895] 2 Ch 649; *Bowman v Secular Society Ltd.* [1917] AC 406; *Re Endacott* [1960] Ch 232.

the controversy has continued for decades. In other jurisdictions matters have been dealt with by legislative reform.

A sociological approach to doctrine in this area attempts to extend established methods of legal thought in new, relatively unfamiliar ways (Cotterrell 1992; 1993). First, it puts the development of doctrine into a far wider historical context, noting the changing social and economic contexts in which trust law as a whole has developed. By this means it suggests that the institution of the trust has been thought of in ways that have changed radically over time. This change becomes recognizable when attention shifts from the development of a particular line of precedents, as in orthodox legal analysis, to changing patterns of legal ideas about the nature of trusting relationships seen as interrelated with broader social, economic and moral ideas. Thus, the inquiry broadens the idea of law as a social phenomenon by treating legal ideas as an aspect of social ideas in development. This is not to reduce the former to the latter, but to see each as inseparable from the other.

Similarly, empirical inquiry is broadened beyond the observation of previous decisions to include much wider observation of the social contexts and implications of these decisions. It considers the relation of the decisions to other legal developments in areas that may be legally distinct from but socially interconnected with private purpose trusts, viewed as a field of legally structured social relationships. Thus sociological inquiry seeks a broader, systematic view of the law by reinterpreting the relationships between ideas which the lawyer identifies. It puts them into an intellectual context that allows the identification of other relationships and other connections. And these in turn help to explain the law as it stands and point to ways of rethinking and developing it.

When sociological inquiry is used in the ways outlined above it ceases to appear as the pursuit of a methodology alien to law, or the invocation of a competing academic discipline with the aim of colonizing law. It is seen as the radical extension and reflexivity of legal participants' understanding of law. Viewed in this way it is a necessary means of broadening legal understanding – the systematic and empirical understanding of a certain aspect of social life recognized as 'legal'.

It proceeds from participant understandings, but because it seeks to *systematize* legal understanding beyond the needs of particular participants it goes beyond their perspectives. For example, it certainly does not reject – but does not treat (for its purposes) as adequate – personal or anecdotal accounts of legal experience, particular narratives which cannot be generalized. Because it treats very seriously the requirement that systematizations of legal or social knowledge must be grounded in *empirical* observation it resists speculations that it considers as taking inadequate account of empirical variation. And because it emphasizes law's character as a *social* phenomenon it examines law's social character far more extensively and broadly than most participants need to do. Hence, for example, it is led to extend its conception of the legal as a social phenomenon beyond the forms of law familiar to lawyers or some other categories of legal participants.[12]

Viewed in this way the enterprise of sociological interpretation of legal ideas is not a desirable supplement but an essential means of legal understanding. Legal ideas are a means of structuring the social world. To appreciate them in this sense and to recognize their power and their limits, is to understand them sociologically.

---

12 Thus, sociological theories of legal pluralism often suggest a vast *diversity* of legal knowledge, consciousness, authority and experience, which tends to be obscured by the typical focus of lawyers' practice and legal education on uniform law applied by state courts. See Chapter 2, above.

Chapter 4

A Legal Concept of Community

How should legal studies envisage the social? The concept of society is less useful than it was. Society is disintegrating into many different networks of social relations in and beyond nation states. A concept of community (as contrasted with society) can indicate social relations that have some stability and moral meaning, yet are not necessarily territorially fixed or limited and may be fluid and transient. Relations of community take diverse forms and a law-and-community approach allows legal scholars to analyse regulatory aspects of different types of social relations. Four basic types of community are introduced in this chapter. They compete and combine in complex ways in actual social conditions. I argue that a rigorous and distinctive concept of community is needed to understand law's relations to different social groups and cultures.

Why Community?

Why is a legal concept of community necessary? My argument is that we need such a concept because, as many writers have suggested, we need to rethink the concept of law itself in pluralistic terms (see, for example, Petersen and Zahle (eds) 1995). That can only be done theoretically with any rigour by developing some such notion as that of community. The long-established 'modern' view has been that law is in essence the law of the nation state (Arnaud 1995). But transnational law – harmonizing legal practices and legal thought across nation state jurisdictions or irrespective of them – is assuming increased importance, especially in Europe. So also are the problems of autonomous or semi-autonomous regulation of regions,[1] localities, groups and enterprises.

The nation state clearly remains the primary focus of legal regulation. But nation states recognize federal or subordinate jurisdictions and they participate in transnational legal regimes or coexist legally with such regimes. Equally, there are now aspirations for more diverse and, in some sense, 'local' processes of creating, interpreting and applying regulation. The aim is to make this regulation more morally meaningful, closer to the lived experience of citizens, than much state law.

These aspirations are not new. In modern social theory they go back at least as far as Durkheim's work at the beginning of the twentieth century. But, as transnational legal developments dislodge an almost exclusive focus on the law of nation states,

---

1 Suggesting a less direct and subordinate relation to a national centre than the older conception of 'provinces': see Anderson 1994.

a space is created for rethinking law in intranational as well as transnational terms. And present globalizing tendencies in economy and society may be responsible for powerfully encouraging localizing tendencies with regard to some cultural aspirations (Axford 1995: 164ff.).

None of this denies the significance of the state as author, interpreter and enforcer of law but it opens up possibilities for conceptualizing law in new ways. Sociology of law has largely been built around the concepts 'law' and 'society'. Sometimes in legal sociology law was theorized as acting on or being acted on by society; the organizing idea was law *and* society. Sometimes law was theorized as an aspect or field of social experience; the corresponding organizing idea was law *in* society. A theme of postmodern writing, however, questions whether we can usefully talk of society as a sociologically identifiable entity any longer (Bauman 1992: Chapter 9; Smart 1993: 57–8). However loosely conceptualized 'society' may be, the concept suggests a unity, a social totality of some sort with boundaries separating it from other such totalities.

What are these boundaries? If we seek to define them in terms other than legal ones (that is, as legal boundaries of jurisdiction, typically associated with the territorial reach of the state) we run into the dilemmas of interpreting so-called postmodern social conditions. The concepts that seem to have to be invoked (for example, nation, province, region, city, neighbourhood; racial, ethnic, religious, economic or cultural group; linguistic community) beg all questions about definition and the specification of boundaries. Which criteria of demarcation are important, or more important than others? Why are they important? The typical postmodern image of 'society' is of a vast, endlessly shifting diversity of interests, values, projects and commitments of individuals, expressed and pursued through multiple, transient memberships of collectivities of many different kinds. Insofar as relatively enduring frameworks for this diversity exist they may be in no way limited in scope to a 'society' in any traditional sociological sense. They may be provided, for example, by financial systems, commercial networks, production and distribution systems or employment markets, of very varied scope and scale; or by complex networks of cultural allegiances.

If this portrayal of social conditions is even partly plausible it has important implications for the concept of law with which legal sociology has typically worked. The modern concept of law and the modern sociological concept of society have common origins in the composite idea of the nation state brought to full realization in the revolutionary period of the late eighteenth century (Woolf 1991). In the shadow of this idea, law and society are almost mutually defining. Society is for many definitional purposes *political* society; that is, a territorially defined arena of social interaction regulated by a specific political system (for example, British society; French society). Society is, thus, significantly delimited by the jurisdictional reach of legal systems (cf. Lacey 1998: 120). This, however, undermines the idea that law is in some sense a product or expression of society. One might put matters the other way around: (political) society is a product of law (Fitzpatrick 1995). If the unity of society is fragmented, so too is that of law as a social phenomenon. The stability of the idea of law as essentially state law, the law of the nation state, has depended on the continued possibility of treating state and nation as coterminous – having the same scope, as in the nation state concept. As long as these conditions prevailed, law could gain its conceptual unity from its inseparability from the idea of the nation, itself treated as simultaneously guaranteeing a social unity (society) and a political unity (the state).[2]

While the concept of community is an 'infuriatingly slippery notion' (Hamilton 1985: 7) its use may be one way of escaping from the modern intertwining of the concept of society (as political society) with that of the state. The idea of 'communities' now can suggest a diversity of social collectivities, commitments and systems of interests, values or beliefs, coexisting, overlapping and interpenetrating. The aim in invoking the idea of community cannot be to hark back to pre-modern ideas of *Gemeinschaft*, but rather to express a sense of complex contemporary variation in the character of social groupings and allegiances and in their reasons for existence. To link law and community is thus to explore continually shifting patterns of social variation expressed or reflected in legal diversity. It is to hold out the possibility of theorizing law as a social phenomenon that is something other or something more than the law of the nation state as a political society.

As Anthony Cohen has argued, a community is best thought of not as a social structure but as a web of understandings about the nature of social relations. While relations of community may well be expressed through institutions and social structure, community in its symbolic dimension 'exists as something for people "to think with". The symbols of community are mental constructs: they provide people with the means to make meaning' (Cohen 1985: 19). Community provides a sense of identity for members within a bounded whole; a 'sense of belonging to a local social context' (Cohen 1985: 9). 'Local' should not necessarily be understood in a geographical sense, but rather in the sense of being rooted in particular contexts of experience. This suggests that community means something different to participants in it and to observers of it, to 'insiders' and 'outsiders'; it can be understood subjectively and objectively (Schutz 1957: 250–7). Law externally observes all such communities except its own; that is, except for the community (the web of understandings about social relations) which law itself inhabits and expresses. National state law, for example, expresses a subjective understanding of community only insofar as the nation state itself can be thought of in terms of community. A fuller, more complex legal recognition of the experience of community requires a plurality of forms of legal consciousness representing in some way the subjective reality of a whole range of communities.

---

2 An illustration of the problems that arise when these relations are unclear is the long-standing, fundamentally ambiguous situation of Scotland, having its own national law (Scots law) and yet not its own law (Scots law being ultimately subordinate to UK law and the legislative will of the UK Parliament). The combination of autonomy and dependence has made indeterminate for a long time (and, for some political purposes, conveniently) the nature of the social/political entity which, as Scotland, law defines.

This is precisely what Georges Gurvitch's (1947) unique, classical legal sociology attempted to show. The complexity of Gurvitch's project provides a warning that practical limits on this rethinking of law are essential. Gurvitch saw legal pluralism as the expression, in a diversity of legal forms, of different kinds of sociality and the innumerable different possible forms of group life. While modern legal sociology has not pursued his ambition (see Belley 1986; 1988) and has largely ignored the unwieldy, seemingly endless taxonomies of law that resulted from it, a contemporary way of reinterpreting Gurvitch's project is to see it as a logical effort to 'sociologize' (to inform with sociological insight) an approach to legal philosophy such as Ronald Dworkin's. Dworkin treats law as webs of understanding about social relations sustained by a community of legal interpreters (Dworkin 1986: Chapter 6). The sociologization of a Dworkinian approach would involve the recognition that there are inevitably *many* interpretive communities. Hence, if we try to pursue in radical ways the link between law and community, there might turn out to be many forms of legal consciousness, many sites and contexts of legal interpretation, and, as Gurvitch argued, many forms of law coexisting in the same social space.

If, however, communities appear differently in the different perspectives of 'insiders' and 'outsiders', the linking of law and community would suggest that legal meaning is also a matter of perspective. Each community may have its own subjective legal understanding and appear as an object in the legal understanding of other communities. The legal outlook of any community is a partial legal perspective; a partial view of the social phenomenon of regulation. There is no way of producing a 'total' legal perspective, except through the unifying coercive power (*voluntas*) of some centralizing political authority, such as the state. Even that, however, does not really create a unified, total perspective. It merely ensures that some legal perspectives *dominate* in practice at the expense of others.

Four Types of Collective Involvement

It has been said that 'people manifestly *believe* in the notion of community, either as ideal or reality, and sometimes as both simultaneously' (Hamilton 1985: 8). If this is so, however, the notion is nevertheless associated with very varied contexts and only the vaguest common reference points. It indicates, at the very least, a situation of collective concern or involvement which is not to be seen merely in terms of the isolated projects of individual lives. Beyond this, following a somewhat Weberian schema, I suggest that community can be associated with at least four distinct ideal typical contexts of interaction and collective involvement. For convenience of reference we will call these *types of community*, although (as will appear) more is required than just the existence of collective involvement for the concept of community to have useful meaning.

Following this schema, community can be associated, first, with habitual or traditional forms of interaction; with the often accidental circumstance that people find themselves coexisting in a shared environment. I call this *traditional community*.

It includes what sociologists often refer to as 'local community' – the coexistence of people in a defined geographical space; a neighbourhood, for example. But an empirical correlate of traditional community is also found in the sharing of language. A linguistic community, in ordinary terminology, is a group of people who have a particular language or dialect in common. Often, of course, local and linguistic groups reinforce each other's identity. Secondly, community may be associated with a convergence of interest among a group. I term this *instrumental community* (or community of interest). Its closest empirical correlate is a typical business community, or perhaps the original European Economic Community. Thirdly, community may refer to the sharing of beliefs or values that stress solidarity and interdependence. I shall refer to this as *community of belief* (or belief-based community, or community of values). Religious congregations, churches or sects of various kinds most obviously approximate this type. Finally, the uniting of individuals by their mutual affection may be thought of in terms of community. This type can be labelled *affective community*. Family and friendship groups may most obviously approximate to it. The legal philosopher John Finnis has noted that this is the kind of community in which 'groupness' in itself is most important; indeed, 'the most intense form of community' is 'the friendship of true friends' (Finnis 1980: 141ff.).[3]

These four types correlate indirectly with Max Weber's four ideal types of social action (Weber 1968: 24–5). Their formulation is an effort to extend Weber's typification of action into a typification of basic forms of collective involvement and interaction. Thus, traditional community correlates with Weber's type of traditional action, instrumental community with purpose-rational action, community of belief with value-rational action, and affective community with affective action. Viewed in Weberian perspective, therefore, they can be seen as a development in terms of collective action of the four fundamental orientations of all individual social action.

They are, themselves, ideal (that is, pure) types of social relationships. In other words, they are expressed in abstract form in terms of the irreducible, most fundamental motivations or conditions that give essential meaning to interactions between individuals. As ideal types they do not indicate actual, empirically identifiable groups that might usefully be labelled 'communities'. In actual social groups or organizations the four abstract types of collective involvement may be combined in an infinity of ways. Particular groups are not, therefore, empirical representations of any of the four ideal types of collective involvement or community. Relationships within a group of traders may be only partly explicable in terms of instrumental community; relationships in a family will not be explicable entirely (if at all) in terms of affective community; a church is certainly not just an empirical manifestation of

---

3   Finnis (1980: 140) treats what he calls relationships of play as fundamentally distinct from business relationships. But the players of a game may well be motivated to associate by a convergence of their individual interests – for example in stretching their wits, exercising their skill, being amused or gaining the various rewards of winning – so that, within my classification of community, their association might be best understood in terms of the ideal type of community of interest.

community of belief. It can be assumed that, as an empirical matter, patterns of social relationships of collective involvement are different in each group or collectivity that might be studied. Thus, the ideal types of community conceptualize the various kinds of social relationships that are combined in complex ways in actual group life.

Nevertheless, my tentative argument is that, like Weber's ideal types of social action, the ideal types of community are comprehensive. Together they encompass *all* the distinct types of collective involvement that can be components of community.

Community: Stability, Attachment, Boundaries

The idea of community must, however, suggest more than just the types of collective involvement identified schematically above. The four ideal types of collective involvement do not, for example, explain when or why actors will feel a sense of community and self-consciously identify themselves as part of a community, adjusting their conduct and expectations in relation to that identity.

Community in this sense seems to require, objectively, some degree of *stable, sustained interaction* (relations of collective involvement must be continuing and reliable). Subjectively, it requires a *sense of attachment* (Anderson 1991: 141ff.) or belonging (Cohen 1985: 15) to others or to something beyond the individual; a degree of mutual concern and involvement; a sense of membership in a 'bounded whole' which confers an identity (Cohen 1985: 9, 12). When these objective and subjective conditions are satisfied a collectivity might be thought of as a communal group – that is, a group that exhibits characteristics of community. But again it is important to recognize that relationships within any particular communal group may be characterized by different types of collective involvement, as discussed earlier. Hence the subjective sense of membership or attachment is not necessarily of the same nature for all individuals who see themselves as members of the group. Reasons for it may vary. Sometimes, in the case of nations thought of as communal groups, this sense of attachment is politically promoted (Anderson 1991: 113–14). At its highest, it may amount to a willingness to sacrifice oneself completely for the survival of the group as a whole (Anderson 1991: 7, 141); a willingness, which in the context of the nation state at war is turned into a legal obligation, supported by the state's coercive power, to fight and if necessary die in battle (Kantorowicz 1957: 232ff.).

It is difficult to say how much or what quality of interaction makes it plausible to talk about the objective existence of community. Geographical *locality* or a shared *language* seems plausible as an identifier of community where it identifies a relatively high intensity of interaction within the population and relatively highly developed communication networks, by comparison with levels of interaction and developed communications of the population in relation to other populations outside it. Convergent *interests* seem plausible identifiers of community when these interests are regularly promoted and expressed in interaction within the group, and through group activity to address perceived threats to them from outside it. Thus, a business or professional community may seem most 'real' to its members through everyday interactions, and to outsiders through its collective lobbying (for example, in Britain, through representative bodies such as the Confederation of British Industry, the Law Society or the British Medical Association).

Again, some *shared values* (for example, of militant individualism) may not provide a basis for community (except in the sense of a common rejection of those not sharing these values). If shared values or beliefs are to provide such a basis they must require an outreach of solidarity to others holding similar values or beliefs. Hence, since most major religions require this, churches and religious groups are easily thought of as communal groups. This may be especially so if, as in the case of most forms of Christianity, they require an outreach even to others who do not share the church's values and beliefs.[4] As for *affective* community, it seems clear that sustained interaction and mutual commitment over time is necessary to enrich and deepen affective relationships and provide them with the roots and resources that enable affective community to become stable and strong.

Beyond stable, sustained interactions and mutual attachments, indicia of community, in the sense of a communal group, are often associated with *attitudes to outsiders*. Community is said to be a relational idea; the use of the word only being occasioned by the need to express a distinction from others not included within the group (Cohen 1985: 12); the identification of 'other' may even be necessary for the identification of self (Neumann 1995: 10ff.; and see Lacey 1998: 112, 124). Georg Simmel argued that the stranger 'is an element in the group itself', playing a role in defining for those within it its collective identity (Simmel 1971: 144). Thus, the nation state is easily seen as gaining its identity in part by its definition of and treatment of 'the alien' (Welsh 1993: 13ff.), a matter which implies a legal concept of the nation as an exclusive community. In Carl Schmitt's stark view, the state bases its very legitimacy on its capacity to identify friend and enemy (Schmitt 1976: 26). In practical terms: 'The insiders in a we-group are in a relation of peace, order, law, government and industry to each other. Their relation to all outsiders, or other-groups, is one of war and plunder, except so far as agreements have modified it' (Hogg and Abrams 1988: 17).

It may, however, be easy to exaggerate the extent to which a communal group's very existence is predicated on a negative attitude to outsiders. Community can refer to networks, needs and conditions of mutual support or a shared sense of collective experience or destiny, which does not have to emphasize a distinction from outsiders, nor indeed focus on relations with outsiders at all. It certainly does not have to imply fear, hostility or exclusiveness with regard to outsiders, though it may attach special importance to resources of mutual support between members and the need to protect these (if necessary against 'outside' interference).

Rather than assuming a certain relationship between insiders and outsiders as theoretically inevitable, it is appropriate to ask the following empirical questions of any collectivity: How far is the experience of those involved in social interaction

---

4   See, for example, *St Matthew's Gospel*, Chapter 5, verses 43–8.

linked to categories of insider and outsider? How significant in experience is such a distinction? Assuming the distinction has significance, what attitudes to outsiders exist? Are they positive or negative, fearful or fearless? What are the typical attitudes of outsiders to the group and to its members? Alfred Schutz emphasizes that a group's identity is given not only by members' perceptions but also by those of outsiders, including (the state's) legal definitions of the group (Schutz 1957: 254–6). The result may be a 'looking-glass effect' in which group self-perceptions are shaped by external perceptions (Schutz 1957: 247). Finally, does the group see itself as wholly or partly *exclusive* (restricting entry from outside) and as *inclusive* (deterring exit from it; for example, through social sanctions against 'marrying out' of a cultural or religious group)?

As regards exclusivity, most communal groups can only maintain themselves by having *some* limitations on freedom of entry, but what kinds of limits for any particular group are likely to be treated as acceptable by outsiders of the group probably depends on the significance of the existence of the group for the lives of the outsiders; in other words, how far they can exist satisfactorily independently of it. As regards inclusivity, it seems essential for peaceful coordination of communities and the protection of personal security of all individual citizens of contemporary nation states that communities should *not* be in any degree inclusive.

An important – if difficult – distinction should also be drawn between *voluntary* and *involuntary* groups (Schutz 1957: 251–2), or at least between a sense of freedom to decide whether to attach oneself or remain attached to others in social relationships, on the one hand, and a lack of such a sense, on the other. For involuntary groups, into which, for example, individuals are born, no choice arises as to whether to enter or not. The member participates in an already constituted group system. Hence, there is no question of committing oneself initially to relationships of mutuality. In voluntary groups – that is, those which actors freely choose whether or not to join – the identity of the group is not pre-constituted but continually reconstituted by the voluntary allegiance of its members. In general, it may be said that voluntary groups are the kinds of groups that best reflect the dynamic, fluid, transient and adaptable aspects of so-called postmodern culture. Their existence is compatible with a unifying cultural value of liberal individualism, expressed for example in contemporary principles of human rights. Involuntary groups represent forms of collectivities that often exist in tension with these conditions. One might go further and say that voluntary groups can be communal groups in a much deeper sense than is possible for involuntary groups, because they provide scope for members to give and withdraw attachment and to regulate deliberately the extent of social interaction. Hence participation in them is more conscious and considered, and potentially richer since it flows from and expresses the member's individuality rather than governing it.

Community and Trust

It must be emphasized that reference to characteristics of groups as such does not identify the determinants of community. The question of when any particular collectivity is properly thought of as a communal group cannot be conclusively answered at a theoretical level. We have seen, however, the main criteria of an answer. They are a matter of the subjective outlooks of members together with objective characterizations of stable, continuing interaction observed from outside the group. But the idea of a social group suggests an identifiable, discrete social phenomenon. I suggested earlier that community is best thought of in terms of webs of shared understanding about social relationships: in Cohen's terms, 'something for people to think with'. This means that the *sense* of community is not limited to or 'imprisoned within' distinct social groups. Community in a broader sense refers to the degree of development of certain aspects of social relationships.

What aspects of social relationships are fundamental to the concept of community in this sense? John Finnis, one of the few recent writers who has attempted to develop a rigorous concept of community for the purposes of legal philosophy, associates it with social interactions coordinated 'over an appreciable span of time ... with a view to a common objective' (Finnis 1980: 153). This chapter's earlier discussion suggests that a common objective is not necessarily associated with typical collective involvement.[5] A mere *convergence* of interests is sufficient for instrumental cooperation, and traditional community or community of belief, as types of collective involvement, are not necessarily associated with any common objective.

The idea of 'an appreciable span of time' in relations of community does seem significant, however. Interactions need to be more than transient. Networks of interaction are important, and interactions as part of extended sequences that recall past interactions and presume future ones. So, community is not, as generally understood, a matter of quickly entered and quickly disconnected relations. It is, typically, slowly and steadily built. The key characteristic of such gradually evolved relations is that they are imbued with a high degree of *trust*, which, in general, can only be securely built over time, with the accumulated experience of past interactions. Trust encourages future interaction and provides the motivation to engage in relatively free, uncalculated relations with others.

I have argued elsewhere, on this basis, that mutual interpersonal trust is the basic element of the idea of community as a web of understandings about social relations (Cotterrell 1995: Chapter 15). Trust provides the common building blocks of the four ideal types of collective involvement referred to earlier. It is the underpinning of all the many experiences of community – strong and weak, organized or diffuse – that occur in social life. In each of the four ideal types of collective involvement or interaction – traditional community, instrumental community, affective community

---

5   In fact, Finnis later (1980: 156) seems to de-emphasize this element in his specification.

and community of belief – trust assumes different typical forms and is expressed in different typical ways. The conditions of its creation or maintenance may be different as may the kinds of regulation necessary for its expression and support. These matters, differentiated in terms of the various components of the idea of community which this chapter has sought to analyse, become central regulatory problems for legal theory to address. A legal concept of community sets an agenda for law; it presents legal analysis with the task of adapting regulation sensitively to current social and cultural diversity.

It is easy to recognize how important mutual interpersonal trust is; how, in fact, all aspects of social life are built to some degree on it.[6] But also apparent is its potential fragility. Niklas Luhmann (1979) has described the process of displacement of interpersonal trust as a feature of contemporary life, in favour of confidence in impersonal systems of communication. Confidence in financial, commercial, scientific, technical, professional and political systems is essential to social interaction in modern complex societies (see Barber 1983). But there is a risk of underestimating the extent to which *impersonal* systems of confidence are underpinned by and, in a sense, modelled on idealized relations of mutual *interpersonal* trust (cf. Cotterrell 1993: 90–5). Confidence in political systems, for example, is built on images of 'the typical politician', shaped in turn by perceptions of actual politicians and judgments of trustworthiness made in relation to them on the basis of reflection on their actions and statements. Today, mass media play a major role in conveying and shaping images on which judgments of trust are made with regard to representative figures in, for example, politics, commerce and the professions.

Law polices systems of confidence in various ways. But the analysis offered earlier of collective involvement or interaction, and of the elements that turn this involvement into community, subjectively experienced and objectively identified, suggests the complexities of this policing process. I have argued that community is best thought of as a web of understandings about social relations and that this web of understandings is built on (in a sense codifies[7]) relations of mutual interpersonal trust. While actual empirical conditions in which these relations develop and are expressed are infinitely varied, we have noted ideal typical instances of collective involvement or interaction (traditional, affectual, instrumental, and founded on belief), reflecting and requiring different patterns of trust relations. Insofar as these trust relations flourish and strengthen, community flourishes as something subjectively experienced in a sense of attachment and objectively identifiable in stable patterns of interaction.

Each such type of collective involvement has its ideal regulatory requirements; that is, ideal for the purpose of expressing and supporting the kind of trusting

---

6   For a survey of the idea of trust as a topic in the literature of social theory, see Misztal 1996.

7   Cohen (1985: 16) is right to argue that conditions of community are 'not reducible to a body of rules'. But informal rules about appropriate behaviour are surely an important expression of the understandings that constitute community.

relationships that are necessary to it. In a radical legal pluralist perspective, it might be said that each kind of community has its own legal needs, and demands its own legal structure, legal consciousness and legal outlook. In practice, however, *state law* dominates with its legal structure, legal consciousness and legal outlook. It does this insofar as the state maintains – as Weber put it – the monopoly of the legitimate use of physical force (Gerth and Mills (eds) 1948: 78). The state can insist, coercively, on the prevalence for many purposes of its legal vision and legal controls. Indeed, the needs of order require that there be such a coordinating power. But it is often seen as the sole significant legal authority. What the state does not control in this way is typically considered legally trivial.

It has been suggested above that impersonal systems of confidence are rooted, however distantly and indirectly, in judgments of interpersonal trust. Law supports confidence, therefore, by supporting trusting relations, not individually in their particularity, but more generally in the typical patterns of collective involvement in which they are expressed. Law guarantees systems of confidence, in the main, indirectly by sustaining and encouraging patterns of trust embodied in ideal typical forms of collective involvement or interaction. Looking at matters in this way offers a different perspective on what Luhmann and others have seen as law's inability to control, or directly influence, other communication systems in society. If we understand these systems as extensions or derivations, at an abstract level, from interpersonal trusting relationships it becomes possible to see that law as a form of regulation of social action operates not on abstract communication systems but only on the kinds of social action that relate to these systems. Actual social relations of interpersonal trust are, by the nature of their intimacy and individuality, removed from external control and depend entirely on subjective understandings between those involved. Hence, law's main support and encouragement of trusting relationships is indirect. It is provided by approving and protecting empirical conditions that facilitate trusting relationships; in other words, by authoritatively defining the character of different kinds of organizations, associations, practices, transactions or institutions that express in their patterns of social relationships the various types of collective involvement or community.

We noted earlier that groups are defined both internally and externally, subjectively by their members and externally by outsiders who observe them. The law of the nation state is an 'external observer' of most groups (treating them as objects of regulation), but an internal, subjective expression of the legal consciousness of the nation state (or of certain elites within it). This is why state legal controls are incapable of fully defining (and controlling) the legal character of community life within the territory of the nation state (or beyond them). State law cannot express the rich diversity of this community life as subjectively experienced. A legal concept of community entails 'a more fragmented conception of the legal' (Lacey 1998: 160). Thus, a pluralist conception of law would require that we recognize not just the legal reality of state law but also the defining role of the legal consciousness of particular groups within the nation state. These groups must somehow coexist within a larger national group regulated by state law. So, it follows that state law has the task of coordinating them, facilitating their coexistence. As noted earlier, it also has a role (but not an exclusive one) in legally defining their character.

Nation and Law

In considering state law we should note a fundamental characteristic of the nation, as the entity whose character is expressed through the law of the nation state. The nation whose political expression is the nation state is not even a loose empirical correlate of any of the pure types of collective involvement considered earlier – traditional, affective, instrumental or belief-based. The nation as a political society certainly presupposes and depends on relationships of community between its citizens. But the nation as an entity is frequently an 'imagined community' (Anderson 1991) seen in terms of all or any of the four pure types of collective involvement. For some purposes it is a traditional community essentially united by the accidents of geography or language, for others a focus of convergent interests of citizens, for yet others a symbol of shared beliefs or a repository of shared values, or an object of veneration and patriotic affection. Consequently state law as law expressing the regulatory needs of the nation reflects the regulatory needs and forms of all the fundamental types of collective involvement. Yet precisely because of the ambiguity of the idea of nation as a community in itself, state law's reflection of these regulatory needs and forms is ambiguous and indirect. State law gains its strongest relationship with community through its support of the various types of collective involvement or interaction as these are combined in actual empirical contexts.

Seeing matters in this way indicates that state law has many different kinds of relationships with community, since community itself, viewed in terms of ideal types, is expressed in diverse forms. In Britain, for example, centralized state control has typically left relatively limited scope for independent democratic decision-making in localities such as cities or regions. Until recently, the governmental outlook of the state has been that the nation, thought of as a geographical entity in terms of *traditional community*, would be threatened by a recognition of a specific legal consciousness of subordinate geographical communities.[8]

Business communities, however, as empirical approximations of the type of *instrumental community*, have often been encouraged towards self-regulation. Their subjective legal needs, outlook and regulatory structures are typically respected by the state. This state policy can be understood as founded on an assumption that the community of interest to which actual business communities approximate expresses the same convergence of interests as those of the nation as a whole, thought of in terms of instrumental community. Thus the recently fashionable slogan 'UK plc', used in discussion of the national economy, conjures up the bizarre image of the nation as a single, giant business corporation.

---

8   New government policies after the election of a Labour administration in May 1997 were aimed at actively promoting a degree of regional self-government within the UK.

By contrast, the relationship of state law to groups approximating the type of *community of belief* is often highly controversial. Familiar issues here include the question of how far particular religious groups should be able to maintain their own educational establishments and systems, how far children should be protected from subjection to their parents' beliefs or values (for example, with regard to 'arranged' marriages, or the use of various medical treatments). The major controversy is how far the unifying values or beliefs of such groups are compatible with those thought to characterize the nation, itself thought of as a community of belief in this context.

Finally, with regard to *affective community*, the family, as an empirical approximation of community in this sense, has long been extensively regulated by state law (for example, as regards marriage formalities, property, marital relations and parental rights). This has occurred despite an important rhetoric of non-involvement by the state in family matters. Indeed, the rhetoric of non-involvement has allowed a highly selective consideration of rights and responsibilities in domestic relationships until relatively recently in most Western nations. The basic issue here would seem to be that affective community refers to the most intimate form of community, whose self-regulation is, for that reason specially highly valued. But domestic relationships are the locus of primary socialization of children to productive citizenship within the nation state, as well as of the orderly intergenerational transmission of wealth. For this reason, if for no other, these relationships have long been too important for the state to ignore. And family loyalties are never allowed to interfere with allegiance to the nation when, as in time of emergency (such as war), it is particularly thought of in terms of affective community. Not only does the nation emotively demand that the son or husband go to risk his life in battle, but the family as a whole is typically shamed unless this demand is met; indeed, unless the parent encourages the son, and the wife the husband, to take up the colours. The nation seen as affective community harnesses, to protect itself, the normal affective regulation of family relationships. It becomes the 'motherland' or 'fatherland'.

A legal concept of community offers a means of rethinking law's relation to the diversity of social groupings and networks of shared understanding that characterize contemporary social life. It does not solve problems of pluralistic regulation in complex societies, but it offers a more flexible and sophisticated framework for conceptualizing those problems. It does so in the context of jurisdictions whose reach can no longer be adequately portrayed in traditional sociological terms of (political) 'society' and traditional legal terms of state sovereignty.

A legal concept of community is devised to highlight the need for regulatory expression of communal relationships of trust; it recognizes the variety of these relationships and the diversity of forms of their expression. Consequently, it facilitates a pluralistic view of law. It recognizes the importance of order and coordination and the present, though not necessarily permanent, dominance of state law in defining and shaping the regulatory conditions of community. Yet its pluralistic vision of law also emphasizes the inevitable inadequacy of state law in this role and the social significance of legal expressions of community other than those offered by state law. It offers a means of rethinking law's role in fostering the kind of highly developed trusting relationships that are fundamental to a society at ease with itself in conditions of rapid change and increasing cultural and social diversity.

PART 2
Applications
(Comparative Law and Culture)

Chapter 5

The Concept of Legal Culture

How can sociolegal theory aid comparative legal studies? All the chapters in Part 2 address this question in one way or another. The idea of legal culture has become prominent in recent work by both comparatists (comparative lawyers) and legal sociologists. It might, therefore, seem useful as a starting point for collaboration between them, but this chapter argues that – as an explanatory tool – it is problematic. 'Culture' has been treated by legal sociologists as a key variable in considering the causes and effects of legal change. But the concept is an inadequate foundation for this kind of inquiry. The idea of culture can be used in legal research in certain ways. But, pushed beyond its strict analytical limits, it is dangerous and misleading.

Introduction

The search for a rigorous concept of legal culture has obvious attractions for a comparative sociology of law – that is, a sociology of law offering general comparisons of different legal systems. A focus on legal culture might, indeed, be seen as a means of fusing the aspirations of sociology of law and comparative law.

Comparative law – 'the comparison of the different legal systems of the world' (Zweigert and Kötz 1998: 2) – offers the example of a scholarly enterprise that has developed explicit conceptual frameworks for comparison between state legal systems. The idea of 'legal families', for example, whatever its difficulties, suggests that different state legal systems, or central elements of legal doctrine within them (including styles of developing and presenting doctrine, and of legal reasoning and interpretation), can be treated as having sufficient similarity to make comparison fruitful. At the same time, it suggests that these comparable systems or system-elements treated as a group can be distinguished from others treated, for certain analytical purposes, as qualitatively more remote (see, for example, Zweigert and Kötz 1998: Chapter 5; David and Brierley 1985: 17–22).

However, the main conceptual mechanisms of comparative law seem inadequate for the purposes of sociology of law, since what is required for the latter is a conceptual framework allowing comparison not of legal doctrine as such, but of legal ideas and practices regarded as inseparable from a broader social context.

One of the enduring problems of comparative law has been its inability to demonstrate convincingly the theoretical value of doctrinal comparisons separated from comparative analysis of the entire political, economic and social (we might call it contextual) matrix in which legal doctrine and procedures exist (cf. Friedman 1975: 201). Comparative law has seemed unable to provide viable frameworks for comparison of laws or legal systems treated as aspects of or elements within a political society (cf. Damaska 1986: 6–7). Indeed, some writers have suggested that the destiny of a comparative law that solves these problems of comparison is, in fact, to become sociology of law (cf. Hall 1963: 10–15; David and Brierley 1985: 13), or at least 'a composite of social knowledge of positive law' contributing to a humanistic sociology of law (Hall 1963: Chapter 2).

The promise held out by the search for a concept of legal culture appropriate to comparative sociology of law is that of an idea that would embrace or recognize all those elements of the contextual matrix that have to be taken into account if comparisons of legal systems and their characteristic elements are to be sociologically meaningful. But the difficulty of any such concept – as of the concept of culture itself – is its imprecision and vagueness, which is a consequence of the demands made upon it and the role in analysis that it is typically required to play.

This chapter examines in general terms the theoretical usefulness of a concept of legal culture. It takes, as its focus, the attempt by the American legal sociologist Lawrence Friedman since the late 1960s to elaborate and apply such a concept. The first main section of the chapter examines Friedman's various formulations and applications, over a period of more than a quarter of a century, of a concept of legal culture, and assesses how far his claims for the explanatory power of this concept are justified. Friedman's work is emphasized here because it is, by far, the most sustained effort to work with an explicit concept of legal culture in recent comparative sociology of law and to defend and elaborate theoretically its use.

My claim is that the concept, as developed and applied in Friedman's work, lacks rigour and appears – in certain crucial respects – ultimately theoretically incoherent. This result should be seen, however, less as a fault of Friedman's particular elaboration of the concept of legal culture than as a reflection of general problems in using culture as an explanatory concept in theoretical analysis of law.

It may, indeed, be impossible to develop a concept of legal culture with sufficient analytical precision to give it substantial utility as a component in legal theory and, especially, to allow it to indicate a significant explanatory variable in empirical research in sociology of law. The remainder of the chapter asks in what circumstances the concept of legal culture may, despite these problems, be valuable in social studies of law and how far some of the theoretical aims for comparative sociology of law sought by developing the concept of legal culture can be pursued by other means.

The main problems that the chapter identifies with the concept of legal culture, as developed in Friedman's work, relate to, first, the definition of the concept; secondly, the varieties of legal culture and their relationships; thirdly, the causal significance and mechanisms of legal culture; and, fourthly, the explanatory significance of the concept. While these problems are fundamental, an examination of them also highlights criteria that should guide analytical frameworks for comparative sociology of law.

Problems of the Concept of Legal Culture

The Definition of the Concept

In Friedman's most extensive theoretical discussion of legal culture he offers a variety of characterizations: legal culture 'refers to public knowledge of and attitudes and behaviour patterns toward the legal system' (1975: 193). Legal cultures may also be 'bodies of *custom* organically related to the culture as a whole' (1975: 194). Legal culture is a part of culture generally: 'those parts of general culture – customs, opinion, ways of doing and thinking – that bend social forces toward or away from the law and in particular ways' (1975: 15). Thus, the emphasis is on clusters both of ideas and of behaviour patterns, intimately related. In later formulations, however, legal culture appears only as ideational; the behavioural elements appear to have been discarded. Legal culture consists of 'attitudes, values, and opinions held in society, with regard to law, the legal system, and its various parts' (1977: 76), 'ideas, attitudes, values, and beliefs that people hold about the legal system' (1986: 17) or 'ideas, attitudes, expectations and opinions about law, held by people in some given society' (1990: 213; 1985a: 31; and see 1994: 118).

The imprecision of these formulations makes it hard to see what exactly the concept covers and what the relationship is between the various elements said to be included within its scope. As long as explanatory significance is not attached to the concept of legal culture and it is used only as a residual category to refer to a general environment of thought, belief, practices and institutions within which law can be considered to exist no serious problems arise. In some discussions of the concept of general culture Friedman seems to imply this approach. Thus, a 'common-sense view' of culture is advocated; culture merely refers to the range of individual variations in a certain environment (1990: 212, 213); national culture is 'a kind of aggregate, hard to compare with other aggregates' (1975: 209). Culture appears, therefore, as a kind of residue; the contingent, even arbitrary, patterning produced by many specific, diverse and possibly unrelated factors.

This view is, however, clearly insufficient for Friedman's purposes. The patterning is held to reflect something, like a shadow of an unseen object (1990: 196); therefore legal culture has significance as more than just an aggregate. As will appear, for Friedman, it is to be understood as itself a causal factor in legal development – it '*makes* the law, at least in some ultimate sense' (1990: 197) – and is therefore an essential component in theoretical explanation in sociology of law. For this reason the concept needs more rigorous specification than it receives. Yet the variety of meanings of legal culture here is strikingly reminiscent of the variety of meanings of the term 'culture' itself that have often been found in anthropologists' writings (cf. Geertz 1973: 4–5).

The Varieties of Legal Culture and their Relationships

Friedman remarks that 'one can speak of legal culture at many levels of abstraction' (1975: 204; cf. 1994: 120). Each nation has a legal culture (1975: 209); legal culture can describe 'underlying traits of a whole legal system – its ruling ideas, its flavour, its style' (1975: 15); each country or society may have its own legal culture and no two are exactly alike (1975: 199). On the other hand, Friedman writes extensively of what he calls the legal culture of modernity, or modern legal culture, which is a characteristic feature of many contemporary societies (1975: 204ff.; 1994); elsewhere he writes of Western legal culture (1990: 198–9), and even of an emergent world legal culture (1975: 220).

Again, however, and especially in his later work, he has strongly emphasized the idea of a plurality of legal cultures – indeed 'a dizzying array of cultures' (1990: 213) – within countries or nations. In the US, for example, there is a legal culture of rich and poor; of blacks, whites or Asians; of steelworkers or accountants; of men, women and children, and so on (1990: 213). 'It should be possible to isolate a pattern for any particular group we might select' (1994: 120). A complex society has a complex legal culture (1990: 96). American legal culture is not one culture but many: 'There are legal conservatives, legal liberals, and all sorts of variants and subgroups. Within specific groups, legal culture consists of particular attitudes which, however, do tend to cohere, to hang together, to form clusters of related attitudes' (1985a: 98; and see 1986: 17).

The concept of legal culture is thus stretched two ways. On the one hand, it points towards broad comparison and the recognition of extremely wide historical tendencies or movements that are certainly not contained by the boundaries of nations or state legal systems. On the other hand, the concept is invoked to recognize familiar themes of legal pluralism as understood in its social scientific sense (cf. Merry 1988). Up to a point, this catholicity of application suggests a concept of considerable subtlety. Legal culture appears not as a unitary concept but indicates an immense, multi-textured overlay of levels and regions of culture, varying in content, scope and influence and in their relation to the institutions, practices and knowledges of state legal systems.

Looked at in another way, however, the highly flexible idea of legal culture presents serious problems for its theoretical application when specific questions are asked about the relationship between legal culture and particular aspects of state legal systems. If legal culture refers to so many levels and regions of culture – with the scope of each of these ultimately indeterminate because of the indeterminacy of the scope of the idea of legal culture itself – the problem of specifying how to use the concept as a theoretical component in comparative sociology of law remains.

Friedman has consistently described a fundamental duality of legal culture which may in some respects cut across the various levels or regions of legal culture noted above. He distinguishes in a broad manner, reminiscent in this respect of Savigny (Savigny 1831: 28–9), between the legal culture of 'those members of society who perform specialised legal tasks' (Friedman 1975: 223) and that of other citizens. The legal culture of legal professionals, which Friedman considers 'specially important' (1975: 194) is 'internal' legal culture. Contrasted with it is what he has variously called 'external' (1975: 223; 1986: 17), 'popular' (1990: 4) or 'lay' (1977: 76) legal culture. The relationship between 'internal' and 'external' legal culture remains, however, very unclear. It is not apparent why internal legal culture *must* be regarded, sociologically, as specially important, nor why exactly the behaviour and attitudes of professionals have a great effect on the pattern of demands in the legal system (cf. Friedman 1975: 194). This is a crucial matter given that, as will appear, the concept of legal culture is intended to explain much that is socially significant about the workings of legal systems.

Lawyers' legal thought, according to Friedman, is necessarily bound to its culture and culture determines the limits within which legal thought can change (1975: 206). Internal legal culture reflects the main traits of lay (or external) legal culture (1977: 79). Nevertheless, in his view, different kinds of professional legal reasoning – if this is taken to mean the formal, authoritative stating of reasons for a legal decision – are socially significant. Legal reasoning may tend towards closure or openness, and towards innovativeness in doctrine or resistance to innovation. Different types of legal system can be classified in terms of the types of reasoning that dominate within them. Such matters as legalism, reliance on legal fictions, the use of reasoning by analogy, and specific aspects of judicial language and style, can be related to these classifications.

It remains unclear from Friedman's discussions, however, just what social consequence these various matters are considered to have, although he clearly considers them to be expressions or products of internal legal culture. Equally, it remains unclear how internal legal culture, in this sense, is to be distinguished from what comparatists (that is, specialists in comparative legal studies) think of as the 'style' of a legal system or legal family (cf. Zweigert and Kötz 1998: 67ff.). Yet Friedman suggests that the idea of legal families is not useful for sociology of law because stylistic differences between legal families do not necessarily correlate with contrasts in socioeconomic conditions of existence of law. Hence, differences between families of law, unlike differences between legal cultures, may be socially relatively insignificant (Friedman 1975: 202; 1977: 75–6). If this is because they are based only on arbitrary aggregations of traits, it seems that this may also be a characteristic of legal culture, at least in some of its forms, since, as has been seen, this can also be considered merely as a range of individual variations, culture itself being 'a kind of aggregate'.

As will appear, the lack of clarity in explaining the sociological relationship between internal and external legal culture has serious consequences for the explanatory usefulness of the concept of legal culture. The cause of this lack of clarity seems easily identifiable, however. While, as has been noted above, Friedman emphasizes the diversity and multiple levels and regions of legal culture, ultimately he continues to use the concept of legal culture in a way that implies unities of what may be extremely diverse elements of ideas, practices, values and traditions. Thus, the use of the concept of legal culture encourages a view of 'internal' legal culture as a unity set against 'external' legal culture.

By contrast, in (for example) Weber's rich analyses of the relationships between styles of legal thought and the social conditions in which they develop, particular strands of influence are traced without the need to assume any uniform idea of culture, or that the infinitely complex historical patterns marking the evolution of ideas, beliefs and values should be conceptualized as more than transient chance encounters between co-present elements from the infinite data of history.

Certainly Weber was concerned with unique, historically significant aggregates of intellectual, moral and social conditions – for example, in such complex phenomena as the spirit of capitalism, the rationality of the West, or the social orientations associated with the dominance of certain religions (see, for example, Gerth and Mills 1948: Chapter 11) – but in no case does culture, as such, seem to be employed as a key variable in explanation. It may be necessary to conceptualize cultural 'aggregates' for the purposes of organizing inquiry (and the use of the method of ideal types in doing this is discussed later in this chapter). But the inquiries themselves are almost always concerned with specific, differentiated elements – for example, particular religious, economic, legal or political orientations of intersubjective action – that can be identified and related within these aggregates.

The Causal Significance and Mechanisms of Legal Culture

What is the concept of legal culture for? For Friedman it specifies a vital element in determining the social circumstances in which legal systems operate. Legal culture 'determines when, why, and where people use law, legal institutions, or legal process; and when they use other institutions or do nothing'; it 'sets everything in motion' and is an essential variable in explaining the workings of law; adding legal culture to the picture of law 'is like winding up a clock or plugging in a machine' (1977: 76). The causal significance of legal culture is thus unequivocally asserted.

Especially in his 1975 book *The Legal System*, Friedman has offered a relatively detailed account of the way he sees legal culture acting to affect the working of legal systems. Social forces create an impetus for change but do not work directly on the legal system (1975: 15, 153; and see 1994: 118). Interests have to be turned into demands and demands must be pressed successfully on the legal system to produce 'legal acts' (for example, new laws). Legal culture achieves or permits the translation of interests into demands (1975: 150, 193) through the attitudes expressed in legal culture that operate to shape demands; and legal culture also determines the manner in which the legal system responds to these demands. In this latter capacity, however, legal culture – presumably both internal and external – operates to build 'structures' (1975: 209). These are structures of the legal system itself – such as systems of rules – as well as of power and influence operating on and around it (1975: 150).

But, while these structural elements operate to resist or accommodate demands, Friedman is anxious to deny the idea that somehow the legal system itself, as a system, responds. 'Real forces, real people' are at work; 'the concrete opposition of interest groups expressed *through* or *in* the legal system' (1975: 155). Nevertheless, the legal system – the procedural and doctrinal structures – 'does make some difference; exactly how much we do not know' (1975: 156). The analogy of the rope in a tug of war is used. The legal system is the rope; it can be stretched to a certain extent; perhaps its weight and bulk also adds some inertia element. But the rope hardly determines who wins the game.

There is, undoubtedly, a great deal of vagueness in the causal mechanisms of legal culture being suggested here. But the general outline of Friedman's view is clear enough. Legal culture controls the pace of production of demands brought before the legal system for specifically legal solutions to problems or protection of interests. And, by more obscure and complex means, legal culture seems also to determine the legal system's responses, partly, it would seem, through the operation of internal legal culture shaping legal structures and partly through 'external' pressures – reflecting social distributions of power and influence – which equally affect the system's responses.

The problem with this account is again the relatively undifferentiated character of legal culture – or at least the difficulty in linking what Friedman has to say about these shaping elements operating on the legal system with the image of an immensely complex interplay of varieties of legal culture as discussed earlier. The concept of legal culture explains too much. Indeed it seems to explain everything that happens or fails to happen within the legal system. Yet, at the same time, it explains very little, because the attribution of so much to legal culture, when legal culture itself embraces such an indeterminate array of elements and operates on such an indeterminate set of levels of generality or specificity, fails to identify any particular factors that can be seen to be making a difference to the situation of law in society for the purposes of inquiry in sociology of law.

The Explanatory Significance of the Concept

Friedman disarmingly admits frequently the vagueness of the concept of legal culture; it is 'an abstraction and a slippery one' (1990: 95). Statements about legal culture 'rest on shaky evidence at best' (1975: 204). Little systematic data on comparative culture exists (1975: 209). 'As it is, I can only estimate, interpret and infer' (1990: 198). An exposition might be 'less an explanation of data than guesswork about what the data might show' (1994: 119).

Why maintain a concept that is so hard to pin down? The answer implicit in Friedman's writings seems to be that the concept serves more of an artistic than a scientific function; it allows impressions of general tendencies to be sketched. Litigation enthusiasm may be an aspect of legal culture in certain countries: 'These are, at any rate, strong impressions' (1975: 212). And, as the issue of citizens' invocation of law in different countries and especially in the US has been returned to in Friedman's writings over the years, the idea that the matter is one of legal culture has allowed him to adjust his accounts of the relevant culture to changing interpretations of the sociological reality of variations in the extent and nature of citizens' involvement with the state legal system in different countries and periods.

Thus the idea of legal culture has been able to embrace the notion that somehow law is seeping into more areas of life and that claims consciousness is extending in certain countries (1975: 210–11); that there is a growing general expectation of justice and recompense (1985a: 43, 144; 1986: 22; 1990: 60); that there is simply more law as a component of social life (1986: 20); and that a culture of choice in which people expect to be able to formulate, express and fulfil personal choices and, if necessary, pursue them through law has become pervasive in the US and elsewhere (1990: 74).

Friedman's discussions on these themes are often avowedly impressionistic; like a painter's portrayal of a landscape, rather than a surveyor's measurement of the terrain. The appeal of the concept of legal culture is that it seems to suggest a way of ranging across important but indeterminate matters – relating especially to the significance of general changes in social beliefs, opinions, values and outlooks – that cannot be easily encapsulated in the kind of testable hypotheses about social action that American law and society research has usually sought. Discussion of legal culture is a means of inferring and suggesting rather than explaining in behavioural terms; of describing general impressions where these cannot easily be supported by systematic empirical analysis.

Legal Culture and Legal Ideology

The problems of Friedman's account of legal culture reflect, in the main, general difficulties with the concept of culture itself. These difficulties seriously limit the utility of the concept for a comparative sociology of law aimed at systematic empirical explanation and the development of theory capable of clarifying general causal or functional relationships between social phenomena.

On the other hand, the concept of culture – and perhaps legal culture – remains useful as a way of referring to clusters of social phenomena (patterns of thought and belief, patterns of action or interaction, characteristic institutions) coexisting in certain social environments, where the exact relationships existing among elements in the cluster are not clear or are not of concern. Culture is a convenient concept with which to refer provisionally to a general environment of social practices, traditions, understandings and values in which law exists. Legal culture, in this sense, may have the same degree of significance for sociology of law that the idea of legal families has for comparative law – a means of using extremely broad and (perhaps) more or less impressionistic terms to characterize large aggregates of distinct elements.

Otherwise, the concept of legal culture might best be replaced in most contexts of analysis with other concepts. Much of what legal culture can embrace might be considered in terms of *ideology*. Like legal culture in Friedman's formulation, legal ideology can be regarded not as a unity but rather as an overlay of currents of ideas, beliefs, values and attitudes embedded in, expressed through and shaped in practice.

Unlike Friedman's concept of legal culture, however, the concept of legal ideology can be considered to be 'tied' in a relatively specific way to legal doctrine. Legal ideology is not legal doctrine but can be regarded as made up of value elements and cognitive ideas presupposed in, expressed through and shaped by the practices of developing, interpreting and applying legal doctrine within a legal system. One advantage which the concept of legal ideology has over that of legal culture is that a more specific idea of the source of legal ideology and the mechanisms of its creation and effects can be offered than seems to be the case for legal culture.

Legal ideology can be seen as significantly generated and sustained by the professional practices of law and diffused through the impact, in one way or another, of institutionalized, professionally developed and applied legal doctrine on citizens' consciousness. This is not to claim that ideology *originates* in these practices and forms of doctrine; legal doctrine itself necessarily reflects ideological currents which it does not control and which themselves deserve analysis by those wishing to understand the development of doctrine. But it seems important to emphasize the intellectual and institutional mechanisms by which legal doctrine may have power to shape 'common-sense' understandings – forms of taken-for-granted knowledge and belief – outside the spheres of professional legal practice. Hence, although the concept of legal ideology embraces a very broad and somewhat indeterminate range of ideas embedded in practices, a specific link between ideology and doctrine can be theoretically specified.

Legal doctrine in contemporary conditions is typically fragmented, intricate and transient; it is in continuous process of reformulation, supplementation and amendment, especially in the light of changing governmental policies. It often combines highly particularistic regulation with extensive authorization of the exercise of official discretion. Legal ideology, by contrast, can be regarded as the repository of all of contemporary legal doctrine's impossible aspirations – in a sense, the 'opposites' of its technical characteristics. Legal ideology embodies, for example, the mirage of legal doctrine as timeless or self-evidently valid principle; of self-sufficient legal logic applicable to solve all legal disputes; of law as a 'gapless', complete code of systematic regulation; or of legal ideas as a coherent embodiment of consistently elaborated values.

The concept of legal ideology provides a focus for important inquiries about the ways in which legal doctrine, transformed in ideological thought, helps to constitute or shape social understandings and structures of beliefs, attitudes and values; and how law as doctrine provides a conduit through which extremely broad currents of thought and belief can be translated into regulatory practices (Cotterrell 1995: 7–14).

Another advantage of using the concept of legal ideology is that it seems easy to think in terms of specific ideologies, or currents of ideology, and to recognize that currents of ideology may conflict with each other and reflect different kinds of social experience. Marxist theories of ideology tended to fall into the trap which we have seen as a real one for the concept of legal culture: that of *assuming* unity in what are no more than possibly arbitrarily identified aggregates. But the concept of ideology lends itself, in less constrained analyses, to use in identifying quite specific systems of values and cognitive ideas.

It allows analysis of the way in which values and ideas can indeed be sustained as systems despite contradictions and incompatibilities within and between them; and it also facilitates recognition of the tenacity of these systems of thought and belief, and of their resistance to modification through experience. It inspires examination of the structure of ideological systems, of the role of rhetoric and symbolism within them, and it allows recognition of the ubiquity of conflict between currents of ideology. Perhaps more clearly than the concept of legal culture, the concept of legal ideology emphasizes the link between social power and currents of thought and belief. It focuses, for example, on the way that the professionalized doctrinal production of legal systems exerts social power through its shaping of such currents.

The concept of legal culture, at least in Friedman's formulation, seems to focus most directly on a diversity of elements that exert influence *on* the production of 'legal acts' within legal systems, and are held to explain differences in the character and orientation of these systems and their responsiveness to interests and demands; Friedman tends to remain vague or agnostic about the power of professionalized legal practices and doctrine to exert influence on the wider contextual environment in which these exist; he focuses broadly on aspects of the whole environment of culture as a determinant of law.

By contrast, analyses of legal ideology may present a more manageable theoretical task insofar as they explore mechanisms by which law – usually in the sense of the professionalized practices of state legal systems – exerts influence on, or translates and thereby helps reinforce, wider structures of values, beliefs and understandings. The task might seem more manageable to the extent that institutionalized, professionally managed legal doctrine is taken as its specific focus, rather than a potentially unlimited diversity of cultural sources of influence on legal systems.

The Use of Ideal Types

The concept of legal ideology, as sketched above, may, however, not be particularly oriented towards those specific tasks of comparative sociology of law that seem to inspire the use by some scholars of the concept of legal culture. These tasks are to consider the social determinants of specific institutional differences in state legal systems, or differences in practice, style and organization, or patterns of citizen involvement with professionalized law and its agencies. Since the focus is on diversity in legal systems the inquiry seems to return to that of the interface between comparative law and sociology of law. But, in this context, an approach such as Mirjan Damaska's (1986), which focuses on the interaction of specific variables related to political structure and political ideology in explaining differences in patterns of legal procedure, seems more promising than one that adopts the concept of legal culture as an explanatory tool.

Damaska (1986: 14) writes about his variables and their interaction as providing 'models' for analysis. Thus, the analysis is based on ideal types of governmental structure and procedural authority, on the one hand, and of orientation towards political authority, on the other. These are to be used to explain elements of what Friedman would call internal legal culture, especially the kinds of differences in legal organization and outlook that are often associated with contrasts between common law and civil law families recognized in comparative law. But Damaska denies an intention to make general claims of causation. The presence in the political and ideological environments of specific legal systems of characteristics approximating the explanatory models is considered to 'justify or support particular clusters of procedural forms', but not usually to determine them (Damaska 1986: 14).

Damaska's effort seems to be, in part, to 'disaggregate' what might be thought of as very general differences in legal culture as between common law and civil law procedural systems.[1] He suggests that the comparative law concept of legal families is inadequate to characterize the distinctive features of procedural systems, first, because of the variety of practices that different systems, even if considered to be within a single family, present and, secondly, because of the seeming lack of relationships between procedural elements that are clustered together as characteristic of one or other legal family.

In Weberian fashion, Damaska seems to recognize the impossibility of characterizing cultural complexity except in terms of the tracing of specific, more or less unique, clusters of historical developments in particular legal systems. These developments are to be understood in terms of certain underlying ideas which they can be considered to express: that is, 'ideas that are capable of moulding forms of justice into recognisable patterns' (Damaska 1986: 5). The logical relationships between these postulated ideas (about governmental organization, including the organization of judicial systems, and about bases of legitimate authority) produce ideal types of procedural systems that can facilitate comparisons between actual procedural systems.

The use of pure or ideal types (that is, logically constructed concepts deliberately designed not to represent empirical reality but to organize interpretation of it) seems to be one important way to combine two vital research requirements in comparative sociology of law. First, it makes possible a recognition of the myriad of elements that might be referred to as legal culture without falling into the trap of thinking of culture as a unity rather than an aggregate. At the same time, secondly, it facilitates comparisons.

The approach has classic origins in Weber's studies of broad cultural aggregates. Indeed, in one sense, the whole of Weber's work might be considered to focus on the characterization of Western culture as a unique aggregate. But the method of ideal types may be the only general method available that makes possible the study of large cultural aggregates without reifying them. An ideal type by its nature assumes, first, that what it designates as a logically unified, self-contained idea created purely

---

1   For a detailed discussion see Goldstein 1995.

for the purposes of intellectual reflection must not be taken to correspond to a logically structured, self-contained empirical reality. Secondly, it assumes that the empirical phenomena which the ideal type is used to organize are no more than a set of data, selected for the specific purposes of research, from the infinity of historical experience.

The price that must be paid for this valuable methodology is that we recognize that culture – and, specifically here, legal culture – has no empirical existence *per se* as something that is, itself, to be measured, observed or experienced. Rather, it is an idea that may yield methods of measuring, observing or experiencing specific social, including legal, phenomena. But this seems to be possible only when the idea of culture is radically transformed into sets of logically elaborated ideal types.

The Study of Cultural Aggregates

There may, however, be certain limited conditions under which the concept of legal culture, in something like Friedman's descriptive and empirical sense, gains a more precise utility. In other words, there may be circumstances in which it is appropriate to identify legal culture as an empirical category, rather than to treat it as merely a set of ideal typical constructions.

It may be feasible in certain conditions not merely to abstract from the infinity of data by means of ideal types by which culture can be characterized but to attempt to describe and record, ethnographically, in all its richness and complexity, a cluster or aggregate of attitudes, values, customs and patterns of social action such as might make up external legal culture in Friedman's sense. But this is likely to be feasible only when relevant cultural aggregates are small-scale and isolated, so that no serious problems of differentiating and distinguishing cultures are encountered.

For example, Bronislaw Malinowski's rich, classic ethnography presents what he certainly could regard as the legal culture of the Trobriand Islanders (Malinowski 1926). The scope of Malinowski's ethnographic study is determined not primarily by the effort to trace specific variables, but by its concern to bring to light social structure, change and continuity and functional relationships in an account of a complex and undifferentiated cultural whole. The limits of the cultural aggregate are here defined, and made manageable for the purposes of ethnographic research, by the geographical isolation of relatively small Melanesian societies.

It should be emphasized, however, that, because the concern is with the cultural aggregate as a totality and with the immensely complex interweaving of diverse elements within it, the legal is necessarily undifferentiated from other aspects of culture, or differentiated only in provisional and variable ways. Hence legal culture is only a certain *aspect* of culture (a point of view on it) as an undifferentiated aggregate. Strictly speaking there is no legal culture, but only culture seen from a certain standpoint of legal relevance to the observer. Still there are unresolved problems with the scope of culture. But 'Malinowski's rather fuzzy concept of culture' (Firth 1988: 16) avoids these insofar as it refers merely to the totality of ethnographically recorded social life within a geographically (thus, from a sociological point of view, arbitrarily) limited space. Only when efforts are made to theorize this totality as an integrated and distinct unity of some kind (cf. Malinowski 1944) does the concept become deeply problematic (Paluch 1988).

These ideas are not irrelevant in considering contemporary large-scale societies, such as those of Europe or North America. The problems of the vagueness of the concept of legal culture and of assessing the causal significance of the numerous layers or regions of legal culture that Friedman indicates as related to change in a legal system might seem less acute in the context of these contemporary societies if the extent of the relevant cultural aggregate could be limited in a manner comparable to that achieved in studies such as Malinowski's.

This is sometimes possible when the focus of attention switches from unified or centralized state legal systems and towards a *plurality of regulatory systems* in contemporary societies; the scope of these plural systems mirroring that of the various kinds of legal culture discussed earlier in relation to Friedman's work. Clearly, this possibility of analysis using the concept of legal culture arises not because the concept in such circumstances acquires a more unified content, but – as with Trobriand 'legal culture' – because as a purely practical matter the diversity of elements in the cultural aggregate, being more local, narrowly confined or limited in scale, may seem more manageable; more apparently amenable, for example, to what the anthropologist Clifford Geertz refers to as 'thick description' (Geertz 1973: Chapter 1).

The focus on legal pluralism in anthropological studies, as well as in some early work in sociology of law such as that of Eugen Ehrlich (1936), goes along with a relatively sharp sensitivity to cultural variation. In Ehrlich's writing the stress on a plurality of systems of legal ordering beyond the legal system of the state is intended to mirror this variation precisely and to show the complexity with which differences in attitudes, values, beliefs and customs might be directly registered in regulatory diversity. It may be, indeed, that the concept of culture is especially appropriate to ethnographic research that aims to portray the interweaving of cognitive structures, systems of values and belief, patterns of social action and regulatory structures as a relatively undifferentiated complex existing in a limited social locality; a complex aggregate which is of interest *as an aggregate*, as a portrayal – as far as practically possible and, indeed, plausible – of the entire, intricate web of social life.

But, as has been noted above, this approach makes it difficult to retain a differentiated theoretical focus on the legal, or on institutional elements that might be treated as equivalent to, or set in the place of, those aspects of social organization that in complex societies would be treated as distinctively legal. To isolate the legal requires an analysis of culture into its components and a specification theoretically of the relation of elements. But this is precisely what the use of the idea of culture as an aggregate seeks to by-pass – or, at least, seems to justify by-passing. It seems significant that as anthropology has developed a concern to study specific regulatory, order-maintaining or dispute-focused aspects of social organization, separating these analytically at least to some extent from other elements of social life, the concept of culture has tended to lack prominence alongside the range of other concepts that the literature has employed (see, for example, Snyder 1981).

Would it be possible to treat internal legal culture in Friedman's sense – that is, the values, attitudes, and perhaps practices (the ambiguity in Friedman's writing was noted earlier) of legal professionals – as a small-scale cultural aggregate? The answer would seem to be generally negative on the basis of the arguments above. Friedman's own uncertainty as to how far internal legal culture can be distinguished from external, and what its independent social significance may be, seems understandable in the light of anthropological approaches to the ethnographic presentation of culture. There seems no obviously satisfactory way of isolating internal legal culture from the larger cultural aggregate within which – insofar as it is to be treated *as* culture – it must be implicated in an immeasurable array of linkages.

Nevertheless, the prospects for using the concept of a cultural aggregate in relation to the analysis of certain aspects of contemporary state legal systems may not be so limited as suggested above. There is some affinity between the use of the concept of culture to synthesize complex aggregates of elements present in small-scale social contexts, and some important efforts to develop sophisticated ethnographic accounts of popular legal consciousness in the US.

This work, particularly associated with members of the Amherst Seminar on Legal Ideology and Legal Processes, explicitly adopts the concept of ideology rather than any idea of culture as indicating the focus of its concerns. In accordance with the orientations of analysis of ideology suggested earlier in this chapter, the focus is more obviously on the power of the state legal system to produce structures of social understandings, attitudes and values among lay citizens, than on the ways in which these kinds of diffuse understandings, attitudes and values shape the workings of the state legal system. On the other hand, some of this writing is in terms of culture, as well as ideology. 'Legal words and practices are cultural constructs which carry powerful meanings not just to those trained in the law or to those who routinely use it to manage their business transactions but to the ordinary person as well' (Merry 1990: 8–9). And much literature stresses the conflicts, tensions and negotiations between popular or lay legal understandings and those of lawyers and other professionals within the state legal system, or the relative integrity of popular legal consciousness.

In general, as might be expected, this kind of research is at its most persuasive when it looks in detail at a wide range of aspects of relatively limited social contexts – for example, specific towns considered as communities (Greenhouse 1986); or social interaction in such settings as lawyers' offices (Sarat and Felstiner 1995), mediation hearings in court (Merry 1990) or social welfare offices (Sarat 1990a) where negotiations around the meaning of law take place. These studies acquire much of their explanatory power from their detailed ethnographic recording of entire complex contexts of social interaction. On the other hand, a specific relation to law is maintained because the state legal system and its practices and processes are treated as the background against which social interaction takes place and in relation to which forms of popular consciousness develop or are shaped.

To this extent, it might be said that these studies are directly concerned with legal culture – and especially the interaction of internal and external legal culture in Friedman's terms. They seem to make a virtue of the character of legal culture as an aggregate of many contingent elements. On the other hand, the use of the concept of ideology maintains a clear focus on the relationship between relative social power and the possibilities for establishing or negotiating legal meaning. The popular legal consciousness literature depends on the general conditions for effective ethnography: especially the restriction of focus to *specific* social contexts. It implies the possible utility of a concept of legal culture in those kinds of contexts.

Equally, however, this literature seems relatively unconcerned with the tracing of social causality or the construction of explanatory theory; neither does it usually attempt the kind of comparative projects that this chapter has taken as central to a specifically comparative sociology of law. Ethnographic accounts of popular legal consciousness and its expression in social action seem to aim to set out complex thick descriptions of specific social settings of law. Yet this literature also generally affirms a commitment to sociology of law as social science (Sarat 1990b).

Conclusion

A general conclusion to be drawn from these reflections on legal culture is that the concept is most useful for its emphasis on the sheer complexity and diversity of the social matrix in which contemporary state legal systems exist. We have noted that legal culture may be understood as a vast diversity of overlapping cultures: some relatively local, some more universal. Yet, in many circumstances, reliance on a general concept of culture also makes problematic the theoretical identification of a specifically *legal* culture.

As social studies in law presently tend to retreat from or reject many traditional understandings of the idea of a specifically social science and adopt, appropriately and necessarily, interpretive methods that deny many positivist implications of the use of the term 'science' in this context, the temptation may be to rely more heavily on relatively vague concepts of culture and legal culture in the interpretation of social phenomena. The argument of this chapter is that this kind of reliance would, except in limited and carefully defined circumstances, be a mistake and that an examination of Friedman's long-term elaboration of implications of the concept of legal culture reveals problems that are probably endemic in its use.

In certain contexts, however, the idea of an undifferentiated aggregate of social elements, co-present in a certain time and place, may be useful and even necessary in social research. This idea is expressed conveniently in the concept of culture. In the study of relatively specific social contexts, the concept of legal culture may also be useful to embrace provisionally an entire contextual matrix in which state law operates.

More generally, it may be appropriate and necessary to refer in terms of culture to clusters of social phenomena whose exact interrelation is not known but whose collective significance is recognizable and requires emphasis. By this means it becomes possible to characterize complex webs of beliefs, values, understandings and practices, which sociological studies employing ethnographic methods may appropriately seek to describe, perhaps as a prelude to more specific inquiries about the ideological significance of legal doctrine and the practices in which it is institutionalized.

Chapter 6

Law in Culture

Chapter 5 questioned the explanatory value of the concept of culture in sociolegal studies, but legal analysis now encounters this concept in many contexts. From so-called cultural defences in criminal law to law's efforts to define, protect or express culture in various ways, the idea of culture is more prominent than ever in law. This chapter surveys a wide range of evidence of this contemporary prominence and asks how the idea of culture can be appropriately dealt with *juristically*. The answer, I argue, is to break 'culture' down into component parts and see it as expressed in different types of social relations of community.

The relationship of law and culture has long been a concern of legal anthropology and sociology of law. But it is recognized today as a central issue in many different kinds of juristic inquiries. All these recent invocations of the concept of culture indicate or imply problems at the boundaries of established thought about either the nature of law or the values that law is thought to express or reflect. The consequence is that legal theory must now systematically take account of the notion of culture. This chapter asks how this might best be done. I argue that a concept of culture, as such, is of limited utility for legal theory because the term 'culture' embraces a too indefinite and disparate range of phenomena. But legal theory needs conceptual resources to consider at a general level the relations of law and culture. This chapter suggests that these resources should include, above all, a rigorous distinguishing of different abstract types of community. What is encompassed by the vague idea of culture is actually the content of different types of social relations of community and the networks (combinations) in which they exist.

Intersections of Law and Culture

In what ways have the relations of law and culture become more prominent in legal scholarship? I shall try initially to sketch the main parameters of juristic concern in this area by outlining six important foci of legal inquiry in which culture is explicitly invoked and made central. Here the term is usually taken to indicate collective beliefs, values, traditions, attachments or outlooks. These are assumed to exist in persistent but not necessarily unchanging combinations, characteristic of particular social populations.

Comparative Law

Developments in comparative law indicate one such focus. Comparatists 'have become increasingly obsessed by notions of "legal culture"'(Ogus 2002: 419). As comparative legal study gains in importance as a practical matter in a world of globalization and perceived cultural diversity, the nature of comparative law as an enterprise is discussed widely.[1] The question of how far law is 'rooted' in, and how far it can 'fly free' of, culture becomes urgent. If comparative law serves the practical purposes of improving regulatory structures and systems, how far should comparatists see law as an adaptable technical instrument and how far as an expression of cultural conditions or *mentalités* (Legrand 1999) which law must acknowledge if it is to have practical significance? The debate on law and culture might seem to hold the key to comparative law's nature as a scholarly field and also to its potential as a source of practical guidance for legal policy – as, for example, in regard to legal transplants (Watson 1993) – and harmonization of law between legal systems. The key issue here is about *law's dependence on culture*. Does legal interpretation depend on cultural understandings? Is legal effectiveness determined ultimately by cultural conditions?

Liberalism and Multiculturalism

In a completely different context, culture presses its demand for consideration as a concept in political philosophy. Efforts to consider in a constructive way the implications of multiculturalism for liberalism are significant here (Kymlicka 1995; Kymlicka 1989; Raz 1998). Can multiculturalism be a liberal concept as, for example, Will Kymlicka proposes? If the rule of law is, in part, the doctrinal recognition of a need for equal treatment of equal cases before uniform, consistently applied law, can this doctrine recognize claims and interests of social groups as such, differentiated from other groups according to persistently reproduced, usually clearly recognizable but often highly complex criteria? These criteria might be defined as cultural: for example, on Kymlicka's (1995: 18) view, if they focus on collective identity associated with language, homeland and history. Can the rule of law recognize groups as cultural persons possessing rights and subject to duties? In the context of this chapter, what is significant is the fact that this large question is being discussed in many legal contexts today (cf. Kymlicka (ed.) 1995: Part 4).

The issue here is of *law's recognition of culture* in its conceptual structures. Is culture necessarily invisible to legal doctrine, at least where that doctrine is built on liberal premises? It might seem so, if law cannot recognize cultural variation or differentiation in any significant way, but assumes cultural uniformity within its jurisdiction. Given such an assumption, law may have no need to consider the nature of this uniform culture. But should culture be invisible? Conversely, should it

---

1   See, for example, Legrand and Munday (eds) 2003; Harding and Örücü (eds) 2002; Nelken and Feest (eds) 2001; Riles (ed.) 2001; Glenn 2004.

become a legal concept? What precise meaning can be given to the idea of culture if it is to assume an enhanced position in mainstream legal and political thought?

Legal Definitions of Culture

Law and culture are also linked in debates about law as 'constitutive'. Both feminism and critical race theory (CRT) have emphasized law's power to shape the meaning of social relationships and social institutions and, indeed, to define personal identity. This is not just a matter of defining legal personality (the juridical nature of the subject or citizen) for the purposes of regulation. Law sometimes also shapes expectations, responsibilities and constraints attaching to social statuses – for example as mother, immigrant, or member of a particular racial or ethnic group (Frug 1992; López 1996) – which thereby help to create the cultural meaning of those statuses. Much discussion (not restricted to feminism and CRT) stresses law's constitutive power – its capacity to create the meaning by which people understand the social environment in which they live, and their place in it. As regards property, Bentham (1970: 255) noted, 'creation of it is the work of law'. The same is surely true, in part, of responsibility, binding agreement, fault, guilt, fiduciary duty, authority, reasonableness and many other concepts that define everyday relationships.

In *Mashpee Tribe* v *Town of Mashpee*[2] an American court took responsibility for deciding whether the Mashpee people of Massachusetts were or were not 'a tribe'. In doing so, it defined their collective identity with dramatic consequences. The definition 'incorporated specific perceptions regarding race, leadership, community and territory that were entirely alien to Mashpee culture' (Torres and Milun 1995: 130). Law, applied in this way, dictates culture, demanding (for specific definitional purposes here related to property claims) that cultural expectations should be adjusted to conform to law's definitions and prescriptions (López 1996: 12–13; and see Sheffield 1997). Law, in these circumstances, polices and confers cultural meanings. The issue is of *law's domination of culture*.

Cultural Defences

A further recent intersection of law and culture occurs in debates around cultural defences in criminal law. 'Simply stated,' writes an American commentator, a cultural defence 'is the use of social customs and beliefs to explain [and so perhaps wholly or partly to justify or excuse from criminal liability] the behaviour of a defendant ... [S]ome cultural defences offer an explanation of how a foreign culture affects a person, usually an immigrant, who currently resides in America, comparing that culture's mores and legal standards with those of the United States. To a less frequent but significant extent, this defence is also used by America's indigenous

---

2   447 F Supp. 940 (D Mass 1978), affd, 592 F 2d 575 (1st Cir), cert denied, 444 US 866 (1979).

peoples and by those who are immersed in the country's non-dominant cultures' (Harris 1997: 241).

From one point of view, when a cultural defence is raised, what is at stake is a demand for differential cultural interpretation of law. Law's interpretive communities may not be restricted to professional communities in which lawyers help law 'work itself pure' through debate on the 'best' reading of legal texts.[3] Non-lawyer citizens are potentially legal interpreters too (Dworkin 1977: Chapter 8; 1985: Chapter 4). At the same time, legal professional communities themselves, in many Western countries, increasingly reflect explicitly proclaimed diversities of gender, race, ethnicity, sexual orientation, etc.[4] Law's interpretive communities now reflect the patterned differentiation of the social, which might also be described as a diversity of cultures. The idea that culture is brought explicitly into legal interpretation is, in a sense, a reversal of the idea of law dominating culture, considered above. Does culture dominate law in the sense that law's meanings cannot be secure except when related to the cultural contexts that inform them? If so, *which* cultural contexts will be treated as significant, or most significant, when these contexts are not uniform?[5]

In this context, then, the issue is about *law as an object of cultural competition* or struggle. Directly comparable matters arise when feminists demand that law be recognized as gendered in its very nature. Does, for example, English criminal law presume responses to violence that are more typically 'male' than 'female', so explaining its difficulty in recognizing the reasonableness of 'slow-burn' (delayed, calculated) reactions to violent provocation (Edwards 1996: Chapter 6)? Does the legal meaning of consent or force in rape or sexual harassment cases presuppose a particular male-oriented view of what is normal in sexual relationships (MacKinnon 1989: 111–13, 172–83)? Does the English law of equitable ownership of the home take a view of property and its modes of acquisition that ignores common types of women's experience?[6] If law is gendered, the parallel claim that law is 'cultured', in the sense of being powerfully shaped by certain cultural assumptions, may raise even more difficult practical problems for legal regulation. This is because law has typically assumed the uniformity of culture and so avoided considering it. But in contemporary conditions of considerable (and perhaps only partly mapped) cultural diversity such a position may no longer be tenable.

---

3   Cf. *Omychund v Barker* (1744) 1 Atk 21, 33.

4   Cf. Cotterrell 2003: Chapter 8, discussing a 'new jurisprudence of difference' arising, in part, from this professional development.

5   Marriage is an example of a concept long taken for granted as having an adequately settled central legal meaning but now, in some societies, a focus of culture conflict focused on law. See, for example, Shah 2005: 120, 121, asking 'how long English law will be able to continue turning a blind eye to ethnic minority legal facts ...'; a legal system must be 'sensitive to the ... ethnicity of the persons that come before it'; plural marriage should 'be accepted as constituting one form of family arrangement within a polyethnic society ...'

6   See, for example, *Lloyd's Bank* v *Rosset* [1991] AC 107; *Burns* v *Burns* [1984] Ch 317.

In Anglo-American legal traditions, the rootedness of law in culture has often been celebrated and treated as of considerable political significance. Coke CJ, early in the seventeenth century, wrote of English common law: 'we are but of yesterday ... our days upon the earth are but as a shadow in respect of the old ancient days and times past, wherein the laws have been ... by long and continual experience ... refined ...'[7] Early in the twentieth century, the American jurist James Carter wrote that, 'Law, Custom, Conduct, Life – different names for almost the same thing – are so inseparably blended together that one cannot even be thought of without the other' (Carter 1907: 320). It would be hard to find a clearer assertion of the total embeddedness of law in culture, the entire dependency of legal meaning on cultural context.

These assumptions seemed, until recently, unproblematic because the unity of culture was an object of faith in classical common law thought. The rise of legal positivism shifted attention from cultural bases of law to its political sources in legislation and obscured the issue of the consequences of cultural change. Only recently, with interpretation elevated to a central concern of legal theory, has the nature of legal interpretive communities attracted sustained attention. Consequently, the patterned differentiation of the social (by gender, class, race, ethnicity, sexual orientation, religion, and so on) has also become a matter for inquiry bearing on the nature of law.

Law and Popular Culture

A fifth example of contemporary research explicitly relating law and culture is the burgeoning literature on 'law and popular culture'. Popular culture in this context is often taken to mean the presentation of images of life through film, television, theatre, novels, magazines, newspapers or advertising (Silbey 2002). The object of much research is to ask how law appears when represented as part of society's general, public self-images, filtered through popular understandings or presented by mass media. The issue is of *law as a cultural projection* – not necessarily understood through any detailed acquaintance with its practice, doctrine or effects but perceived in terms of constructed images or fictional narratives. The media of popular culture, portraying law, shape this portrayal to existing cultural presuppositions.

Closely related for the purposes of this chapter's categorizations is recent research on law and 'popular consciousness' (such as Ewick and Silbey 1998; Merry 1990; Yngvesson 1993) which examines how citizens in various contexts understand law and experience it, often in ways radically at odds with lawyers' professional understandings and experience of law. This literature, however, usually asks how popular experience and perceptions of law raise possibilities for resistance to law's domination of culture.

One theme is that law (as professionalized juristic doctrine), encountering the rich variety of cultural experience, is faced with cultural conditions that it may not

---

7   *Calvin's Case* (1608) 7 Co Rep 1, 3.

be able either to understand or regulate comprehensively. 'Popular consciousness' may not succeed in redefining law in defiance of professional juristic interpretations but culture's rich, uncontrollable diversity may provide opportunities to resist these interpretations. Research in this area aims at capturing cultural richness and holistic experience. So, it often uses narrative accounts that can provide, through many incidental insights, thick descriptions (Geertz 1973) of culture. By such means, law in popular consciousness is often shown to be entirely different in character from law as professional knowledge and practice. Law as a cultural projection (rather than as juristic expertise) is multifaceted and hard to define in precise prescriptions or procedures. It is a matter of diverse, complex experiences, in which the legal and the non-legal are often hard to separate.

Law and Cultural Heritage

A final example of the law–culture link is law's role as protector of 'cultural heritage'. This includes the protection of historic sites, control of the export of works of art, the use of legally regulated incentives to protect local film industries or other enterprises seen as representing national or minority cultures, and the use of laws to promote or preserve the use of national languages. Here the issue is of *law's stewardship of culture*. Often this culture is presumed to be a collective possession of the entire society which law regulates. Sometimes it is seen as the collective possession of minority groups, whose distinctive culture is considered in turn to be part of the collective cultural wealth of society as a whole.

Sociolegal Components of Culture

The examples above suggest the pervasiveness and diversity of issues about law's contemporary relation to culture. But they should also suggest how confused this relationship generally is in legal scholarship. Mainly this is because the concept of culture is vague in much legal literature. Though it is widely recognized that links between law and culture should be explored, the question of what it is that law is to be linked to in this exploration often remains unclearly answered. As a consequence, links between law and culture are portrayed in many seemingly incompatible ways – law sometimes appearing to be dependent on culture, sometimes dominating and controlling it; sometimes ignoring it, sometimes promoting or protecting it; sometimes expressing it, sometimes being expressed by it.

The remainder of this chapter sketches ideas as to how this problem might be addressed. A starting point is to note that culture, in the examples of legal inquiries referred to above, typically embraces traditions (a sense of shared cultural inheritance of some kind) and values or beliefs (a sense of convergence or commonality in ways of thinking, commitments, outlooks or attitudes in a population). Overlaying these components of culture are often affective (emotional) elements that colour shared traditions, value-commitments, attitudes or outlooks. When law is seen as rooted in or impacting on culture it is usually some such aspects of culture that are being emphasized.

At the very beginning of the era of modern code-based European law, Savigny (1831) proclaimed the deep embeddedness of law in culture, understood as the spirit of the people (*Volksgeist*), closely related to common language. Shared language can, indeed, be seen as a form of cultural tradition, an *inheritance* that shapes and expresses a sense of cultural unity. In a Savignian perspective – which is close in some respects to the classical English common law outlook made explicit by such as Edward Coke and Matthew Hale (Cotterrell 2003: Chapter 2) – law too is a symbol of cultural inheritance. Like language, law evolves and grows. Yet, according to this view, it also necessarily retains a sense of cultural homogeneity and gains its essential meanings (its implicit criteria of interpretation and evaluation) from its rootedness in the traditional cultural matrix – the inherited environment.

As it appears in this perspective, law cannot fly free of its cultural foundations. Yet *because* of its cultural rootedness it has considerable power. It is a carrier of culture (perhaps the most important carrier) and is given force by this responsibility. Lawyers, for Savigny, are interpreters of culture, in important respects its professional guardians and definers. In classical English common law thought, the 'artificial reason' of the law is accessible only to lawyers – and then only through long experience, not merely by reading books (Sommerville 1999: 84, 89; Postema 1986: 32–3). It gains a peculiarly unassailable strength from being both arcane, esoteric knowledge *and* the assumed collective experience of the community (here meaning the nation, realm or people). The important point is that law can be portrayed in this kind of reasoning as utterly dependent on inherited cultural conditions, yet, at the same time, immensely powerful because of this cultural basis.

Alongside this traditional component of culture is a different (though often interrelated) one that focuses on common *mentalité*, shared ultimate values or beliefs, significant attitudes held in common, or a collective general outlook. Though such common ways of thinking, feeling and evaluating (and the practices that embody them) will often be a received inheritance, this traditional basis may be emphasized less than the current strength and integrity of the beliefs or values assumed to be held in common and their differentiation from others assumed to be typical of outsiders of the cultural group. Again, such an assumed basis of culture, related to law, makes it possible to portray law as both strong and weak, dominating and dominated.

Thus, Pierre Legrand's (1999) recent work in comparative law stresses the importance of legal culture as a *mentalité* informing law, and in which legal practices and doctrines exist and are given meaning. One consequence of law's embeddedness in legal culture, for Legrand (2001), is that legal transplants between different cultural milieux of law are, strictly speaking, impossible – law's capacity as a directive instrument, a technique for steering social change, seems dramatically scaled down. On the other hand, law is shown as something much more significant than a technical instrument of control. It is part of a way of life, a means of interpreting social relationships, a component of an entire outlook, deeply rooted in all kinds of experience (not only juristic). Law rooted in culture has the strength to maintain its identity in the face of political efforts to instrumentalize it. In fact, like Savigny's assertion of law's cultural rootedness, Legrand's new version of this old claim may give a distorted view in some respects of the nature of law as a cultural phenomenon. This is because (like Savigny) it tends to assume a monolithic character of culture, rather than recognizing the fragmented, complex, shifting nature of cultural phenomena (see further, Chapter 8, below). But the key point is that, again, law in culture is portrayed as *both* powerful and dependent and as having (moral) characteristics not directly affected by political conditions of the creation, interpretation and enforcement of law.

Culture in relation to law is thus highly paradoxical: weak and strong, dependent and independent, expressed in different ways, embedded in or encompassing many different things. While culture is usually assumed to be a unity of some kind, it actually refers to a fragmented diversity of influences, experiences, understandings, environments, expectations and constraints. In this situation it may be most helpful to see culture – as regards its relation to legal regulation – as a matter of various contrasting criteria that define social relations of community.

For example, culture is certainly, in part, a matter of tradition. Where this is so, it is expressed in social relations of community that are themselves traditional in character. These relations may, for example, be based merely on common language, or common territorial location, inherited environment or customs, or common historical experience. Culture is also, in part, a matter of beliefs or values held in common, shared outlooks, ways of understanding or world views. Where this is so, it is expressed in social relations of community founded on a real or assumed shared commitment to certain ultimate values or beliefs. But, in addition, culture can embrace an affective (emotional) bond that may be extremely hard to define or understand: a sense of attachment that is diffuse, not rationally explicable or capable of being conclusively related to particular phenomena, but often evoked symbolically (for example, through cuisine, landscape, buildings, works of art, items of popular culture, experience of particular events). Culture can therefore be expressed in affective social relations of community.

Earlier, in Chapter 4, I discussed how law can relate to community of belief (or values), traditional community or affective community, treating these as ideal types. As explained there, four types of community can be identified by drawing on Max Weber's sociology, and in combination they exhaust all the possible forms of stable, cooperative social relations (see also Cotterrell 2003: 257–61). The fourth type of community, to be added alongside the traditional, belief-based and affective types, is instrumental community – social relations based purely on the pursuit of common or convergent purposes (often but not exclusively economic).

From one point of view it might seem plausible to exclude instrumental community from consideration in relation to culture. Instrumental relations survive just as long as the purposes for which those relations have been entered into. For that reason they may not have the enduring character that is often associated with cultural phenomena. Once the purposes have been fulfilled, social relations come to an end. Indeed, the idea of culture, as it is generally invoked in relation to law today, does often imply a meaning that embraces affective, belief-based and traditional relations of community (combined in complex networks), rather than instrumental relations. So, globalization is usually associated with the internationalization and transnationalization of instrumental (mainly economic) relations. And it is often viewed as set against considerations of culture. Culture, in fact, is often seen as needing protection against globalization.

But from another point of view, globalization carries its own culture which might be thought of as, in many ways, one that values instrumental relations and seeks to harmonize and stabilize the conditions for establishing and maintaining them in transnational environments. So, culture can sometimes be expressed in terms of instrumental community, too. Once culture is reinterpreted in terms of the four ideal types of community, interrelated in practice in innumerable ways in complex networks of community, the possibility is opened for more productive analyses in legal theory of the relations of law and culture. For one thing, the separation of the idea of culture into several distinctive ideal types of social relations of community makes it possible to see how culture can be and often is in conflict with itself: that is, different types of social relations of community may conflict with each other.

Law's relation to each of these types of community is different. Hence law's role in culture conflicts is complex. The often-noted potential conflict between globalization and the protection of distinct cultures is frequently a clash between the transnational proliferation of instrumental relations of community and the more local promotion of other types of community. But it can also be a matter of the transnational promotion of a particular community of belief or values (stressing, for example, the ultimate values of freedom, democracy or human rights, or, indeed, of market relations as a specially valuable form of social relations).

Culture and Regulatory Complexity

The significance here of a typology of relations of community is to provide a vehicle for arguing that, for the purposes of legal theory, the concept of culture should be broken down into distinct components and its vagueness and indeterminacy thereby reduced. Relations of law and culture are now a very important focus for legal inquiries. But the concept of culture is too vague to be useful in this context. Law's diverse relations with community can, however, be productively analysed in terms of ideal types. Up to a point, different kinds of law can be associated with different types of community and, in general terms, law's regulatory potential and some general problems of its use can be considered (and differentiated) in connection with each of these types (for a detailed discussion see Chapter 9, below). All law exists in culture but, because it shapes relations of community, law shapes culture.

This approach might be clarified by returning to the issue of cultural defences in criminal law. Martin Golding has recently argued that while cultural evidence 'may have a role to play in conjunction with the standard excuses and with sentencing considerations' a free-standing cultural defence to criminal liability should not be accepted (Golding 2002: 157). His analysis emphasizes the kind of mental states (in particular, knowledge of circumstances and of the propriety of acts) that criminal law normally requires for liability. A key issue is what it is reasonable for the defendant to know and think about the legal situation, the act and the context of action. The problem with a cultural defence is that it seeks to locate 'reasonableness' in cultural understandings that may be entirely unreasonable from law's usual standpoints. Fundamental, intractable, practical questions arise. What are the conditions for and limitations on the invocation of 'culture'? What defines the specificity of any particular culture and what should determine when 'cultural' considerations should or should not apply? The difficulty is ultimately that of the vagueness of the concept of culture.

A law-and-community analysis also leads to scepticism about general cultural defences while similarly advocating sensitivity to cultural evidence. But it adopts a different approach to the issues. The focus is not on culture as such but on the nature of the specific social relations to be regulated. Their quality and meaning are to be judged by reference to the types of community these social relations embody. Three American local jurisdiction cases,[8] which Golding refers to, illustrate situations in which the issues may arise. In *People* v *Moua* (1985) the defendant, charged with the kidnapping and rape of a woman he had abducted, pleaded that the marriage-by-capture practice of his Laotian tribal culture authorized both the woman's abduction and her protests, which demonstrated her virtuousness. He was convicted of the lesser offence of false imprisonment. In *People* v *Chen* (1988) the defendant killed his adulterous wife. The court held him guilty of manslaughter rather than murder, finding that he was 'driven to violence by traditional Chinese values about adultery and loss of manhood'. An unnamed Nebraska case debated the liability of an Iraqi immigrant father for the forced arranged marriages of his two daughters, aged 13 and 14, as well as the liability of their 'husbands' for unlawful sexual relations with them. The practice of arranged marriage was understood by all the defendants as normal, proper and sanctioned by long tradition.

What is at issue in these cases is the nature of the social relations that law must regulate. And it is important to consider both the 'external' legal classification and interpretation of the type of social relationship involved and the 'internal' perceptions of the relationship by the participants in it. As Golding notes, law properly seeks evidence of these perceptions and this may involve what is termed cultural evidence. But the danger in using the term 'culture' here is in reifying perceptions (treating them as positive phenomena given by membership of a certain culture), instead of recognizing that invoking culture cannot do the work of assessing individuals' subjective understandings of their relationships. It is no accident that issues of culture are often raised in cases involving domestic or sexual relations. In these cases, relations of affective community may be very relevant. But of all types of community, affective community is often the hardest for law to regulate. This is mainly because of the difficulty of fixing – in the form of rational rules – parameters

---

8   Details are in Golding 2002: 148–51.

of expectation, obligation and understanding that govern emotional ties. Invoking culture cannot solve the problem and may disguise it.

Central to the three cases are issues about *force* and *consent*. But these are matters of variable, sometimes indeterminate meaning depending on context. Law hardly approaches them consistently. Dominant communities of belief, however, in contemporary Western societies emphasize the ultimate value of human dignity and autonomy (expressed most clearly and directly in invocations of human rights). In representing this type of community, law struggles to define meanings of dignity and autonomy that can be generalized as common values underlying all forms of social relations. These values also imply how force and consent are to be understood and regulated in various contexts.

Ultimately at issue in the cases above is law's stance on this particular value system – either insisting on its non-negotiable character or negotiating its interplay with *different* understandings of human autonomy and dignity. Invoking culture in this context might help to identify some 'local' community of values having a different view of issues of dignity and autonomy. But invoking culture also implies reasons – often indeterminate and unexpressed – why this local community of values should be *respected* by law: reasons typically linked to tradition, group interests or group solidarity.

Law cannot, however, allow defences, exceptions or justifications under some blanket category of culture. It must make judgments about the acceptability of each component of culture (whether seen as a matter of interests, of ultimate values and beliefs, of traditions or of affective ties). A law-and-community approach sees law as rooted in community life; as an ever-changing web of norms expressing and influencing the interactions of many different networks of community. Law is not neutral about these networks. It judges the particular norms arising in them, in terms of its existing doctrine, and it represses, adopts, integrates, modifies or compromises with these norms.

In the three cases above, traditional community should also be seen as a factor to be taken into account. In pleading cultural defences, appeal is made to inherited ways, customary practices and familiar experience. What, then, is the legal significance of tradition as a component of culture? Law recognizes traditional practices and understandings, treating tradition mainly as accumulated experience. Law's appeals to 'reasonableness', for example, depend largely on the existence of this experience. The regulation of traditional community aims at securing basic requirements for coexistence. But law is also often required to help people escape tradition, giving them freedom to find new projects and relationships (Santos 2002: 177). So, in dominant contemporary Western understandings, legal policy emphasizes the value of security but also the need to escape inertia: law should respect tradition insofar as it gives orientation to people's lives, but not so as to make projects and instrumental relations atrophy and not so as to allow affective relations to become oppressive. Thus, because tradition is of ambiguous virtue, having both positive and negative aspects, its regulation must be governed by the evolving content of the dominant communities of values that law also serves.

Conclusion

This chapter's purpose has been to suggest that relations of law and culture should be re-conceptualized. They should be considered as problems of legal regulation bearing on different types of community with which law is concerned and the networks of social relations in which these types are combined.

Because social relations of community are diverse and their nature and significance are understood in diverse ways, law can never represent in a harmonious, integrated way all of these relations. In representing and shaping culture by these means, law is influenced by power in communities and between them. Hence it is not paradoxical to see law as simultaneously depending on and dominating culture, being insensitive to and ignorant of it, while seemingly promoting or protecting it, expressing it and being expressed in it. Culture is important for law. But community, defined in terms of a strictly limited number of ideal types, may be the most powerful concept available to legal theory to help unravel the complexities of the law–culture relation.

Chapter 7

Is There a Logic of Legal Transplants?

Alan Watson and William Ewald have suggested a new relationship between comparative law and legal sociology. But they portray it in a way that denies the important contributions these fields of scholarship can make to each other. Using the typology of community introduced in Chapter 4, this chapter examines the core of Watson's influential approach to comparative law – his theses about transplantation of law between legal systems. I argue that the law-and-community approach allows a nuanced, realistic analysis of the possibilities of successful legal transplants. It also suggests how success here should be understood.

This chapter takes as its departure point some provocative ideas about the relation of sociology of law to comparative legal studies. William Ewald has advanced them in defending and explaining Alan Watson's influential theses about comparative law (Ewald 1995b). My purpose in the first half of the chapter is to criticize the problematic Ewald and Watson set up for relations between comparative law and legal sociology. I argue that this problematic is unhelpful. It deters productive interaction between these fields. The remainder of the chapter suggests a new conceptual framework for that interaction. It does so by rethinking the idea on which Watson's work focuses: legal transplantation – the transferring or borrowing of law between legal systems.

Watson's 'Sociology-free' Comparative Law

Ewald argues that if Watson's claims about legal development are shorn of extreme formulations they are not only fundamental for comparative law but should inspire major changes in legal sociology. In Ewald's view, Watson 'sets new methodological standards for sociological speculation about the nature of law' and new tasks for 'speculative legal sociologists' in considering the relation of legal and social change; indeed, unless Watson's challenge is taken up, legal sociology's speculations here 'will be (as so often in the past) little more than a fable' (Ewald 1995b: 509, 510).

The challenge involves entirely discarding what Ewald terms 'mirror theories' of law and social change. These postulate that, in some way, law mirrors society or some aspect of it in a consistent, theoretically specifiable way. Mirror theories are incompatible with Watson's most important general claims about the processes of legal change, documented and illustrated in many publications (e.g. Watson 1977, 1985a, 1985b, 1991, 1993). These claims include the following:

1. that the growth of law is principally to be explained by the transplantation of legal rules between legal systems, or by the elaboration of existing legal ideas within systems so as to apply them by analogy to new circumstances;
2. that social need does not necessarily, or even often, bring about legal development and that laws that serve no apparent social needs survive for generations and sometimes centuries;
3. that the mechanisms of legal change are largely controlled 'internally' within legal systems by legal professional elites such as makers of codes or drafters of legislation (Watson 1988: Chapters 1 and 2), judges or jurists;
4. that legal rules survive over long periods with 'extraordinary persistence' (Ewald 1995b: 490, 496) despite significant variation in the social context on which they operate; and
5. that the development of at least some important bodies of law (notably major structures of European civil law) is wholly or largely the result of 'purely legal history' and can be explained without reference to social, political or economic factors (Ewald 1995b: 500).

Stronger, more general assertions about law's 'insulation' from society can be found in Watson's work. For example, he sometimes suggests, as Ewald puts it, 'that there is *no* interesting relationship to be discovered between law and society' or 'that law is radically insulated from economics, sociology, and politics' (1995b: 509). But Ewald discards these extreme views as being atypical of Watson's general outlook on legal development, gathered from his work as a whole.

Ewald emphasizes the radical implications of Watson's ideas for legal theory, by systematizing and generalizing them. This is necessary because 'Watson himself has presented his theory in a somewhat loose and intuitive fashion'(Ewald 1995b: 491). Ewald wants to harness Watson's ideas to do more than explain particular occurrences in legal history. Watson presents 'an original and contentious view of the relationship between law and society' and 'opens the door to a view of law ... subtler and more nuanced than any of the theories that have hitherto prevailed' (Ewald 1995b: 490, 509). His work suggests that causal relationships between law and society 'will prove to be reciprocal, interactive and multi-layered'; they will not be straightforward. On the other hand, his approach also raises the possibility that 'the phenomena may be too complex for a tidy description, even in principle' and that 'no satisfactory theory can be given' (1995b: 508, 509).

Thus, if Watson's theses about the autonomy of law from society hold good, doubt might be cast on any general theory of law and society. The matter might simply be too complex to theorize. A legal theory must grow out of 'a careful study of the data, rather than being imposed on them a priori' (Ewald 1995b: 510). Criticizing legal sociology, Watson claims that, 'as it is usually practised,' it 'provides the least help [by comparison with legal history and 'traditional comparative law'] in understanding legal change and the relationship between legal rules and the society in which they operate' (Watson 1991: 72). This is because it lacks historical perspective on the pace of law's response (if any) to changed circumstances; also, its focus on law-in-action 'leads to a discounting of the importance of legal rules and to a lack of awareness of their imperfections and their impact' (1991: 72).

No further exemplification or qualification of these statements is given, however, and so they amount to painting with a very broad brush. It is hard to claim that Max Weber's (1968) work, to take a single major example, lacks a historical dimension or discounts the importance of legal rules.[1] Watson (1977) quotes a very diverse group of writers including Savigny, Roscoe Pound and Marx, for claims that law corresponds with some constant feature of society, or expresses social interests or needs. Ewald sees such writers as propounding 'mirror theories'. The term seems inspired by Lawrence Friedman's claim that law is 'a mirror of society' or 'a mirror held up against life' and 'moulded by economy and society' (Friedman 1985b: 12, 595). Both Ewald and Watson quote similar passages from Friedman to characterize the sociological theories to be challenged (Ewald 1995b: 492; Watson 1991: 82–3; and see Wise 1990: 2). But neither of them looks in any detail at the theories to consider their variety and the specificity of their claims. Thus, Watson has justifiably been accused of setting up a straw man, caricaturing what he wishes to attack (Abel 1982b: 790); he ignores the detail of the arguments of these theories and their qualifications and conditions.

While Ewald treats mirror theories as a class he provides no definitive list of the theories included in this class. Sometimes he refers simply to '*the* mirror theory' as '*the* theory that law is the mirror of some set of forces (social, political, economic, whatever) external to the law' (1995b: 491, my emphasis). What is meant by law 'mirroring' society is never addressed and Friedman's quoted words seem the only justification for using this terminology. Ewald does note that different theories postulate different 'strengths' of determination of law by society (or whatever social factor the theory addresses) and that sometimes a variety of factors is seen as determining (1995b: 493–4). But these variables do not prevent Ewald treating the theories generically or even as a single compendium theory.

The suspicion that this amounts to a drawing of the shutters against all sociolegal theory is strengthened by Watson's own comments. He treats all sociological and anthropological theories of legal development as functional theories (Watson 1991: 85, 86) and claims that they cannot recognize the often dysfunctional character of law (as legal rules). Hence, he admits that he thinks it impossible to develop any general theory of law from a sociological or anthropological standpoint (1991: 86). Yet he also claims, in the same essay, that 'the sociological perspective is necessary for any understanding of legal development' and his approach 'does not dismiss the theoretical framework of sociology of law, rather it sidesteps it for the time being' (1991: 72, 92).

Why should it be necessary to arrive at such unclear but essentially negative positions? Are, for example, no social theories of law acceptable to Watsonian comparatists, even if they try (as they are enjoined to do) to take account of law's processes of apparently 'internal' development or 'purely legal history'? Should it

---

1　Aspects of Weber's work are discussed in Watson 1981: Chapter 3.

not be emphasized that Watson's 'weak' theses (the ones Ewald wishes to defend), as opposed to his more extreme pronouncements, do not deny that much legal development is brought about by social factors of some kind? Surely it should be recognized that many social scientific theories of law are not functional theories; that is, they do not assume that the social phenomena they study must be interpreted in terms of their functions? And, above all, surely it should be recognized that there is, in fact, *no meaningful category of mirror theories* but rather an immense variety of theories addressing different aspects of law as a social phenomenon? Should it not also be noticed that the relation of law to society is not obviously the main focus of sociological approaches to law today? Rather, law may be seen as an aspect of society, or as a field of social experience, its 'internal' processes, in themselves, being seen as social processes, so that – as noted in Chapters 2 and 3, above – the internal–external distinction in relation to law appears, sociologically, to be of very doubtful utility.

A Logic in Search of a Theory

Watson's theoretical aim seems to be only to show that other theories are wrong, not to state a general theory of his own. It would certainly be significant to argue that particular social theories – for example, of Marx or Montesquieu – invoked by comparatists are wrong, but this could not be done by claiming that they do not explain *every* legal development, or rule pattern in every legal system, or even every important development or pattern. That might show only that the theories need supplementing. Proving these theories wrong would involve showing that they explain *nothing*, or nothing significant. But because Ewald wishes to present only Watson's more moderate theses, he gives the legal sociologist little to confront. It is, after all, a commonplace of legal sociology that, as Watson claims (Watson 1977: 8; and see Ewald 1995b: 499–500, 503), legal professional elites are important (the question is how important). They are often able to control to some extent the patterns of development of legal doctrine, and lawyers act to preserve their professional prerogatives and interests in the face of pressures arising from sources external to their professional groups.

   While the legal sociologist is given little to address, Watson's logic, as defended by Ewald, puts Watson himself in an even more difficult position. His task is to confront the entire fictitious category of mirror theories but only with his 'weak' thesis. In other words, Watson must show that at least *some* important legal developments have occurred without any reason for them that can be found in 'society' (that is, excluding the possible reasons of self-interest, inertia, conservatism or professional pride of the class of law-makers themselves who are treated for this purpose as not being part of society). Alternatively – and this is, it seems, often preferable for Watson – the task is to show that some particular law or body of legal doctrine has survived for some considerable time despite the fact that it serves the interests of no social group or section of society, its lack of utility is known and it could be changed (Watson 1991: 91; Ewald 1995b: 502, 507).

Either approach presents logically impossible tasks. How is it possible to prove that *no* interests of any kind are served by a law? Or that there could be *no* social reason for it? The problem of proving an absolute negative is obvious. And the practical difficulties even of some plausible demonstration must be great for ancient societies where evidence of many potentially relevant matters is limited. Further, if such a proof were seriously to be undertaken it would involve a social scientific inquiry of some kind in order to understand in depth the situation of social groups or patterns of social relationships in the context of the law.

Again, as Watson recognizes, a survival of socially dysfunctional law is significant only if the law nevertheless has important effects. His tendency is to assume that laws relating to an area of obvious social importance (such as land tenure or contracting) must, in themselves, be important in their effects. He emphasizes that laws frame social institutions; legal institutions, for him, are social institutions given legal effectiveness and seen from a legal viewpoint (Watson 1985b: 68). But it has long been recognized that particular legal forms (for example, of property holding or of recognition of collectivities) may sometimes have limited significance, in themselves, even where they relate to matters of undeniable social importance (see, for example, Renner 1949; Friedmann 1967: Chapter 34). The matter can only be addressed satisfactorily through empirical study of patterns of social organization and social relations (Friedman 1979: 127). But Watson is uninterested in pursuing such inquiries. Their necessity, however, demolishes the claim that, even for the particular laws he focuses on, legal change (or its absence) can be fully understood without resort to empirical inquiries about the nature of society.

The essential difficulty is in Watson's negative logic of legal transplants. As Richard Abel suggests, 'it is hard to conceive of a theory of law in society grounded on the principle of absurdity, irrationality, and disconnection' (1982b: 791). Watson willingly affirms his lack of concern with functional theories. But this admission hides the fact that, as Abel claims (1982b: 793), he is unconcerned with the rigorous construction of *any* theory.

Ewald, however, sees Watson's approach as 'a major theoretical advance' (Ewald 1995b: 491). Ultimately the advance seems to be to clear the way for a philosophical approach to comparative law, freeing it from any need for interdisciplinary cooperation in the social sciences. This contrasts strongly with the important tradition of openness to these disciplines and of locating law in a broad historical context that influences much work in comparative law and has been regularly and explicitly defended by many prominent comparatists.[2] Ewald declares the priority of philosophy over other disciplines in relation to comparative law. Indeed, comparative law is an essentially philosophical enterprise at the stage of execution and 'inherently a single-track activity' (1995a: 1946–7, 1951). But this seems doubtful. An interdependence of

---

2   See, especially, Zweigert 1975; Zweigert and Kötz 1998: 10–12; David and Brierley 1985: 13; Hall 1963: Chapter 2; Sacco 1991: 388–90.

legal sociology and comparative law seems indicated by the empirical questions that the operationalization of Watson's theses, as interpreted by Ewald, consistently provokes.

It seems to me, indeed, that viewed broadly, comparative law and sociology of law are committed to a single enterprise of understanding law as a social phenomenon. Rodolfo Sacco suggests that the 'primary and essential aim of comparative law as a science ... is better knowledge of legal rules and institutions ... The interest of the jurist should be aroused ... wherever he finds rules to study' (Sacco 1991: 5, 9). If this is so, it would seem that both comparative law and legal sociology are concerned with law as ideas and as practice, as institutionalized doctrine in some sense.

Thus, Watson's approach, systematized by Ewald, misunderstands legal sociology while making its own fundamental sociological assumptions. Nevertheless, Watson provides informed reflections on important aspects of legal experience. Legal sociology must explain and integrate Watson's theses in a broader perspective that re-opens avenues for effective cooperation with comparatists. In particular, legal sociology must examine carefully Watson's conceptualization and explanation of legal transplants.

As Watson inadvertently shows, however, the question of how law is to be conceptualized underlies many problems in using the idea of legal transplants. Watson remarks that in his work 'I was ... primarily concerned with positive rules of law' (1991: 86–7). While law-in-action is obviously important, positive law or law-in-the-books is to be emphasized. For Joachim Zekoll (1996: 2747), Watson's 'positivism stands in stark contrast to traditional comparative scholarship'[3] which seeks to put law into a context of its practical application and cultural resonance. For Lawrence Friedman (1979: 128), Watson treats law as 'words strung out on paper, not a living process'.

But Watson also insists that law is 'part of culture'. Law is part of the different cultures of law-makers ('that elite group who in a particular society have their hands on the levers of legal change'), lawyers in general and 'the population at large' (1991: 100). It is essential, he claims, to recognize the 'enormous power' and 'autonomy' of legal culture (1991: 102). What is important for Watson is what Friedman (1975) calls internal legal culture; that is, the outlook, practices, knowledge and values of legal professionals or people performing specialized legal tasks. Watson (1995) uses the concept of legal formants to describe contexts in which law comes into being and gains its meaning. This term, defined by Sacco, 'recognises ... that living law contains many different elements such as statutory rules, the formulations of scholars, and the decisions of judges', so that it encompasses not only rules but also implicit, taken-for-granted or underlying features of law in particular contexts (Sacco 1991: 22, 384, 388). For Watson, law must be understood broadly to recognize fully its processes of development by law-makers: 'a rule cannot become law without being subjected to legal culture' (Watson 1991: 101).

---

3   See, however, Watson 1988: Chapter 5, which offers a spirited critique of positivist legal theory.

On the other hand, it seems that he thinks an emphasis on positive rules is adequate in considering law's impact beyond this professionalized sphere. Thus, he asserts, without supplying any evidence, that to 'a very considerable extent the behaviour of lesser officials is hemmed in and restricted by rules of positive law, and the behaviour of individuals is also affected by legal rules' (1991: 87).

These positions are important because they show a crucial ambiguity as to what counts as law in Watson's work. Sometimes positive legal rules are emphasized; sometimes wider but indeterminate ideas of legal culture. The rule emphasis might suggest, as in Watson's approach, that legal borrowing from other systems is *simple*; if law-makers have the will and skill they might simply choose from the most technically sophisticated and legally prestigious sources available. It becomes a separate issue to consider how any borrowed rule once received operates in its new environment (Watson 1993: 20). On the other hand, an emphasis on legal culture might highlight the *difficulty* or even impossibility of transplants, since a legal culture is not easily replaced by a different one and legal rules are understood in relation to legal cultures (Legrand 2001).

Legal culture here could be interpreted by different writers as encompassing different elements, and – as we saw in Chapter 5, above – the concept often seems highly indeterminate. So, an entire spectrum of views on the feasibility of legal transplants is easily encouraged. But implicitly, at least, legal culture, in many discussions, tends to mean aspects of professionalized legal thought and practice, especially those typically considered by comparatists as characterizing the style, outlook or tradition of legal systems.

Viewed sociologically, this professional environment of legal ideas and practices requires empirical study. Research on the development of international commercial arbitration practice in various countries vividly shows lawyers' legal cultures conflicting in the development of important new markets for legal services (Dezalay and Garth 1996). This research understands these cultures in terms of lawyers' traditional practices, views of law and styles of work. But it also shows the way legal cultures, in this empirically definable sense, are reformed and reorganized under the pressure of economic developments and transnational influences and, above all, competition in markets for legal services (see also Garapon 1995). The contrast could not be more stark between such an empirical approach recognizing diversity and continuous change in lawyers' roles, outlooks and organizational strategies in relation to legal doctrine, and Watson's use of a non-empirical and therefore seemingly static idea of professional legal culture.

Thus, it is important to Watson's theses on legal development's relative insulation from social pressures that law 'is treated [by lawyers] as existing in its own right'; that 'the means of creating law, the sources of law, come to be regarded as a given, almost as something sacrosanct, and change in these even when they are obviously deeply flawed is extremely difficult to achieve'; again, for lawyers 'law has to be justified in its own terms; hence authority has to be sought and found. That authority ... must already exist; hence law is typically backward-looking' (Watson 1985b: 119). Undoubtedly these observations are plausible, but whether they characterize lawyers' style and outlook in all important contexts of legal practice or legal development is very doubtful, especially in contemporary conditions of rapid legal change, policy-driven law and transnational pressures on legal regulation. Legal traditions are the traditions of specific legal communities, whose conditions of existence can and should be studied empirically.

The way law is conceptualized – for example, as rules, as ideas embedded in legal culture, as a part of culture in some wider sense, or as an instrument for particular purposes – colours the way that the success (indeed, the very possibility) of legal borrowing is judged. An emphasis on law as positive rules might make transplantation seem unproblematic, as noted earlier. Mere official promulgation of the borrowed law might be treated as transplantation: concern is 'with the existence of the rule, not with how it operates within the society as a result of academic or judicial interpretation' (Watson 1993: 20) or popular invocation or acceptance. By contrast, an emphasis on law as an instrument necessarily directs attention to law-in-action. A legal transplant will not be considered significant (or perhaps as occurring at all) unless law can be shown to have social effects in the recipient society. The success of the transplant will be judged by whether or not it has the effects intended, which were the reason for it. Similarly, where law is seen as an expression or aspect of culture in the sense of shared traditions, values or beliefs (either of lawyers, of society generally or of some part of it), a legal transplant will be considered successful only if it proves consistent with these matters of culture in the recipient environment or reshapes them in conformity with the cultural presuppositions of the transplanted law.

Given these complexities it is tempting to say that no logic of legal transplants is possible; the concept of legal transplant itself is unclear, the matters to be addressed too complex, the variables too numerous, or too often insufficiently defined. Yet important sociological ideas have been put forward as to why transfers of law succeed or fail. What seems necessary is to try to integrate these ideas with those of recent work that emphasizes the strength of legal professional traditions, styles, discourses, outlooks and practices in different legal systems.

Legal Transplants and Law's Communities

In the older literature, generalizations about legal transplantation often rely on simple categorizations of law. Thus, Ernst Levy claims that not all types of law are equally amenable to reception:

> Least inclined to give up its traditional feature is the law of the family including the rules on intestate succession. Second in order is the law of real property, especially as far as rural land is concerned. On the other hand, more loosely connected with a people's past and therefore more easily copied is the law of personal property, notably that of commercial goods, and consequently most of the law of contracts. These fungible provinces of the law, which are controlled by economic interests rather than national customs or sentiments, have at all times offered the readiest seed ground for a reception (Levy 1950: 244).

Kurt Lipstein (1957: 72) similarly sees 'marriage, divorce, land law and succession' as 'those branches of a legal system in which the national character of a people expresses itself much more vividly than in the practice of commercial law, contracts, and the law of procedure'. Yet, relying on analyses of the famous Turkish reception of the Swiss civil code in 1926, he concludes: 'While it has always been assumed that legislation ... cannot exist in the teeth of conflicting local traditions and convictions, the Turkish experiment proves the contrary'; success or failure in transplantation may depend ultimately on organization, education and a flexible system of administration and judicial practice to adapt unfamiliar ideas to local conditions (Lipstein 1957: 80–1) and perhaps to maximize incentives and remove disincentives to popular invocation of new legal ideas.

The simple distinction between, broadly, instrumental law and culturally-based law contains a germ of insight. But this cannot be developed without entirely recasting the terms of discussion. In particular, rather than seeing matters in the old terms of law's impact or non-impact on society, it is important to see law as always rooted in communities. Law is a part of the life of these communities, an aspect of their social experience.

Even for Watson's view of legal transplants this idea is important. He sees law as rooted in and shaped by elite legal professional communities. He seeks to emphasize and illustrate their influence on the possibility and nature of legal transplants by reconstructing some of their historical practices (see, for example, Watson 1995; 1996). For Watson the professional community determines where new law is borrowed from. This community resists external pressures for change, determines its own criteria of legal excellence, or shields its law (by obfuscation, monopolization of knowledge, or other means) from outside influence for its own reasons (Watson 1977: 7–8; 1985b: 72ff.; 1995). I stressed earlier that the nature of any such community must be examined empirically and not assumed. But it is likely, in many cases, to be one strongly governed by shared interests and by tradition – inherited styles of working, customary practices and common historical experience; the kind of lawyers' community in which professional legal culture is nurtured and sustained.

In a wider sociological view other kinds of tradition-based communities apart from professional communities of lawyers might be important as locations of law, or as locations which law is intended to enter and become embedded in or to transform. A classic example in the literature of legal sociology is provided by Gregory Massell's (1968) account of attempts in the 1920s and 1930s to use law to transform traditional rural society in Soviet Central Asia. Much of the idea of cultural resistance to legal change, in fact, assumes more than just tradition as the unifying element of culture in these contexts. Massell writes of 'old unities based on kinship, custom and belief' persisting in the traditional environments which Soviet law was intended to reshape. Often, therefore, culture as the resistant element which, according to the old stereotypical view, hampers the transfer of culturally based law such as family law, is a vague amalgam of customary practices, structures of family organization, and religious or other beliefs.

For these and other reasons, the concept of culture seems too broad and vague to identify variables relevant in considering the conditions under which transferred law can or cannot embed itself in a social environment to which it is brought. It would be better to separate, in theoretical analysis, different bases of community associated with the persistence of culture. Massell's unities of 'kinship, custom and belief' imply three kinds of community: community based on affective ties such as those associated with kinship; community based purely on common location, experience or traditions; and community based on shared values or beliefs, such as those of Islam in the territories to which Massell's study relates. These should not be thought of as communities in a physical sense, but as abstract types of bonds informing social relationships; different kinds of links creating a sense of identity, solidarity or cooperation between people.

In the stereotypical view of culturally-based law as hard to transplant each of these three kinds of community appears as a potential site or source of opposition to legal change. But it is simplistic to think that they necessarily resist new law. Each kind of community may facilitate or deter legal change in its own way. Perhaps Watson's most important contribution is to show that professional legal communities, defined in part by their reverence for their own traditions and their ease with familiar, inherited styles of working, nevertheless engineer ambitious legal change through legal transplants ('massive voluntary legal borrowing': Watson 1985b: 97) and extensively develop existing law by analogy or other means. What is important, it seems, is that new developments are seen as consistent with tradition; they should, as far as possible, appear as organic developments appealing to traditional understandings of legal excellence, appropriateness, justice or practicality.

The stereotypical contrasting view of instrumental (especially contract and commercial) law as easy to transplant implies that a tie to 'economic interests rather than national customs or sentiments' (as Levy puts it) does not hold law to specific communities but allows it to move relatively freely beyond and between them. But economic interests that inspire legal change are often the interests of business elites or commercial communities. Otherwise they are interests binding people together generally in purely instrumental relationships, for example as producers, consumers, traders or exchangers of services. There seems no reason to assume that such economic communities will always welcome reform, for example of commercial or contract law. There may well be strong interests in modernization and in the facilitation of economic relations that new law might bring. But there may also be resistance to new law that upsets practices on which people (for example, operating businesses) have come to rely as serving their collective interests.[4] But interest-based or instrumental community clearly needs to be recognized as a further type of community to which transplanted law may relate.

---

4   See, for example, the discussion of initial resistance of moneylenders to the transplantation of bankruptcy law and debt enforcement law in Turkey after reception of the Swiss civil code in Belgesay 1957: 50–1.

Thus, I think it is useful to propose, as a conceptual framework for understanding legal borrowing, the four pure types of community (instrumental, traditional, belief-based and affective) introduced in Chapter 4. The last of these refers, in this context, to relations of intimacy, privacy and uncalculated concern often (but not exclusively) associated in some degree with aspects of family life. The idea of law as embedded, in some sense, in relations of community might help in clarifying parameters of legal transplantation – that is, the range of circumstances and variables that present themselves when transfers of law between societies are considered sociologically. In the final section of this chapter I shall try to illustrate why this framework might be helpful. But initially, the four abstract types of community need further clarification.

I explained them earlier as derived from Max Weber's four pure types of social action and it is essential to recognize their abstract nature as pure or ideal types themselves. Invoking the idea of affective community does not, for example, require that any actually existing group such as a family be thought of as a community founded purely on emotional relationships. Any such group might be founded on or sustained by instrumental relations as much as affective ones, or by the mere familiarity and custom of traditional relations. The idea of affective community highlights, however, aspects of social relationships that are intimate, uncalculated, diffuse and strongly shaped by emotion or friendship. Because affective community is an abstraction, like the other types of community, law does not relate directly to it but rather to actual social relations in all their complexity. Any given pattern of social relations will be informed by the interplay of the pure types of community. Nevertheless, in legal terms affective community is specially relevant in considering organizational problems where the affective aspect of relations is usually significant: for example, in marriage and divorce, inheritance in families, and sexual and fiduciary relations.

Similarly, the concept of instrumental community does not presuppose that, for example, contractual relations are entirely or necessarily governed by instrumental considerations. But it highlights the instrumental aspects of social relations and, when related to law, the specific legal problems of regulating such relations, for example in fields such as contract, corporate, industrial or commercial law. Again, traditional community embraces not only relations based on tradition or custom but, more abstractly, all aspects of relationships based merely on chance proximity or common experience. Thus it refers to relationships that arise merely through living in the same locality, but also to those that derive from sharing a language or dialect, or a common history or experience. Legally, it can be related most obviously to regulation providing minimum conditions for peaceful coexistence; for example, general criminal and tort law, and aspects of property law. Finally, belief-based community (community of belief or values) focuses on aspects of social relationships defined by shared beliefs or commitment to certain values for their 'own sake' (Weber 1968: 25). In contemporary Western societies its main legal reference points may be with human rights or other law seen as expressing moral individualism in

Durkheim's (1975a) sense; that is, the idea of autonomy and dignity of the individual as fundamental values worthy of legal protection.

This typology of community does not allow any neat classification of laws as hard or easy to transplant. But it provides possibilities for linking law to different kinds of needs and problems associated with different kinds of social relationships. Certainly, when laws are transplanted, the transplant is likely to be linked in the perceptions of the transplanters with patterns of social relations they associate with the law. These may be, for example, admired patterns of practice which a law-making elite in the borrowing society associates with a community of law-makers elsewhere (Levy 1950: 245); or thriving economic life associated with nations whose commercial or corporate law is to be imported (Ajani 1995; Waelde and Gunderson 1994); or perhaps a secular society of individualist values, providing a model for those wishing to borrow that society's law to achieve secularization and 'modernization' in their own society (Kubali 1957; Starr 1992).

The emphasis in recent literature on legal transplants seems to vary greatly depending on geographical focus. In contemporary Western Europe the dominant debate is around the 'convergence' (or lack of it) of European legal systems. Perhaps an assumption of relative economic, social and cultural homogeneity between Western European societies leads to a particular concern with transnational influences on law's relations to instrumental community and traditional community.

The focus on instrumental community is most obviously, but not exclusively, a focus on the economic utility of legal innovations, or on the adaptation of law to economic circumstances and needs. The focus is illustrated by Gunther Teubner's (1998) discussion of the likely adaptation of continental principles of good faith in contracting to a British context, partly by comparing the different structures of economic organizations in the German and British contexts. Much discussion of legal transfers in Western Europe focuses, however, on law's relations with traditional community, treated in this case as a matter of lawyers' guarding of traditional professional styles of working with law. Discussion focuses on the effects of lawyers' professional legal culture on the meaning which law receives when it crosses the borders of nation state jurisdictions, or, indeed, on the possibilities of a genuine convergence of legal thought around a common European law or legal culture (Legrand 1996, 1997; Van Gerven 1996; Van Hoecke and Ost 1997).

In recent legal transplant literature relating to the post-Communist states of Eastern and Central Europe or the former Soviet Union the emphasis is different, although traditional and instrumental community are still key implicit foci. Tradition shows its power in what Gianmaria Ajani calls the 'myth of civil law codes among Central and Eastern European countries that, since the early Nineties, has made codification a priority in the legal reform agenda. The myth dates back to the socialist age, when virtually all countries in the area codified and recodified civil law' (Ajani 1995: 106). Codification symbolizes a legal tradition influencing contemporary approaches. At the same time, however, law-making elites in Eastern and Central Europe and former Soviet states are not necessarily unified by traditions, because strong pressures, even in a civil law climate of thought and practice, arise to accept 'common law solutions, because of the insistence of proponents and commentators who are more familiar with such solutions' (Ajani 1995: 113). Tradition is not necessarily a uniform force because law may be linked to different traditional communities, even where these can be thought of, in modern terms, as legal professional communities.

Social Frameworks of Legal Change

Legal Transplants and Traditional Community

How far is it possible to generalize about the relation of types of community to legal change? Applied to modern conditions, the concept of traditional community may often suggest relatively weak, because limited, social relationships. The mere contingency of residence in a particular locality, for example, does not in itself necessarily create a significant positive social bond between residents. Similarly, the bond of legal tradition carried by lawyers in modern conditions is probably weaker than Watson sometimes implies. Ajani points out that modernizing economic pressures in post-Communist states urgently demand new regulatory frameworks to support very rapid economic and related changes. 'In Western societies civil codes lasted for decades, sometimes for centuries. In the socialist experience their life was shorter. In the post-socialist experience the old "pretension to eternity" of the civil codes has to face the changing framework of the economy during the period of transition' (Ajani 1995: 116). Waelde and Gunderson (1994: 376) argue that the most appropriate law in such circumstances is 'interim law'; that is, law 'for, around and subsequent to individual major transactions' (see also Ajani 1995: 105).

Thus, just as tradition generally has been outflanked by social change, so legal professions seeking to preserve traditions are forced to adapt continually. Professional relationships may be dominated by an instrumental rather than traditional type of community as lawyers jostle for new markets for services and ally themselves with particular interest groups. On the other hand, even if (and because) traditional community is weak, the law it inspires can, in some respects, be strong. Thus, laws concerned only to provide minimal conditions of coexistence in a certain environment (such as basic criminal, tort or property law) are often relatively well defined and settled (like the social environment to which they relate), and their basic ideas are recognized in popular consciousness. This strength of law arises from its limited scope and foundational character. Essentially, law focused on traditional community is minimal regulation needed for sustaining existing order, security and stability in an established environment. Its justification is a simple, easily understood need for order.

Insofar as professional law-making elites can themselves be thought of as exemplifying a type of traditional community, their legal influence may be especially to help to make legal doctrine itself orderly, secure and stable in terms of (professionally) familiar, established legal traditions. Lawyers, sustaining relations of traditional community, infuse basic order into legal thought and practice; that is, the order that long familiarity with their customary practices makes 'obviously' appropriate and congenial. Thus, even in the rapidly changing contexts of Eastern or Central European societies, law-makers seek to frame new law in relation to established traditions, whether of civil or common law. It seems necessary to link law to tradition, to find a framework for its stable interpretation and development. Thus it is claimed that interim law, useful in the short term, will nevertheless give way to something more stable and firmly linked to interpretive traditions (Waelde and Gunderson 1994: 377), even if a struggle remains, as more generally in European law, over which traditions will prevail and in what form (cf. Dezalay and Garth 1996: Chapter 5; Legrand 1996).

The influence of traditional community on law should presumably be at its strongest when other types of community are least involved. There are, as Sacco (1991: 392) points out, 'no known cases in which the dissolution of class antagonism changes the side of the road on which motor vehicles have to drive'. In other words, when beliefs, interests or emotions are not engaged, all that remains is the legal rule, determined or sustained by tradition or inertia. Where the question of which rule to adopt is not finally settled in other terms, adherence to one legal tradition or another may supply the answer. When other factors had been considered, for example, was the final choice of the Swiss civil code for Turkey's modernizing legal system the result, as has been claimed, only of the particular kind of legal education received by particular law reformers (Findikoglu 1957: 13–14; Lipstein 1957: 74)?

Legal Transplants and Instrumental Community

Some of law's potentially important relations to instrumental community are illustrated in recent literature on legal transplants in post-Communist transitional economies of Eastern and Central Europe. The prestige of models for transplanted law reflects the 'widely accepted belief that with the introduction of the formal elements of democracy and of the legal pillars of market economies a "happy end" to the transition will have followed' and borrowing law is 'a prerequisite for the creation of a free market' (Ajani 1995: 96, 103). Ajani details the areas of commercial, corporate, competition, intellectual property, labour, consumer protection, tax, banking, insurance, investment, international trade and other law affected (1995: 104). Of particular interest is the variety of views as to which law best serves instrumental needs. As noted above, *ad hoc* interim regulation is sometimes advocated. On the other hand, some economists suggest that a 'comprehensive and permanent legal framework for the exchange of goods, services and capital' in code form is needed to 'prevent chaos' and provide essential technical guarantees. Comprehensive legal change will make producers and consumers adapt without waiting to see whether current policies will be reversed (Ajani 1995: 107). Thus, from one viewpoint, a firm legal tradition best serves instrumental community; from another, it may hamper it and interim law is required, at least in the short term.

Equally important is the point that law may relate to groups or networks that are different, competing or even incompatible expressions of instrumental community (just as groups expressing traditional community compete). Pressures for legal change come not just or even mainly from economic groups or interests in the society receiving new law. Competing legal models are presented by international banking and credit organizations (IMF, World Bank, EBRD, etc.) anxious to encourage economic opportunities. They come also from European Union bodies, transnational law firms, multinational corporations, universities, the American Bar Association and other organizations. These assist in drafting legislation or training legal personnel, or give policy advice (Ajani 1995: 110–13). Thus, it becomes hard to think of legal elites in Watson's narrow sense controlling legal development. Instead, a wide range of actors, with varying influence, promote legal development to serve the needs of national, sub-national and transnational groups pursuing diverse interests.

Considered abstractly, however, instrumental community is (like traditional community but for different reasons) mainly a matter of relatively weak social bonds. If traditional community is a residue of weak social ties over which stronger ones (of common or convergent interests, shared beliefs or emotional commitment) are superimposed, instrumental community is a matter of relationships lasting only as long as the particular purposes of the actors involved in them converge. Yet the law relating to instrumental community, like that of traditional community, is often strong. Because of its relatively limited purposes (defined by the limits of instrumental relations) it may lend itself to technical efficiency and predictability. This surely explains the germ of truth in the stereotypical legal transplants thesis that instrumental law travels well. Where this is so, the reason may be that its relative precision derives from the limited social ties it represents which need little cultural context to make them meaningful when expressed in legal terms. But those ties may provoke resistance to law that does not appear to serve them.

Legal Transplants and Community of Belief

It remains to consider, if only briefly and selectively, community of belief and affective community in relation to legal transplants. A group or society seeing itself in terms of community of belief may resist any significant reshaping through imported law associated with fundamentally different values or beliefs. Shared values or beliefs can create a strong social bond so that perceived challenges to them may be disruptive. Thus, fundamental problems have been shown to arise when transplanted law presupposes (as, for example, in the idea of the reasonable man of English common law in some societies in which common law was imposed) a community of belief foreign to the society in which the law is set down (see, for example, Seidman 1965; Keedy 1951).

On the other hand, it is important to note that law's relation to community of belief may often be relatively weak (in frequent contrast to its relation to instrumental or traditional community), if only because of ambiguities and interpretive leeways that can arise in translating values into specific legal provisions, or of specifying uncontroversially the value-orientations of particular laws.[5] Thus, socialist ideology in Central and Eastern European states did not prevent the borrowing of non-socialist legal forms on a large scale or the superimposition of socialist values over traditional 'bourgeois' legal rules and institutions (Ajani 1995: 99–101). A tendency, indeed, may be for legal interpretation to avoid debate on values or beliefs and focus on instrumental considerations or basic ('traditional') requirements of stability and order, as practical, 'down to earth' considerations. Labelling laws as embodiments of shared values or beliefs might open them to particular controversy without resolving issues of interpretation. Where law's relation to values or beliefs is consciously emphasized this is sometimes a deliberate strategy to use law to reaffirm the identity of a group or society in terms of community of belief (cf. Amin 1985: 14–15). Nevertheless, the strategy is risky. Where particular laws are seen as symbolizing, however vaguely, fundamental values or shared beliefs, these laws can become foci of intense value conflict where different sections of society (or different societies such as those supplying or receiving legal transplants) see themselves as communities of belief opposing each other. Abortion laws are an obvious modern example of laws symbolizing, to varying degrees in different societies, such a 'clash of absolutes' (see, for example, Tribe 1992).

Legal Transplants and Affective Community

Finally, what of affective community? The concept of affective community emphasizes the intimacy and multifaceted nature of affective relationships, and the elusiveness of the parameters defining emotional or friendly ties. The general problem for law is that these relations – in, for example, family and domestic settings, but also fiduciary, care and dependency, or mutual support relationships – are hard to define in terms of specific rights and obligations or appropriate criteria for acceptable conduct. To some extent, they resist clear legal specification or control. Thus, fiduciary obligations, defined in law, tend to have vague parameters.[6] Marital relations, similarly, resist full definition in terms of rule-based obligations and rights. Finally, affective community, especially in family settings, encompasses relationships typically removed from public view. The problems for legal regulation posed by the nature of affective community are thus different from those posed by tradition, beliefs or interests. They are often practical problems of lack of legal visibility of social relations, or in legally defining what is to be regulated, or in fixing criteria for regulating intimate relations having elusive parameters.

Thus, while affective community is often a matter of strong social bonds its relations with law are typically weak, like those of community of belief, but for

---

5   For a classic discussion see Arnold 1935.

6   Surveying fiduciary law, Paul Finn (1989: 54) concludes: 'All that the writer would venture is this: a person will be a fiduciary in his relationship with another when and insofar as that other is entitled to expect that he will act in that other's or in their joint interest to the exclusion of his own several interest'.

different reasons. Whereas the difficulty of law's relation to community of belief lies in ambiguities of translating values into legal form or of interpreting law in terms of values, the main difficulty of law's relation to affective community lies in the elusiveness and resistance to legal definition of affective community itself as a matter of social relationships. This latter difficulty surely bears on the old stereotypical view that transplants of family or inheritance law tend to be ineffective.

In fact, many successful transplants of these kinds of law have occurred, not restricted to transfers between Western legal systems (see, for example, Kahn-Freund 1974; Starr 1992: 92). In any case, this law is not to be understood merely in terms of links with affective community. Yet some legal transplants relating to family relations might have to confront general legal problems of addressing or interpreting affective relationships. These are reflected, for example, in legal difficulties of interpreting situations of coercion and consent in sexual relationships or in defining aspects of fiduciary duty, and in the often alien or irrelevant character of law as seen from within affective relationships, even when (as in domestic violence cases) legal protection or help in escaping from the relationship is clearly necessary. Law's difficulties in regulating family or sexual relationships often arise from a reluctance or inability of victims of these relationships to invoke it, and the frequent inappropriateness or insensitivity of its responses.

Consequently, law's impact on family relationships is often shown in legal transplant literature to depend on special motivations for invoking law. For example, long after the Turkish Westernization of marriage law, marriages continued to be contracted informally and privately according to customary practice. The situation began to change, in favour of formally regulated marriage under the new law, in part because a population previously resistant to or disinterested in the law recognized that family welfare or dependency benefits, guaranteed through state law, could be obtained only if formal family relationships could be proved (Timur 1957; cf. Starr 1992: 92). Massell's (1968) study of revolutionary law in Soviet Central Asia showed that, insofar as the law reshaped traditional family relationships, it did so mainly because it gave women a possibility of securing their individual interests outside repressive forms of affective community, or of serving as a vanguard of the new socialist community of belief. Similarly, in Turkey, strenuous propaganda encouraged women to invoke the Westernized law to improve their social situation. Their use of it (especially in relation to divorce, and later domestic violence) advanced its broad impact on traditional patterns of rural and family life (Starr 1992: Chapter 5).

Conclusion

The law-and-community approach does not yield a general logic of legal transplants but rather contributes towards a framework for examining the borrowing of law in particular contexts. No unambiguous correlation of areas of law with ideal types of community is possible. Law's relevance to them is complex, diverse and variable.

Thus, no claim is made here that the links this chapter identifies between law and each of the types of community are the only significant ones, or that they are always significant. They illustrate the way the types can be used to aid analysis of law as an aspect of social life in particular empirical settings. Again, each type of community is not necessarily to be identified with any particular empirically identifiable social institutions; they are superimposed on each other in particular contexts and interact in complex ways; each of the four types may reinforce or disrupt any of the others in particular empirical settings.

Conflicts between different types of community in practice are, however, easily associated with different group interests. Hence Otto Kahn-Freund's (1974) idea that politics or power is an important factor in determining the feasibility of legal transplants has merit. But power operates not just in and through political systems but especially in conflicts between sections of society whose unity or identity is given in terms of the types of community. Conflicts over law are often conflicts between expressions of instrumental, affective or traditional community or community of belief, or between social groups, societies or sections of societies that, in some sense, see themselves or are seen as 'owning' or 'disowning' the law in dispute.

What should be made of the question of comparative law's relations with legal sociology from which this chapter began? A focus on law's links to the types of community makes it possible to retain the important insight of Watson's work that the ways of working and thinking of professional law-makers as an elite are an important consideration in analysing legal transplants. But the law-and-community approach allows this insight to be treated sociologically, with a focus on conditions enabling tradition to operate. Thus, emphasis is on the 'internal' legal culture of lawyers and law-makers, for the study of which comparative law offers powerful and well-developed resources. But emphasis is also on the effects of the common experience or common environment of other social groups or sections of society, or of a society as a whole.

Beyond matters of tradition, other types of social bonds or groupings can and should also be considered, as has been seen. By treating these in terms of abstract ideas of community it is possible to appreciate the complexity of any logic of legal transplants. Such a logic can be developed only in relation to particular social contexts and has to focus on the complex interplay of tradition, belief, affect and instrumentality in particular empirical settings as fundamental bases of social bonds.

Chapter 8

Sociology and Comparative Law

From its modern beginnings, comparative law has been closely involved with legal sociology. Early sociology relied extensively on comparatists' work. Over the years, they, in turn, often stressed the closeness of their field to sociology of law. But the promise of collaboration has rarely been fulfilled. Setting the issues in historical perspective, I argue here that legal sociology and comparative law can be closely compatible. Legal sociologists should use research in comparative law. Comparatists, for their part, need to be aware of sociological problems and presuppositions in their work.

An Unfulfilled Relationship?

The relationship between comparative law and sociology has been paradoxical for at least a century. Since the inauguration of modern comparative law as a distinctive field of scholarly practice, conventionally traced to the Paris International Congress of Comparative Law of 1900, the closeness and necessity of this relationship has been frequently asserted by comparatists. Comparative law and sociology of law have often been said by comparatists to be inseparable. Sometimes, as regards an important part of its activity or aspirations, comparative law has been claimed to be a type of sociology of law or even identical with sociology of law. Yet the nature of this relationship has rarely been examined in detail. In general, the need to explore it rigorously has been avoided both by comparatists and legal sociologists.

In some ways this avoidance is understandable. Few scholars claim detailed knowledge of the whole range of the literature of both comparative law and sociology. Few are likely to have sufficient interest in both fields to motivate such an inquiry. And the orientations of comparatists and legal sociologists are often significantly different. The theoretical and empirical concerns of legal sociology go beyond those that interest most comparatists. Comparatists do not necessarily share sociology's ambitions to explain theoretically social change or social stability, or to characterize the nature of social life using abstract concepts such as 'structure' or 'system'. They often prefer specific, seemingly far more practical inquiries closely related to the detail of legal practice and legal doctrine in particular systems. Whereas legal sociology ultimately must put no limits on the range and diversity of legal experience from which it tries to gather empirical material to support its efforts at generalization and theoretical analysis, comparatists tend to distrust broad social or legal theory that might purport to offer matrices for the widest legal and social comparisons.

Even comparatists strongly sympathetic to sociology and who see comparative law as itself a social science tend to urge caution, stressing the limits of objectivity in social research and the danger of mistaking ideology for theory (Zweigert 1975: 83–4).

For the legal sociologist, comparative law should provide an indispensable resource of detail about doctrinal and institutional characteristics of legal systems. But the categories of comparison that comparatists have typically used – for example, those of legal styles or 'families' of law – may seem unhelpful to legal sociologists. Some even dismiss these categories as reflecting 'mandarin' preoccupations with lawyers' professional traditions or outlook, and having no clear relation to law as experienced in its effects in social life beyond the courtroom or lawyer's office (Friedman 1997). Legal sociologists question what and why comparatists compare and how far comparisons of legal doctrine or institutions in isolation from *systematic* study of their social contexts can yield useful knowledge (Carbonnier 1969; Abel 1978).

If these differences of outlook are easy to identify, why has the link between comparative law and sociology, especially legal sociology, been so strongly affirmed by many comparatists, at the same time as they have usually avoided exploring it in depth? The main reason, I think, lies in enduring uncertainties about the nature of comparative law as a research enterprise. An attraction for some comparatists has been to claim for comparative law a special status as social science, distancing it from other legal studies seen as having less fundamental 'scientific' concerns. More crucial, however, is the attraction of assuming that comparative law can presuppose or ally itself with certain sociological understandings about the nature of social inquiry (including inquiry about law as a social phenomenon) and so avoid being enmeshed in broad epistemological and ontological questions.

Epistemological questions here relate to the *purposes* of comparing social phenomena. What kind of knowledge does comparison give? What makes this knowledge valid? Ontological questions relate to what is to be compared, what can be treated as comparable *entities* or appropriate empirical foci of research. In comparative law, foci of comparison might be, for example, legal rules or institutions; or legal styles, traditions or cultures; or social problems (such as 'crime' or 'industrial conflict') addressed by law; or social institutions (for example, 'the family', 'inheritance' or 'the business enterprise') regulated legally.

Sociology has developed concepts that have been useful to comparatists at various times in dealing with these epistemological and ontological problems of comparative law. They have been useful because their provenance from or association with social science has meant that comparatists have not themselves felt the need to engage in social theoretical inquiries to validate these concepts.

Probably the concept most widely appealed to in this way has been that of function. It has often been argued that rules or institutions should be compared in terms of their objectively identifiable functions – the contribution they make to wider social processes or the specific, differentiated task that they can be seen to be fulfilling in society – for example, regulating specific aspects of domestic relations, commerce, or property regimes. Max Rheinstein, writing in 1938, saw comparative law as focused on functional comparison of legal rules and the 'social function of law in general'. 'In this sense,' he suggested, 'comparative law is synonymous with sociology of law' (1938: 296, 298, 301).[1] Legal sociology hardly existed as a distinct field of sociological inquiry at the time Rheinstein wrote, though the idea of functional analysis of law was well established in sociology, mainly through the influence of Emile Durkheim's (1982; 1984) work. So, it was easy to claim, as many earlier writers had done, that comparative law encompassed sociology of law in some sense. Part of comparative law's legitimacy was thus as a division of social science, its distinctiveness given by its specifically legal focus.

Comparative law has appealed, at various times over the past century, to ideas of 'function' (Zweigert and Kötz 1998: 34–6, 62; Curran 1998: 67–8), legal and social 'evolution' (Hall 1963: 16–17),[2] and 'social facts' (Lepaulle 1922).[3] It has referred to social institutions, interests, needs or problems as ideas borrowed from social science or assumed to be validated by sociological discourse. It has done this often to identify what could legitimately be compared and to specify scientific purposes of comparison (cf. Zweigert and Kötz 1998: 10–11). On the other hand, this strategy always had an unsatisfactory aspect. To make part of the foundations of comparative law dependent on reference (even if only implicitly or in the most general terms) to a different discipline offers many hostages to fortune. Perhaps partly for this reason, many comparatists have strongly stressed purposes of comparison having no particular link to sociological inquiries. Often they have defined the projects of comparative law in ways that require no reference to social science. Sometimes they have declared sociological perspectives (as contrasted with historical or philosophical ones) largely unnecessary to comparative law's main concerns (Watson 1993; Ewald 1995b).

These considerations, I think, map the ambivalence of comparatists' views of sociology, and specifically of sociology of law. In the following sections of this chapter I shall try to explore this ambivalence in more detail, suggesting that, in some measure, difficulties in the relations of legal sociology and comparative law arise from difficulties in conceptualizing the scope of each of these enterprises, and from changes over time in the way each of them has been understood. My argument, ultimately, is that comparative law and legal sociology are interdependent and, while each of these research enterprises has a wide variety of appropriate aims, their central, most general and most ambitious scientific projects – to understand law in its development and its variety as an aspect of social life – are identical.

---

1   Rheinstein actively promoted early legal sociology. He directed the English translation of Max Weber's writings on law and wrote extensively about the work of Weber, Ehrlich, Timasheff, Gurvitch and other legal sociologists. See generally Rheinstein 1979: Chapter 1.

2   And see Gutteridge (1949: 73), on the importance of the 'stage of development' (not mere chronology) as a basis for comparison.

3   Lepaulle's (1922) paper, partly a critique of Roscoe Pound's sociological jurisprudence, shows the strong influence of Durkheimian sociology.

The Opposite of Breaking New Ground?

The literature of comparative law suggests an immense range of possible justifications for the enterprise. Comparison of law might be pursued:

1. to find ideas useful in improving or clarifying one's own legal system (Watson 1993: 17; David and Brierley 1985: 6–7; Zweigert and Kötz 1998: 18–19; Markesinis 1990);
2. to aid detailed communication between lawyers of different systems (Abel 1978: 220), for example in interpreting a uniquely common law institution such as the trust in civil law contexts;
3. to explain legal development in particular systems by tracing lines of legal borrowing and influence (Watson 1993);
4. to harmonize or unify areas of law on a transnational basis to promote trade or economic activity across borders or for other reasons (for example, Bonell 1995);
5. to provide legal solutions to causes of international conflicts and so promote international understanding (Lepaulle 1922: 855; David and Brierley 1985: 8);
6. to give law students and legal scholars a more distanced view of their own system (Zweigert and Kötz 1998: 21), challenging the sense of naturalness and inevitability of its particular legal arrangements (Lepaulle 1922: 858; Gutteridge 1949: 19–20) and promoting appreciation of 'difference' (Legrand 1999: 10, 11, 134; Curran 1998: 44);
7. to understand the power of legal cultures (Legrand 1999: 73–4, 134), for example as barriers to harmonization of law;
8. to find a 'common trunk' of legal ideas to express 'the awakening of an international legal consciousness' (Lambert 1931: 127); or
9. to contribute towards knowledge of the social world through study of its legal aspects (Hall 1963).

Other professed aims of comparative law are found in the literature but their diversity is sufficiently illustrated above. They might be arranged on a scale extending from intensely practical concerns with solving specific and immediate legal problems, for example in current case-law (such as Markesinis 1990), to the most abstract ideal of contributing to broad theoretical knowledge of the social world. It is important to note that sociology has also exhibited a somewhat similar range. It has included, at least in the British context, what Philip Abrams (1985) terms a 'policy-science conception', which sees sociology as concerned to provide practical knowledge for rational social planning, and a 'socio-technics conception', treating sociologists as technical assistants to policy-makers or negotiators with them, providing 'basic information, analytic data, advice on data-gathering, technical problem-solving, identification of technically best courses of action or evaluation of the effectiveness of policy after the event'. But sociology, according to Abrams, has also been understood in terms of three other conceptions: 'clarification' (reformulating problems by elucidating assumptions, dispelling illusions or unmasking myths), 'advocacy' (linking good evidence to good causes as a matter of political persuasion) and 'education' (providing gradual enlightenment about the nature of the social world unconnected directly to immediate policy, advocacy or short-term problem-solving) (Abrams 1985: 183, 184, 185).

It is not difficult to link each of these conceptions to corresponding conceptions of the aims of comparative law. The parallels reinforce the point that, from a certain perspective, comparative legal scholarship and sociology can be seen as engaged in very similar multifaceted enterprises of ordering and making sense of the social world, understanding its normative regulation and evaluating and comparing the different ways in which different societies have organized that regulation.

Probably, this closeness was never more apparent than at the time of the 1900 Congress. It has been said that 'the principal emphasis in the meeting was on comparative law viewed as a social science, even then called the sociology of law' and what 'bulks large ... is the enormous influence of nineteenth-century sociology on the Continental scholars' (Hall 1963: 17, 18). In the turn-of-the-century mood of optimism and belief in scientific progress, comparative law, like sociology, presented itself in its most ambitious forms. Both fields, in their furthest extension, appeared to embrace the same overarching intellectual project, differences of emphasis being given only by a degree of specialization.

The great comparatist Edouard Lambert, writing in an intellectual climate in France strongly shaped by Emile Durkheim's sociological ideas, recognized comparative legal history as one of three divisions of the broad enterprise of comparative legal studies (Lambert 1903: 913–16; 1931), and described it in a way entirely consistent with Durkheim's understanding of it as a major branch of sociology (Cotterrell 1999: 7–8).[4] Comparative legal history, according to Lambert, aims to create 'a universal history of law' to reveal 'the rhythms or natural laws of the succession of social phenomena, which direct the evolution of legal institutions'. Its practitioners had been 'up to the present principally interested in the reconstitution of the most obscure phases of the legal history of human societies'(Lambert 1931: 127) and Lambert criticized the speculative nature of their work (1903: 886–91),[5] often compromised by naive assumptions about legal and social evolution. He wished to direct comparative law as a juristic enterprise away from these seemingly arcane sociological inquiries about the genesis of law.

Nevertheless the project of comparative legal history was one to which many of Durkheim's closest collaborators – including Lambert's brilliant young colleague in

---

4   Durkheim, in a review of Lambert's (1903) seminal comparative law text, even treats comparative legal history as synonymous with legal sociology: see Durkheim 1975d: 266. Lambert (1931), correspondingly, cites Durkheim's *L'Année sociologique* as a primary locus of comparative legal scholarship of this kind.

5   But he also carefully noted (1903: 891) sociology's great promise for legal studies. See also Jamin 2000.

the Lyon law faculty, the Romanist Paul Huvelin[6] – devoted themselves, combining the study of legal texts with ethnographic, literary and historical materials (Cotterrell 1999: Chapters 6, 8 and 9). Durkheimian sociologists made much use of jurists' comparative studies. Potentially, at least, links at this time between comparatists and sociologists were intimate, even if comparatists might often regard sociologists' inquiries as impractical, ill-informed and too speculative, and sociologists might see comparatists' work as unsystematic, atheoretical and intellectually narrow. Certainly, for the Durkheimians, it was immaterial whether researchers called themselves jurists or sociologists if their work was sociological in orientation.

The early links between comparative law and sociological inquiry at this most ambitious level find faint echoes in the rich texture and broad sweep of some later comparatists' writings. But presenting comparative legal analysis in a contextual matrix embracing entire cultures is a task suited only to those few who can command with assurance the vast range of historical and sociological reference required.[7] Today, the great classics of sociology – writings of Max Weber, Durkheim and a few of his followers, for example – are still read for this range and for the insight and panache with which they embrace it. But comprehensive comparison of laws, societies or cultures to create panoramic systems of social or legal knowledge has largely ceased to be an objective in either sociology or comparative law. A much more modest stress on comparative law as 'method', distancing itself from broad substantive aims and focusing on multifaceted technical utility, corresponds to some extent with Abrams' socio-technics conception in sociology. Yet objectives of comparative law are still often proclaimed in terms related to Abrams' sociological conception of enlightenment through education. Comparative law and sociology have largely put to one side the broadest ambitions that might have allied them as parts of a project of interpreting history and social variation in the elaborate, asymmetrical patterns of its evolution. But it would be regrettable if these ambitions were discarded entirely.

There has been only one attempt in Anglo-American literature in relatively recent times to re-open a sustained argument for a general union of comparative law and legal sociology. Jerome Hall's *Comparative Law and Social Theory*, published in 1963, tries to recover the old project of an integrated social science in which comparative law would play a major part. But Hall insists that comparative law is an entirely different enterprise from what he sees as the scientific theory-building of much modern sociology, its methods of observation and data collection modelled partly on those of the natural sciences. Comparative law, like all interpretive legal study, must, in Hall's view, understand and give full account of the values, ideals

---

6 On Huvelin's strikingly imaginative sociolegal scholarship see Cotterrell 2005. Lambert often cites Huvelin's writings on early Roman law approvingly in his comparative law text: see, for example, Lambert 1903: 644, 646. The Lyon law faculty also included another key member of Durkheim's sociological group, the radical jurist Emmanuel Lévy, whose work Lambert admired and actively promoted: see Lambert 1926.

7 Cf. Curran 1998, noting a narrowing of vision over time in American comparative law.

and ideas of law. A social science modelled on natural science cannot do this. Again, as 'a composite of social knowledge of law' (Hall 1963: 33), comparative law must study not just positive legal rules but also official action and styles of analysis of legal problems, as well as social practices that relate to law and give it meaning in citizens' experience. As a lawyer, Hall clearly wants to insist that all such matters must be understood interpretively, from a Hartian internal aspect, and in terms of values as well as through observation of law as a social phenomenon. For this reason, comparative law could be part only of a *humanistic* legal sociology that stresses interpretive, evaluative aspects of law. It 'could never be reduced to a sociology comprised only of descriptive causal generalizations. For comparative law holds fast to the distinctiveness, autonomy and value of legal ideas' (1963: 67).

In hindsight, the responses Hall's book attracted are as interesting as the work itself. Some reviews were friendly if bland, but several were very hostile. Hall was criticized for failing to recognize the range of comparatists aims, or the scope and variety of their work, and for focusing only on 'one possible objective of comparative law scholarship, its potential contribution to social theory' (Von Mehren 1965: 188; and see Hazard 1964; Schlesinger 1965); he was asking the impossible, that comparatists should understand the evolution of the social sciences as well as all developments in their own field (Wagner 1964). One critic agreed that comparative legal study should help towards understanding societies but insisted that most comparatists were already engaged on the task (Hazard 1964). From the sociologists' side, a leading scholar wrote that 'whatever the opposite of breaking new ground is, Jerome Hall has done it in this book' (Schwartz 1965); he had failed to see the range of work being done in legal sociology. More good research and a comprehensive theoretical framework were needed but the book gave 'reasons for doubting the possibility of either' and the reasons were unconvincing (Schwartz 1965: 291). Some reviews found the book deeply perplexing, with key arguments very hard to understand (Wagner 1964; Wasserstrom 1964). Richard Wasserstrom identified what he saw as a basic confusion. For Hall, the natural science model was inappropriate in studying legal systems because account had to be taken of human purposes, ideals and reasons. But, Wasserstrom (1964: 109) noted, it is entirely possible to make general, non-normative scientific statements about, for example, people's ideals. These matters, treated as recordable attitudes or preferences, are not outside the scope of a scientific legal sociology.

Such reactions show that sociology and comparative law had travelled far apart by the 1960s. Their agendas were complex and it was easy to criticize Hall for simplifying or distorting them. In contrast to earlier proclamations from both comparatists and sociologists of the closeness or interdependence of the two fields, it seemed misguided to propose any general connection between them. Links could only be for specific purposes and projects. But Hall was right to criticize the limitations of sociology's dominant orientations (functionalism, positivism and scientism) at the time he wrote. Wasserstrom's critique missed the point in claiming that social science could treat values and motivations as data. Hall's book demands exactly the reverse: that social science must appreciate the 'internal', interpretive aspects of law, not just reduce them to measurable data.

Hall calls for a non-positivist project of social science in which comparative law could have a recognized, secure and valuable place. But he wrote before the so-called interpretive turn in legal theory and social research and so lacked the means to clarify his project sufficiently. There is, indeed, much to be said for the aim of integrating some projects of comparative law and sociology. Given developments in both legal theory and social science, this is far more feasible than at the time Hall wrote. It presumes that there need ultimately be no radical opposition between comparatists' and legal sociologists' perspectives despite the great diversity of objectives of research in their fields; that lawyers' comparative perspectives on legal experience can be informed by broader sociological perspectives; and that sociological perspectives on law must ultimately embrace, interpret, preserve, interact with and contextualize the diverse, varied perspectives of lawyers as legal participants and legal observers. The result should not be a resurrection of sociological jurisprudence (legal practice coloured by social scientific rhetoric) but a heightened awareness of relationships between the innumerable forms of practical participation in, and observation of, law.

These claims become clearer in their implications if the terms 'sociology' and 'legal sociology' in this context are themselves clarified. One reason why Hall's project of integrative social science embracing comparative law attracted fierce criticism was surely its implication that comparatists must master some other (social science) discipline beyond legal studies, or else see their work as subservient to it. In an earlier era, a main reason why jurists were suspicious of the kind of sociology Durkheim proposed and of the enthusiasm with which he and his colleagues advocated cooperation between jurists and sociologists (Cotterrell 1999: 37) was that sociology as a discipline appeared shamelessly imperialistic. 'My aim,' wrote Durkheim (1982: 260), 'has been precisely to introduce ... [the sociological] idea into those disciplines [such as legal studies] from which it was absent and thereby to make them branches of sociology.'

Such an idea can be made acceptable to comparatists and to other sociologically minded legal scholars only if sociology, for the purposes of legal inquiry, is understood not as a discipline but solely as a process of and aspiration towards systematic, theoretically oriented and empirically grounded understanding of social life. This process and aspiration is not the monopoly of any particular academic discipline. Sociological perspectives on law use theory, methods, data and research traditions from the social sciences (and other disciplines). Thus, as argued earlier in Chapter 3, legal sociology must be seen as an interdisciplinary project, like comparative law itself, focused on empirical and theoretical study of what we choose to identify as the legal aspects of social life. The focus is firmly on law – that is, law not just as lawyers know it professionally in their distinct jurisdictions but law as an aspect or field of social experience more generally. Provisionally conceptualizing this aspect or field is a task for social analysis.[8]

Legal sociology seeks perspectives that, unlike those of comparative law, directly apply social theory and contribute to it. As argued in Chapter 2, legal sociology is explicitly and systematically focused on exploring the nature of the social, the broader setting of legal doctrine and institutions. Comparative law is less concerned with this. But, in fact, that exploration may be very important in answering comparatists' questions as to how far unification or harmonization of law is desirable or feasible, and in relation to what kinds of regulation and what kinds of regulated communities.

In fact, the question of what the social should be taken to be is complex for contemporary law. Legal sociology has a major role in conceptualizing the various aspects or regions of the social. Its task is to show their general significance as environments of legal regulation in relation to which law finds its meaning. Legal sociology provides theories and interpretations of the nature of law within these environments, embedded in and inseparable from them. In that way, it can help to clarify epistemological and ontological puzzles that still haunt comparative law as a field of study: questions about what to compare, and about the validity of comparisons made. Correspondingly, comparative law's recording and interpretation of legal practices, institutions and ideas are essential to legal sociology. They provide a variety of juristic perspectives on law that must be incorporated into those developed by legal sociology.

In my view, these general ideas should determine comparative law's relations with legal sociology. Legal sociology's most important potential contribution to comparative law is to clarify the nature of the social, the contextual settings of law and legal institutions in relation to which comparison can usefully take place. How then can it do this in relation to current orientations of comparative law? The remainder of this chapter considers three such orientations (Alan Watson's legal transplants thesis, the application of autopoiesis theory to comparative law, and the recent use by some comparative lawyers of the concept of legal culture) as a basis for examining what a sociological perspective can offer comparatists today.

'Internal' Processes of Legal Development

In the present context the most striking aspect of Watson's work is its determined attempt to avoid any dependence of comparative law on sociology. Watson recognizes that legal problems (for example 'rent restriction' or 'alimony on divorce') cannot be formulated as a basis for comparison without study of the social context in which the problems arise and which ultimately defines their nature. Thus, 'the weight of the investigation will always be primarily on the comparability of the problem, only

---

8   A problem in doing that is to take account of socially important regulatory systems that reflect cultural traditions fundamentally alien to Western legal thought and experience: see Menski 2006.

secondarily on the comparability of the law; and any discipline founded on such a starting point will be sociology rather than law' (Watson 1993: 5).[9] Watson's solution is to reject comparison entirely and focus instead on the processes of reasoning by analogy and borrowing of legal ideas from other systems which he sees as the keys to explaining legal development. Comparative law, for Watson, is thus 'the study of the relationship of one legal system and its rules with another' (1993: 6). It looks to legal history and jurisprudence as sister disciplines, since its focus is on the nature of law and its development (1993: 7).

In Chapter 7 I discussed Watson's claims about legal sociology and his legal transplants thesis. As noted there, Watson sees legal change as an essentially 'internal' process,[10] managed by lawyers, and treats sociological influences on legal development as generally unimportant. So, comparative law is free of any reliance on such sociologically dependent concepts as function, evolution, legal or social problems or interests. But these claims, taken at face value, raise two fundamental issues which, despite Watson's best efforts, draw legal sociology back into the comparatist's range of vision. First, assuming that legal transplants are fundamentally important to legal development, what is transplanted and what is the test of success in transplantation? Second, what are the internal processes of legal development which determine whether legal transplants or adaptations take place?

Taking the second of these first, Watson claims that lawyers with their professional needs, interests, prerogatives and judgments of prestige mainly control the processes of legal development. Sociological perspectives are excluded, therefore, only by assuming that legal sociology has nothing important to say about lawyers and legal practice. In fact, however, the sociology of legal professions and legal practice is one of the central, most highly developed fields of empirical inquiry in legal sociology. Very important studies of the role of lawyers' professional practices in shaping legal change have been undertaken (such as Dezalay and Garth 1996). If 'external' social influences (that is, influences other than from lawyers themselves) on legal change are (very controversially)[11] to be excluded from serious consideration, 'internal' influences nevertheless require sociological inquiry. Indeed, on Watson's own arguments it would seem impossible to understand why and when legal development occurs without sociological study of the practices, interests, strategies and politics of legal elites who, he argues, play an overwhelmingly important, usually crucial role in this development.[12]

---

9   The problem is discussed in some detail but inconclusively in Péteri 1970, especially at pp. 90–3.

10   He writes, for example, of an 'internal legal logic' or 'the internal logic of the legal tradition' governing legal development: see Watson 1985b: 21, 22.

11   For an early critique of Watson's approach by a legal sociologist see Seidman (1975: 683): 'Because he has already abjured any study of societal factors as "sociology" and not "law", when he is forced to take these factors into account he does so without any careful analysis or testing of hypotheses'.

12   Watson often cites admiration for a foreign legal system as an important independent factor in the decision to adopt legal doctrine from it (see, for example, 1985b: 109, 118).

Furthermore, his purported distinction between internal and external forces of legal development is *incoherent* if the internal is identified with the practices or interests of legal elites. These surely relate to the interests of client groups that lawyers serve, and lawyers' concerns need to be understood, at least partly, in terms of their position in society. So, their professional interests cannot be separated from conditions in the wider society that provide the settings for their practices. Equally, we need not think only in terms of interests to challenge the internal–external distinction. We can refer, for example, to understanding, interpretation or experience of law. Legal sociology, from its earliest development, has had much to say on these matters. Here, it is important to insist that none of them is the prerogative of legal elites (however defined). Nor are they uniform or invariant for these elites. The ways in which law is understood, interpreted and experienced in different regions of the social are complex, varied, ever-changing matters that can be examined only by combining juristic analysis and sociological inquiry.

A way of avoiding the collapse of any internal-external distinction that excludes sociology from explanations of legal development might be through the use of systems theory. Autopoiesis theory, whose implications for comparative law have been explored by Gunther Teubner (1998), proposes that law in certain modern conditions can be treated as a distinct, self-renewing system of communication. Teubner criticizes Watson for attaching far too much importance to lawyers' professional practices as such. Teubner sees these practices not as, in themselves, the motor of law's development, but rather as the necessary consequence of law's modern character as a distinctive discourse focused specifically on producing decisions that define what is legal or illegal. Because this legal/illegal coding – and not, for example, judgments about morality, efficiency, scientific or historical truth – is law's essential focus as an independent discourse, it cannot be governed by social developments of the kind sociology studies. It may react to these developments but it will always do so in its own terms. What Watson sees as the autonomous law-making of legal elites, adherents of autopoiesis theory see as the working out of law's independent destiny as a highly specialized, functionally distinctive communication system (Teubner 1993; and see Přibáň and Nelken (eds) 2001).

Law as a communication system in society is linked to other systems (such as the economy) but not through patterns of direct influence. What autopoiesis theory terms 'structural coupling' refers to a much more indirect and contingent set of relations between these systems. And in different societies the 'coupling' takes different forms. This has very important consequences for comparative law's interests in the transplantation of law. Legal rules (for example, governing good faith in the law

---

'Admirableness', like 'prestige', remains, however, an entirely opaque concept for explanatory purposes unless the elements that produce it are identified and the relation of these elements explained. Lawyers' ideas about the relative prestige of foreign sources of law are juristic shorthand for reference to a vast sociological portfolio of interests, value commitments, affective ties and historical experiences which, in various combinations, influence choices of models for law reform.

of contracts) might be taken from one legal system and imported into another, or imposed generally through European legal harmonization. But, whereas Watson's thesis suggests this may be an easy process, Teubner claims that the meaning of legal ideas may change dramatically during transfer. This is because, apart from any differences in styles and traditions of legal interpretation and conceptualization in different legal systems, the coupling of the system to the economy and other social systems may vary in different national contexts, and vary in its 'tightness' or 'looseness' for different areas of law. Autopoiesis theory assumes that movement is occurring towards a global legal discourse (Teubner 1997; King 1997) but it also recognizes, at least in Teubner's interpretation, major incompatibilities between legal systems arising from their specific social settings. Because this makes the result of transfers of legal ideas between systems theoretically indeterminate, Teubner (1998) sees not so much legal transplants as legal 'irritants' occurring, causing unpredictable changes in recipient legal systems.

Implicitly, Teubner's thesis entirely rejects Watson's effort to exclude sociology from the logic of legal transplants, and so from the heart of comparative law. For Teubner, law's coupling with other systems in society puts important limits on the ambitions of comparatists for unification or harmonization of law. To understand what is possible in the transfer of legal ideas between legal systems, social scientific knowledge of the legal context is undoubtedly needed. But, from another point of view, autopoiesis theory gives little guidance as to how empirical legal sociology can help comparatists. Law's resistance to 'external' social influence is not, as with Watson's thesis, seen as an effect of lawyers' behaviour that could be studied sociologically. It is the consequence of law's self-sufficient, self-producing and self-reproducing discursive character which autopoiesis theory claims to identify.

Autopoiesis theory has been applied not just to law but to the study of social systems of communication generally (including, for example, economic and administrative systems). Niklas Luhmann, who has pioneered these applications, treats the theory as a basis for all general sociological analysis of social systems and their mutual relations (Luhmann 1995). But its theoretical claims about law's autonomy are very powerful postulates, presented in advance of (and even, perhaps, in place of) the kind of detailed empirical study of social and legal change that comparatists and most legal sociologists are likely to favour. The postulates of autopoiesis theory do not so much guide empirical research as explain conclusively how to interpret whatever this research may discover. Comparatists and (most) legal sociologists might well want to ask why the particular discursive character of law that autopoiesis theory insists on must be taken as the starting point for analysis; why, for example, it is to be *assumed* that any direct influence of legal ideas between legal systems is likely to be impossible, and why modern law is *necessarily* to be seen as merely 'coupled' to (rather than linked in mutual influence with) the economy, or other aspects of social life. In other words, comparatists and legal sociologists might be well advised to join forces to ask for more attention to open-minded empirical inquiry and for theory that imports less initial scepticism about the richness and profundity of law's social embeddedness.

Legal Culture and Comparative Law

In a legal transplant, what is transplanted and what is the test of successful transplantation? This is the other question that was suggested earlier as left open by Watson's transplants thesis. If all that is involved is a transfer of certain rules of positive law, a transplant need be no more than the formal enacting of those rules by the recipient legal system. And if enactment in itself is seen as transplantation, without any concern for who actually uses the rules, who knows about them or whether they influence social or economic life in any way, mere enactment constitutes success. Insofar as Watson's thesis is concerned with lawyers' borrowing of foreign rules and enacting them or adopting them formally in legal practice, his claims about the ease with which successful transplants can occur reduce almost to tautology. If a transplant is merely the putting of a foreign rule on the statute book or its adoption in the practice of courts, success in legal transplantation is entirely in the hands of those legal elites that control courts or legislatures. It has nothing to do with what may or may not happen in society beyond the world of professional legal or legislative practice.[13] By definition, sociology (treated by Watson as the study of everything social except lawyers' own practices) becomes irrelevant: transplants cannot be other than – as Watson (1993: 95) puts it – 'socially easy'.

Sometimes, however, Watson has used the term 'legal culture' to refer to conditions governing successful transplantation (see, for example, Watson 1991: 100–2; 1993: 108, 115, 117–18). These conditions are the outlook, practices, knowledge, values and traditions of the legal elite of the recipient legal system. Sometimes, in fact, he refers to 'the lawyers' culture' (1985b: 117–18). Watson sees legal culture in this sense as a major determinant of law's internal processes of development. But to refer to culture is to appeal to an idea that has for a long time been an important focus of social science (especially anthropology). It refers to a compendium of matters of social experience, understanding and practice that clearly invite social scientific analysis and clarification. Again the problem of the internal/external dichotomy presents itself. If these matters of outlook, values, etc. are important among Watson's legal elites, why are they not important among other social groups that might be crucial in determining whether transplanted law is invoked, applied or enforced?

Here, interesting contrasts with developments in legal sociology can be noted. In Chapter 5 we considered how the concept of legal culture has been used in sociology of law, especially by Lawrence Friedman, to refer to attitudes, ideas, beliefs and expectations related to law. Watson's use of the term corresponds to what Friedman calls internal (lawyers') legal culture. But Friedman's main concern (like that of many legal sociologists) is with external (non-lawyers') legal culture. He rejects comparatists' typical categorizations of legal styles or legal systems precisely because these take insufficient account of differences or similarities in external legal culture which he sees as crucial determinants of law's social meaning and significance

---

13 However, Watson (1991: 87) assumes, without supplying evidence, that transplanted law will normally strongly control 'lesser officials' and affected citizens.

(Friedman 1997). But comparatists might be strongly justified in criticizing the legal sociologists' focus on culture here for its conceptual vagueness and potentially unlimited scope of inquiry. As argued in Chapter 5, the study of legal culture in this sense embraces potentially all kinds of social differentiation without indicating means of defining or relating them or judging their independent significance. A tie to law is given only by *some* attitudinal focus on the official legal system or on something else (for example, disputing, complaining or official behaviour) that might be seen as in some way related to it. The concept of culture in *this* usage is hopelessly vague and comparatists would do well to avoid it.[14]

The contemporary focus on legal culture by some comparatists is clearly different from Friedman's, or from the use of the term by other legal sociologists to refer not to attitudinal matters but to measurable behavioural patterns related to law (for example, as indicated by litigation rates: see Blankenberg 1997). Interestingly, Pierre Legrand's approach contextualizes the traditional comparative law concern for contrasting legal styles of different families of law into a much broader focus on legal cultures as distinctive *mentalités* – 'modes of understanding reality' (Legrand 1999: 11) – informing all aspects of the particular civilization in which law is embedded in a specific time and place.

Because Legrand's main concern as a comparatist in using the concept of legal culture in this way is to appreciate and highlight *difference* (Legrand 1999: Chapter 1) between the styles and outlooks of jurists, rather than to make causal claims as with Friedman's legal sociology, his use of the idea of culture seems much less vulnerable to criticism of its vagueness and indeterminate scope. I see it as a provisional interpretive concept of the kind Jerome Hall might have approved for comparative law as humanistic legal sociology, rather than as an explanatory concept of a scientific, theory-building sociology seeking generalizations about social and legal development. The concept of legal culture in this usage can evoke a sense of rich and complex difference that is important in appreciating, *in a general, preliminary way*, variation between modes of legal understanding or legal styles of analysis and interpretation, even if the elements of difference remain aggregated, diffuse or indistinct and ultimately of unspecified individual significance.

From a sociological point of view, the difficulties with any concept of legal culture of this kind are likely to arise only when it is treated as a sufficient basis of predictions about social (including legal) development. Legal culture, in Legrand's depiction, is focused on the accumulated professional traditions, styles of thought and habits of practice of lawyers but (far more subtly than in Watson's use of the concept) it extends beyond these to stress their roots and resonances in wider aspects of cultural experience. As an aggregate of variables, with its elements not rigorously differentiated, legal culture in this sense can, however, run into the same difficulties as the legal sociologists' concept does when it is used in social explanation. It may

---

14 For a careful assessment of the sociological potential of the concept in a variety of contexts, see Nelken 1995.

cover too much and focus clearly on too little to allow it to be used convincingly in explaining social phenomena.

Just as autopoiesis theory encourages us to see law as immune from direct external influence because of its impenetrability as a normatively self-sufficient discourse, so a focus on legal culture as an all-embracing *mentalité* can suggest similar immunities (cf. Legrand 1996; 2001). In both cases the suggestion of immunity is not necessarily empirically warranted but is the result of presenting a vast diversity of contingently related phenomena as if it were a complex, rather solid *unity*. In autopoiesis theory, law's very diverse forms of knowledge, reasoning and practice are presented as a single, unique discourse. Similarly, in some conceptions of legal culture, the aggregate of extremely diverse elements of experience that might, taken together, be labelled as culture is treated as though it were an integrated unity capable of resisting other cultures, conceived as opposing unities.

No doubt 'each person's cultural context is unique to some extent' (Curran 1998: 49) and perfect communication across cultural contexts may be impossible – as the illustration of language translation so well shows (Curran 1998: 54–9; Legrand 1999: 3–4). From a social scientific standpoint, one valuable effect of the recent emphasis among comparatists on legal culture is the degree of harmonization on matters of method that it may promote, for certain purposes, between comparative law and social science. An awareness of 'irreducible incomparables' and of deep cultural differences, the components of which remain undifferentiated in any conclusive way, points to a 'need to accept that others have different truths' from ourselves (Curran 1998: 91).[15]

But this does not mean that communication or comparison is impossible. It means rather that communication and comparison demand thick description (Geertz 1973: Chapter 1; 1983: Chapter 3) – rich, multi-layered and detailed accounts of social experience to convey the complexity of cultural difference, to identify points of empathy and thereby to provide some keys of entry into the understanding and appreciation of different cultures. Vivian Curran calls this method for comparative law 'immersion comparison'. It involves studying not just legal rules, but what attaches to them: values, traditions and beliefs; and collective memories, understandings, aspirations and emotions. 'It contemplates a slow pushing against cultural barriers toward an ideal of mutual comprehension, a striving to reach comprehension, and a recognition that some distances will remain' (Curran 1998: 91).

---

15 Ethnocentrism (one kind of failure to accept this) is at least as serious a danger for legal sociologists as for comparatists. For example, the 'law and development' movement, a heavily-funded social science initiative in comparative legal research in the 1960s and 1970s, failed in part because it 'was largely a parochial expression of the American legal style' (Merryman 1977: 479). On the ethnocentrism issue see also Alford 1986.

Conclusion

If social science has messages of value for comparative law today, I think they can be summed up in the following way. Comparison is more difficult in some contexts and for some purposes than has often been thought in the past, and what is to be compared must be conceptualized in much more complex and subtle ways than previously. The social milieux of regulation need to be understood systematically, empirically and interpretively in their detail and complexity.

Can legal sociology help this understanding? Earlier in this chapter, reference was made to a need to conceptualize and clarify the different aspects or regions of the social in relation to law. Most legal study is still focused strongly on the law of nation states, but the political society of the nation state is much less obviously, than in the recent past, the social of law – its environment of significance and authority (see, for example, Glenn 2003). Legal sociology has long been concerned to study forms of regulation that have jurisdictions different from those of state law. It has a large literature on legal pluralism. It has sometimes tried to show (often with polemical intent) how law is created and sustained in patterns of social relations that have very little to do with the state's regulatory activity (Ehrlich 1936). And it has tried to understand the varieties of legal experience as forms of subjective social experience (Gurvitch 1935).

In contemporary contexts, these sociolegal orientations become concerns with the interrelation of different types of community.[16] Instrumental community, expressed especially in business relations, extends, with increasing frequency, beyond state boundaries, as in trade and financial systems. Community of belief is expressed, for example, in movements supporting international human rights. Many social relations remain strongly territorial in focus, linked to and defined by specific localities that, again, may or may not be coterminous with nation state jurisdictional boundaries. Others are focused on family or friendship groups. The social is thus complex and varied.

All of this is important for comparative law's efforts to survey and compare systems of regulation that express these manifestations of the social, or are struggling to emerge so as to do so. And a concern with types of community must involve the effort to appreciate how people *subjectively experience* community and its legal expressions. This is what makes thick description and immersion comparison valuable and old ideas of, for example, function, evolution and social problems inadequate for some tasks of comparative study. Despite these complexities, however, comparison of legal systems remains possible and necessary, whether to pursue socio-technics, education (to borrow Abrams' terms), or other aims. It is not to be jettisoned from

---

16 As discussed in Chapter 4, above. Georges Gurvitch (1947: 49) uses the term 'sociality' to convey a similar idea of abstract types of community that can be expressed in diverse ways in actual social relations. But his particular typology of the 'forms of sociality' is, in my view, too intricate and often too obscure in its empirical reference to be generally useful in sociolegal analysis.

the heart of the legal comparatist's enterprise because it often implies difficult links with and dependences on social scientific ideas.

Nor do these links demand or suggest any subordination of one academic discipline to another in a hierarchy of explanation. Legal sociology and comparative law are, for many (but not all) important purposes, interdependent co-workers in the empirical study of law. One aspect of this is that law ought not to be conceptualized (for example, as an autopoietic system or self-contained cultural sphere) in ways that make it harder to see the intricacy and intimacy of influence, interaction and interpenetration between different elements of social life and legal experience. Legal sociologists, no less than comparatists, should take on board these principles and frame their researches in the light of them. If this is done it may not be over-optimistic to suggest that a part, at least, of the great aspirations of the past for the unselfconscious integration of comparative law and legal sociology around ambitious projects of comparative study will eventually be realized.

Chapter 9

Interpretation in Comparative Law

Comparatists use interpretive methods broadly similar to those of other lawyers, but interpretation in comparative law is not usually controlled by ultimate judicial or legislative authority. This chapter argues that the authority of interpretation in comparative legal studies usually comes directly from social sources in the different networks of community that legal regulation serves. This has an important bearing on comparatists' preferences for harmonizing law, on the one hand, or celebrating legal difference, on the other. It helps to explain when and why comparatists should lean towards one or other of these preferences.

Introduction

Comparative legal studies now cover a vast range of subject matter and have very diverse aims. These aims and the means of pursuing them are themselves discussed in a large literature. Today, there is little point in trying to specify what comparative law should be, because it already is many different things. Its importance is clear and growing, a fact illustrated by its use in many practical current contexts.

Despite this importance, two theoretical problems haunt comparative law. The first is an epistemological problem: Why compare? What is the nature of the knowledge comparison gives? What is its status as knowledge? Knowledge for what and subject to what conditions? The other is an ontological problem: What can properly be compared – legal rules, principles, cultures, systems, families, functions, styles? Or should comparison be of legal responses to social needs, interests or problems? What ensures that the entities chosen for comparison really are comparable? In other words, what is the necessary subject matter of comparative law?

These problems are closely related. It has often been suggested that their existence makes comparative law a different kind of research enterprise from the analysis of law in a single legal system (Zweigert 1975: 84; Legrand 1999: 11–12). The problems seem sufficiently serious to some writers to make them argue that comparative law should give up comparison altogether: its aim should be to study adaptation and development in particular legal systems. The comparative element in what would otherwise be an inquiry in legal history or jurisprudence is given by a focus on the way legal systems borrow rules or institutions from other systems (Watson 1993; Ewald 1995b).

Other writers accept that purely technical comparison of rules unrelated to a wider context may be of limited or indeterminate value and so comparison must usually be of sociolegal phenomena including but extending beyond legal rules. They advocate alliance with social science, or see comparative law as a social science itself (Hall 1963; Zweigert and Kötz 1998: 45). Thus, Konrad Zweigert and Hein Kötz claim that comparative law and sociology of law 'use much the same methods' (1998: 10). Clearly this cannot be said generally of doctrinal studies limited to a single legal system. Although sociolegal studies have made great headway, they have not influenced doctrinal legal studies to such an extent that most jurists can be said to 'use much the same methods' as legal sociologists. The dimension of 'internationalism' (Zweigert and Kötz 1998: 2) is said to make the difference as regards the methods of comparative law. And, undoubtedly, for some comparatists, the attraction of comparative legal study is that it is a means of 'putting legal science on a sure and realistic basis' (Zweigert and Kötz 1998: 33), because it demands the study of law in a broad context. On one view, while comparative law is a social science, the study of national law is an 'interpretive human science' (Zweigert 1975: 84), or not even a science at all because its subject matter is limited arbitrarily on a territorial basis (Zweigert and Kötz 1998: 15).

Comparative Law and Legal Interpretation

But matters are more complex than this. The assertion of a close link between legal sociology and comparative law has often presupposed (wrongly in my view)[1] the continuing dominance of positivist methods in both – the positivist aim being to describe and explain law as social fact in some sense. Explaining law as a social phenomenon that presents itself in different ways in different national contexts may seem significantly different from municipal lawyers' efforts to interpret law in their own legal system. But if comparative law's task is not only to describe positivistically but also to interpret law on a comparative basis, to seek the most appropriate legal ideas or understandings in particular contexts, its close relationship with other doctrinal legal studies is reaffirmed. *All* such studies involve comparison (Curran 1998: 45) – the linking or contrasting of rules, the creative comparison of their wording and meanings and the effort to relate them or distinguish them. For Vivian Curran (1998: 45), comparative legal analysis is 'a paradigm for legal analysis in general, and is distinguishable from general legal analysis more in name than in substance'. Like some other contemporary comparatists, Curran sees a main purpose of comparison as being appreciation of difference.[2] But this can, of course, only be a

---

1   See Chapter 8, above, for the argument that comparative law and legal sociology can be closely interrelated as *interpretive* practices.

2   Curran (1998: 44) writes that comparative law 'is the one field which by definition has always dealt with and analysed the *other*, the different'. Pierre Legrand (1999: 11, 13) argues that comparatists should 'cherish difference' and have an 'empathy for alterity' rather than 'obstinately pursue similarity and consensus as if confined to a groove'.

matter of emphasis. The identification of likeness and difference go together in legal interpretation generally: jurists order and integrate doctrine by making distinctions in it, and general categories indicate necessary distinctions.

In all modern legal interpretation, however, the search for unity, integrity or consistency of meaning is usually privileged in certain ways over the identification of difference.[3] For example, common lawyers usually try hard to reconcile precedents and only if they fail do they admit the existence of judicial disagreements or differences of interpretation. Certainly, it is not satisfactory to declare too often that a past decision must be confined to its own unique facts (to recognize that it does not fit other cases, that it represents an irreconcilably different view). The task is to decide how past decisions can best be generalized to play their part in a larger body of legal doctrine. Where legal rules relate without referring to each other and appear to conflict, interpretive effort often aims to show how their interrelation gives new subtleties of meaning in their application together as a doctrinal unity. This is different from (and perhaps more highly prized than) the often unavoidable task of merely recognizing conflict between rules or seeing one rule as derogating from another.

Similarly, in comparative law, it is certainly important to stress the value of appreciating difference between legal rules, solutions, styles, cultures and systems through comparative study and to ask in what circumstances difference is important, inevitable or even desirable. But this strong emphasis is valuable partly because historically so much effort has been devoted by comparatists to projects of integrating or unifying law (Graveson 1977; Gutteridge 1949: Chapters 11 and 12). In this traditional emphasis, comparatists have been no different from other modern lawyers in typically preferring to seek unity and consistency of legal meaning, rather than contrast and differentiation (Legrand 1999: 12–13). Where this unity and consistency is elusive, comparatists have often seen their task as that of trying to build it in programmes of transnational 'uniform law', just as jurists of municipal legal systems have tended in modern times to see the task of expounding law as being to construct order from, or superimpose it on, the varied doctrinal detail given by legislation, case law or other sources. To write of the lawyers' preference here is not to imply that this exists independently of powerful client pressures (for example, from governmental and commercial interests) as well as lawyers' own need to legitimize their professional knowledge and practice (Cotterrell 2003: 8–13). A range of considerations of regulatory efficiency and legitimation no doubt gives comparatists a powerful impetus to work towards uniform law just as it powerfully

---

3   Another way of putting this is in terms of the balance of the *systematic* and the *empirical* (see Chapter 3, above) in legal interpretation. If all legal interpretation involves balancing a need to systematize doctrine, on the one hand, and to address it empirically to particular cases, on the other, modern approaches to legal interpretation ultimately always tilt in favour of systematization. Every effort is made to justify particular decisions in terms of legal principles, or at least explain how they relate to these. A legal decision, however just it seems on the facts, appears juristically unsatisfactory if it cannot be rationally linked to what lawyers see as broader patterns of legal doctrine governing its field.

promotes lawyers' efforts to build system and unity in the doctrine of modern state legal systems.

Seeking similarity versus *appreciating difference*: we could speak also of 'achieving integration' contrasted with 'delineating boundaries'. I want to argue in this chapter that determining the balance between these is one of comparative law's hardest but most important practical tasks and that this task must be understood in relation to the activity of legal interpretation more generally.

In legal interpretation, delineating boundaries can refer to the fixing of boundaries of *meaning* (for example, the meaning of one rule limited by that of another, or of a word or phrase in a statute, or of an entire style of thought or way of understanding that informs law). Equally, it can refer to the extent of the *authority* of law (limits of jurisdiction), whether this concerns a specific rule, a set of procedures (such as those of a particular court or administrative agency) or a legal system. And it can be a matter of defining spheres of devolved or federal regulatory authority within a state legal system, or marking jurisdictional relations between systems.

Integration of law involves removing contradictions between rules or other elements of legal doctrine. This can be done by fiat (for example, a superior court declaring invalid an inconsistent rule laid down by a lower court). Here law's politically guaranteed authority determines matters conclusively. Or it can be done by persuasion as where a community of legal interpreters (for example, lawyers drafting a code, a panel of judges hearing a case, juristic commentators) reaches agreement on the best meaning to give to particular elements of legal doctrine or the most appropriate rule to apply in a particular context. Integration can also involve establishing uniform legal authority by merging jurisdictions or setting a uniform legal regime over a diversity of others (as with the creation of a supranational European legal order or various transnational regimes of trade regulation or human rights). Thus, integration and differentiation of law involve a continuum of comparisons which, in their essential nature, concern comparatists and municipal lawyers alike.

If the activity of comparing as such does not fundamentally distinguish comparative law from other legal studies, what does? Legal interpretation of rules or judicial decisions usually assumes a single structure of legal authority to which all these materials can be related: a structure explicable theoretically using, for example, ideas of sovereignty, rule of recognition or basic norm, which identify its apex or centre. By contrast, comparative law involves comparisons not limited within any single system of established legal authority (such as that of the legal system of a nation state).

The absence of a common structure of legal authority embracing the elements to be compared produces the epistemological and ontological problems of comparative law referred to earlier. In legal interpretation related to a single legal system, the answer to the question 'Why compare?' is usually simply: to expound and clarify what is at a certain time valid law in that legal system (perhaps as a prelude to evaluating it). The answer to the question 'What is to be compared?' is: whatever can be recognized, according to established understandings within the relevant legal professional community, as legal rules, principles or concepts coexisting in the system. The task of comparison is to integrate and differentiate these various legal materials so as to establish plausible conclusions about the legal position in relation to a particular regulatory field or problem. Of course, this in no way suggests that comparison is itself simple. Nevertheless it is usually limited and directed by settled juristic criteria and practices in a way that does not apply in the same way in comparative law.

In most legal interpretation, law's politically guaranteed authority or *voluntas* (for example, the authority of a sovereign legislature or a superior court over an inferior one) limits debates on the rational meaning (*ratio*) of legal doctrine and structures their relevance at all times (see Neumann 1996). And debates on *ratio* are given urgency and point by the assumption that the meanings of legal doctrine arrived at will represent valid law. But, in comparative law, no common legal authority exists to produce these effects. So, comparatists' elaborations of law's *ratio* on a transnational basis, as in efforts at creating uniform law, are often persuasive rather than authoritative (Bonell 1995: 73–4), though they may be adopted by international agreement (Gutteridge 1949: Chapter 13).

The Comparatist's Authority

What, then, makes for good interpretation of legal doctrine in comparative law? For example, in seeking similarity, what makes similarity worth seeking? In appreciating difference, what makes difference worth appreciating? When and under what conditions? What is to be compared? And what is comparison for?

To set these questions, as has been done here, in the context of a discussion of general legal interpretation emphasizes how crucial 'authority' is in determining answers to them. What makes comparatists' search for uniform law or harmonization of law, or their welcome of legal 'convergence', appropriate? The answer may be greater regulatory efficiency (for example, economic utility), as is often claimed for projects of unifying commercial laws. Or it may be that law is thereby made to represent, symbolize or give effect to shared values or beliefs, as in the claim that uniform human rights laws express universal civilized values associated with respect for the autonomy or dignity of all human beings. Again, the answer may lie in the simplicity, predictability or security of a uniform law, as where the same rules (whatever they may be) are applied consistently across a certain geographical area (or in a region of shared language, traditions or historical experience). Finally, a uniform legal solution might be appropriate because it seems congruent with, or a public expression of, widely shared feelings. One of the best known theoretical arguments for uniform law on this basis is Savigny's (1831) invocation of the spirit of the people as the source of law – an impenetrable and mystical idea and therefore dangerous, but powerful in some circumstances (as in the politically disunited Germany of Savigny's era). More recently, the fear of extreme nationalist feelings and the wish to marginalize them and prevent future war has been a spur to efforts to harmonize or unify law on a transnational basis, especially in Europe.

These criteria of appropriateness might pragmatically influence international agreement or the decisions of particular states. In any case, they serve as potential substitutes, in comparative law, for a settled (legal) authority (*voluntas*) that can put an end to debate about law's *ratio*: that is, about its principled justification and appropriate meaning.

Conversely, what is it that makes diverse legal solutions – the appreciation of difference – appropriate? Comparatists have recently tended to answer this question by invoking conceptions of legal culture, or urging a broad recognition of cultural differences underlying different legal styles or systems. These are identified mainly in lawyers' outlook, practices and traditions but they, in turn, are often seen as 'intimately linked to our civilisation and ways of thinking' (David and Brierley 1985: 19). What constitutes cultural difference here is usually mysterious but the claim is sometimes that cultural 'features of the law ... can only be changed at the slow rhythm at which the civilisation of the country itself, the sense of justice of its citizens, its economic structure, language and social manners themselves are changed' (David and Brierley 1985: 19).

The cultural authority invoked to justify difference is often ambiguous and undifferentiated. As has been seen in earlier chapters, the elements of culture might include ultimate values or beliefs (such as those that underpin the distinctiveness of religious legal systems) or traditions (for example, common language or historical experience). The traditions that some comparatists see as most powerful in determining differences between legal systems, styles or cultures are those of professional legal elites (see, for example, Watson 1985b), rather than of the wider society. Otherwise, a justification for legal difference may lie in distinctive collective interests (for example, national economic interests) that require special legal protection. Finally, what remains as a potential cultural justification of difference is the difficult idea of collective sentiments: feelings, for example, about the 'nation' or the 'people' and its character or destiny – the hard-to-analyse but often very powerful sense of patriotism, nationalism or group identification (Gutteridge 1949: 158). The authority of culture as a guide for comparative law is thus a compendium of diverse elements (beliefs, traditions, interests, sentiments), some of which cannot be defined in any conclusive way.

These ideas merely illustrate the kinds of authority that comparatists typically invoke to justify, underpin or explain their legal interpretations. This is not a matter of the legal authority of *voluntas* but of the persuasive 'authority' of instrumental utility, appeal to shared beliefs or ultimate values, tradition or shared sentiment. These kinds of authority point to a logic of sociolegal analysis that, I shall argue, makes the methods and outlook of comparative law specially appropriate to confront the changing environment of contemporary law.

What is most important about this changing environment? The general forces of change in it that are most significant for present purposes are indicated by the terms 'globalization' and 'localization', which have many diverse and often contradictory meanings. Here I take globalization simply to mean tendencies (however interpreted) towards transnational uniformity in economic or social arrangements, institutions and values. Localization refers here to counter-tendencies (of whatever kind) towards protection, assertion or facilitation of diversity, difference, independence, separation or autonomy of groups, nations or territories, most often in matters of government or common values or traditions. Without referring to the extensive debates about these tendencies it can at least be said that, in social life beyond its specifically legal aspects, the tension between seeking similarity and appreciating difference clearly exists, writ large in major social movements that are still imperfectly understood. Globalization seems pre-eminently to be about seeking similarity by unifying social, economic and often legal arrangements. Localization seems to be about appreciating difference by creating, preserving or rediscovering conditions in which difference (for example, political or cultural) can flourish and be respected.

Because the focus of comparative law is not restricted to the law of any particular nation state it is better fitted than other doctrinal legal studies to take full account of the dynamics of social change represented by the conflicts of globalization and localization. Comparative law's long-professed but still inchoate relationship with legal sociology can be exploited and developed to enable it to observe and interpret the changing economic and social contexts of regulation. Certainly, the epistemological and ontological problems of comparative law should force it, in seeking to solve them, to take account of these contexts in pursuing many, though not all, of its aims. Comparative law's commonly adopted focus on legal and social 'functions', 'problems' or 'interests' (see, for example, Zweigert and Kötz 1998: 10) as bases of comparison ought to point it towards serious concern with analysis of the social environments in relation to which legal doctrine must establish its meaning. For example, comparatists have long recognized that power relations between nation states can strongly affect legal change (Gutteridge 1949: 160) and legal sociologists have begun to demonstrate some mechanisms of this influence (see, for example, Dezalay and Garth 1996). Indeed, power relations in and between regulated groups and communities should be a major focus of attention.

On the other hand, comparatists have understandably not wished to become sociologists or to see their focus on legal comparison dissolve away into sociological inquiries (Péteri 1970: 90–3). So, they have held back from exploring some implications of comparative law's dependence on social criteria of legal interpretation (discussed above in terms of instrumental efficiency, shared values or beliefs, traditions and affective considerations). To explore these criteria more rigorously and to understand their interaction in relation to comparative law's tasks, much more cooperation between comparatists and legal sociologists is needed.

A further difficulty is more serious because solving it may not be merely a matter of productive academic alliances. In an important sense, the primary contemporary agenda of comparative law is obviously not set by comparatists. It is determined particularly by those engaged in and seeking to benefit from projects of European integration, the opening of trade and commerce on an ever-wider transnational basis, the development of international banking and financial systems, the worldwide control and exploitation of intellectual property, the development of the Internet, and the control of transnational crime of many kinds. All of these projects are seen to require, for their efficient pursuit, significant harmonization of the laws of nation states or the creation of new transnational regulatory regimes (Wiener 1999). Viewed in these contexts, the great recent resurgence of interest and activity in comparative law is in no way neutrally situated between the appreciation of difference and the search for similarity. Comparative law is powerfully driven now, as through much of its history, by the urge to unify or harmonize law. Recognizing difference does not, in these contexts, lead to its celebration but to devising means of removing it.

To this extent, the coordination of law by unification or harmonization that comparative law has always sporadically pursued (Gutteridge 1949: Chapter 11) has now become, for some major interest groups, an urgent priority. The question is not 'whether or when?', but 'how and on what model?' The predominantly economic process of globalization is like a whirlwind carrying comparative law along. 'It is ... the mechanism of the market which now takes upon itself the role of the judge, the opinion-maker, the verifier of values. Intellectuals have been expropriated again' (Bauman 1987: 124). Comparative law's task is apparently to aid processes of unstoppable change, to identify sources of friction (perhaps embedded in some way in what is seen as culture) and to find the most efficient means of removing or by-passing them. Perhaps it can ease the pain of transition by inventively smoothing out legal differences, creatively interpreting legal change to those who must accept it, or preserving familiar forms, concepts and styles of legal practice and thought while adjusting their effects to meet transnational requirements.

With transnational organization of economic activity in many fields, some see a 'retreat of the state' (Strange 1996) so that law's *voluntas* in many areas of regulation is slowly being detached from its dependence on the political guarantee that the state provides. Nevertheless, for the present, much harmonization of law is still accomplished by adjusting the private and public law regimes of nation states (Wiener 1999). Hence, a huge scope for comparative law opens up. Yet, strictly speaking, the task assigned to it as a facilitator of globalization in these contexts will be neither to appreciate difference nor even to seek similarity between the legal systems, styles or cultures of nation states. Instead, the object will be to make legal adjustments, as needed, to avoid tension and friction in governance systems that seek as far as possible to free themselves from significant moorings in or dependency on the law of any particular nation state.

In at least one area – human rights – appreciation of difference alongside a search for uniformity seems widely recognized as a continuing necessity. While the drive to universalize human rights is as powerful in many respects as the whirlwind of economic globalization (and in some respects promoted by it), the dynamics of legal development are clearly different. Economic globalization serves primarily instrumental aims. In the terms I have sketched earlier, the persuasive authority for unifying or harmonizing law is that of greater efficiency in commercial or related activities (though this can have major consequences on wider fronts). By contrast, the universalization of human rights is a matter of the export, reception or transplanting of fundamental values or beliefs (for example, about the essential nature of humanity) in legal form. These values can be variously interpreted, or confronted by opposing values, in certain settings. Hence the drive for universalism, seeking similarity in human rights jurisdictions, is challenged by a cultural relativism that demands the appreciation of difference (Steiner and Alston 2000: 366–402). Nonetheless, the drive for legal uniformity is very strong, given that the universality of the values to be represented in human rights law is powerfully championed. So, respect for human rights is said to be 'the only regulative principle of state organization which unites every country, race and creed in the world ... the ideology at the "end of history"' (Douzinas 1996: 115).

The Regions of the Social

If comparative law is to set its own agenda of finding appropriate balances between the search for similarity and the appreciation of difference in legal phenomena, it will need powerful theoretical resources to help with this. In their absence, the residual assumption is likely to be that the aim of all contemporary comparative scholarship must be to facilitate legal uniformity on the widest possible scale. The reason is that, while it is now widely accepted that national economic survival and success depend on transnational regulatory harmonization, other kinds of persuasive authority for or against harmonizing or unifying different areas of law remain insufficiently analysed. In such circumstances, most legal differences are likely to be judged negatively: as failures of or challenges to harmonization, or as occasions for ranking so that one legal solution is necessarily seen as worse or better than another, or simply incomprehensible.

But law can be, for example, a means of protecting or symbolizing collective identity in various ways. It must serve the needs not only of economic communities but of other kinds of community too, and it can serve, in some respects, as a normative expression of their nature. It can provide 'rights to roots' that give groundings of identity and solidarity, as well as 'rights to options' that allow the greatest scope for free personal initiative and choice (Santos 2002: 177). Thus, interests in harmonizing or unifying law can be confronted with other interests that require law to express or preserve difference.

Debates around cultural relativism in human rights show that, in some contemporary circumstances, this kind of confrontation is recognized and the invocation of culture as a powerful marker of difference is surely significant in these debates. In a very different context from the human rights debates, the idea of culture has also been invoked to focus attention on the appreciation of difference generally in comparative law. Recent efforts to develop a concept of legal culture as *mentalité* – the entire law-related outlook of a community – are an attempt to work towards theoretical conceptions of difference powerful enough to confront assumptions about the significance (and even inevitability) of convergence, harmonization or unification (Legrand 1996; 1999; 2001; Curran 1998).

I argued earlier, especially in Chapters 6 and 7, that the idea of culture in comparative law scholarship should be broken down into distinct components. It is hard to invoke culture or legal culture as a reason for appreciating rather than condemning or dismissing difference, because these terms refer to an indeterminate number of variables, mostly undifferentiated, so that their relative importance cannot be gauged in specific contexts of regulation. We need, instead, to distinguish the distinct types of community which law regulates, and so identify, for regulatory purposes, different aspects or regions of the social. In this way the components of culture can be examined systematically.

Today, in legal studies, the social can no longer be thought of as an undifferentiated entity of some sort. We can no longer speak of law's functions in relation to 'society' as though law and society are monolithic entities confronting each other. If, as previous chapters have suggested, different kinds or areas of law relate to different types of community, it is clear that much pressure for harmonization of law has always arisen through perceptions of law's role in regulating *instrumental* community. But this is only one kind of community and if law serves it exclusively at the expense of protecting and promoting the well-being of other kinds of social bonds, other types of community, it fails to meet some important demands. The law of instrumental community (most obviously, for example, contract, commercial, financial and corporate regulation) is powerful because it can be tailored to serve precise instrumental objectives. But it serves social groups (especially commercial enterprises, trade networks and economic interest groups) that mutate rapidly as national and international markets alter. These are weak patterns of community. Law serves them mainly by providing rights to options – patterns of regulation geared to flexibility, growth and change, and to facilitating innumerable convergent deals. These bring people together in relationships that are relatively transient or focused mainly on limited objectives that are shared or congruent.

The grand historical ideal of unifying law, now most likely to be pursued by articulating convergences and strategies of harmonization, is skewed and partial if it serves relations of community subsisting only in these limited, loose social groupings. So, comparative law, in alliance with legal sociology, needs to pay special attention to law's contributions to *other* types of community that tend to be marginalized in the whirlwind of globalization. These correspond to other types of justifications, referred to earlier, for seeking similarity and appreciating difference through comparative law. As we have noted, traditional, belief-based or affective kinds of community life do not necessarily demand either that their legal protection and promotion be increasingly globalized, on the one hand, or resolutely localized, on the other. They do not inevitably point the law that serves them towards seeking similarity by unifying or harmonizing law across jurisdictions, or towards appreciating difference and favouring legal particularity and distinctiveness. But they raise these issues in quite different ways from the way they are raised (and usually resolved atheoretically) in many of comparative law's projects of uniform law or harmonization to serve the needs of instrumental community.

Regulating Non-instrumental Relations of Community

Regulating Community of Belief or Values

Take, for example, law's role in expressing shared ultimate values or beliefs. Specifically belief-based community life is usually strong. People cling to ultimate values they recognize as their own. It is painful to discard them or see them fundamentally challenged. But because values are often ambiguous in their implications when translated into specific regulatory demands, law seen as the expression of fundamental values or beliefs is typically weak and problematic. Thus, human rights as legal ideas are not, to use Jeremy Bentham's term, nonsense upon stilts, but they can have very different practical meanings in different contexts and be subject to controversial interpretation. It is not difficult for them to be subordinated or adapted to the regulatory requirements of instrumental community, which give rise to clearer, more specific law that defines freedom of action in economically related fields. And because community of belief is often a strong kind of bonding when present in group life, harmonization or unification of the law expressing it is often difficult or impossible between groups whose fundamental values or beliefs are claimed to differ. This is why comparatists and legal sociologists have long recognized that, in many cases, law seen as expressing values or beliefs (for example, with strong religious overtones) is hard to replace effectively with law transplanted from environments where beliefs or values are significantly different (Levy 1950; Massell 1968; Starr and Pool 1974).

Even in societies strongly wedded, as regards official pronouncements at least, to legal protection of the dignity and autonomy of individual human life, considerable differences in the interpretation of these values in legal form exist. For example, many Americans are strongly wedded to the maintenance of capital punishment within the framework of a belief system that strongly enshrines the values of individual autonomy. But this stance attracts popular 'disgust' in European countries, and is said to have damaged 'America's image as a bastion of freedom' (Kettle 2000). This is not only a transnational issue which makes appreciating differences between national legal systems necessary, but an intranational one too, because significant value-conflict exists around it in many individual European countries and particular states of the US. The same can be said of many other issues that arise in interpreting values of human dignity and autonomy: for example, issues relating to abortion, euthanasia or genetic research.

These considerations highlight the important point that the choice between seeking similarity and appreciating difference is not only to be made with regard to different national conditions taken as unities. A focus on law's relation to community, rather than to political society treated as a single entity, requires that full account be taken of the complex interrelations of different kinds of community life within the territory of state legal systems. People have allegiances, with varying degrees of transience or permanence, at different times and in different ways, and often simultaneously, to different groups and social relations involving intricate overlapping of the different types of community life – instrumental, traditional, belief-based and affective. Sometimes law, faced with impenetrable complexity (especially, perhaps, in the interplay of values and beliefs), steps aside and regulates in the most limited, neutral, locally pragmatic way possible, or not at all. For comparatists, the task in relation to these legal areas may sometimes be neither to seek similarity nor to appreciate difference, but only to recognize the appropriateness of leaving well alone.

Regulating Traditional Community

Relationships founded on traditional community are limited ones that arise from mere proximity: not necessarily physical proximity, as in the case of coexistence in a particular territory, but also, for example, the proximity of shared language or common historical experience. They are often, but not always, weak bonds getting weaker in the era of globalization.[4] Santos' rights to options may be, above all, the right to move freely from place to place and seize opportunities wherever they arise. Hence, the most powerful drives towards economic development on a transnational base weaken the significance of territorial roots for many people (who merely follow the job, the project or the enterprise to whatever location is most appropriate). Instrumental community, although limited and transient as a basis of group life, undermines traditional community.

Language, from this standpoint, becomes an obstacle to be overcome rather than a basis of group allegiance. English is pragmatically adopted most often as the transnational language through which rights to options are realized. But instrumental community life is not always or even mainly realized in transnational groups and relations, and traditional community, while attenuated and instrumentally transformed for some people, remains powerfully significant for many others. These include, most obviously, individuals who do not move their place of work or residence frequently, if ever, and have no second language which frees them from the ties of their native language group. It also includes others who deliberately affirm tradition as a basis of community, for example by reviving and nurturing the previously neglected distinctive language or customs of their group.

Law's relations with traditional community are focused on providing basic conditions for coexistence (rather than facilitating the pursuit of projects or expressing shared ultimate values or beliefs). We might see tort law and much basic criminal law as central to these regulatory aims, although categories of law cannot be linked exactly to types of community life. Crime obviously threatens the coexistence of individuals and groups. Its control is a prerequisite for any stable community life. Thus, although traditional community is weak in perhaps an increasing range of conditions, the law that protects it most fundamentally is typically strong and

---

4   But the dynamics are complex. As local territorial settings seem less important bases of social relations, global, or at least transnational, ones (recognized, for example, in international environmental legal concerns) achieve more prominence. The recognition of threats to global coexistence is providing new foci of traditional community.

must be so. It deals primarily with a bare social minimum – basic requirements of peaceful coexistence – and this minimum is likely to be similar in societies having broadly similar levels of social complexity. For these reasons the regulation of traditional community is often similar in different legal systems. So, comparatists understandably and appropriately tend to seek similarity, rather than to appreciate difference, in this field of legal regulation.

To the extent that instrumental community life expresses itself increasingly in transnational relationships and groups, the requirements of basic coexistence also acquire an increasingly strong transnational dimension. Hence the special importance and urgency of current efforts to develop transnational criminal law. Modern legal regulation for coexistence also increasingly covers health and safety, hygiene and the environment – at least there are strong demands that it should. But it is in these areas that some instrumental economic relations tend to conflict most obviously with regulatory demands of traditional community, as where interpretations of transnational trade laws or agreements hamper national health-related controls on food products, or in other ways frustrate or deter local environmental regulation, or where transnational demands for environmental or health regulation impose restrictions on local industries or even national economies.

As has been widely recognized, lawyers as a group, operating in different legal systems, themselves show many characteristics of traditional community. Tradition shows itself in the persistence of distinctive styles of practice and legal thought, purely because these are familiar and close at hand. The tendency in comparative law scholarship has been to attach much significance to tradition in this sense, as a condition to be taken into account in considering legal transplantation (Watson 1985b), or perhaps as a key element in legal culture causing special problems for convergence or harmonization of law (Legrand 1996; 2001).

From a legal sociological perspective it is hard to generalize about the significance of tradition in this kind of context. But the dynamics of change may be similar to those of traditional community more generally. In other words, tradition, despite some appearances, is often a relatively weak basis of community. The admittedly transient and fluid bonds of instrumental community tend to transform or weaken the bonds of tradition. Hence instrumental need can bring about remarkable transitions in traditional allegiances and practices, especially when transnational groups and relationships cut across all boundaries of local tradition (see, for example, Dezalay and Garth 1996). Hence as lawyers travel and practise transnationally, it seems very likely that traditions of practice will be radically transformed.

Regulating Affective Community

As noted in Chapter 7 above, affectively based community life is, for many reasons, particularly hard to interpret in legal terms. For Max Weber, affective action was clearly irrational, by which he meant not governed by any consciously recognized principles (Weber 1968: 24–6). Similarly, the *Volksgeist* idea, associated with Savigny's work, has often been condemned as irrational. Certainly, affective bonds have an unpredictability and analytical impenetrability which makes it hard to frame or recognize them with any real precision in law. But these bonds are often strong: people may be prepared to die for family, friends or nation when love ties them to these groups or relationships. I think comparatists have always clearly recognized the significance of affective community in considering prospects for unifying law. Usually, national feeling has been judged negatively as a dangerous or regrettable barrier to legal unity, since it has so often led not to transnational cooperation but to tension, conflict and war.

If, however, we take seriously the idea that individuals in contemporary conditions seek both rights to options and rights to roots, it is easy to see that the notion of roots can have strongly *emotional* connotations. A place or group may be just a site of coexistence (as with traditional community), a setting for current projects (as with instrumental community), or seen as an environment 'where people think like me and believe what I believe' (as in community of belief). But it may also be a setting of sentimental attachment which gives powerful, if intangible and ultimately mysterious bases of security, identity or meaningful existence. National identity may be a combination of traditional attachments (for example, to locality, language and literature, or shared historical experience), collective pursuit of economic well-being (measured, for example, in gross national product) and adherence to values or beliefs ('we hold these truths to be self-evident ...'). But these elements can be overlaid by purely sentimental national pride or patriotism. And this can substitute for any of them.

Nationalism clearly remains significant. While it has in the past sometimes inspired legal unification, today it is usually a powerful force for localization (taken in this setting as the promotion through law of specific national interests and prerogatives) in opposition to globalization. Because of its history as a begetter of wars and its frequent inclusion of an apparently purely emotional component, it is a morally and intellectually inadequate opponent of globalization, even if a powerful affective focus. Indeed, often it pragmatically allies itself with globalization insofar as transnational economic objectives or the spread of certain fundamental values are seen to support national interests.

Conclusion

If comparative law develops a systematic concern with the interrelation of types of community, as this chapter has proposed, a new view of the global–local dynamic is possible. Comparative law's central focus should be to balance the promotion of similarity in legal arrangements between legal systems, on the one hand, and the defence of differences in legal arrangements, styles, outlooks and ideas, on the other. But it can do this only if it understands systematically the nature of the social.

Celebration of legal difference may be, as some comparatists have long affirmed (Gutteridge 1949: 156–7), at least as important in some circumstances as unification or harmonization. But there is no point in simply defending, in generalized, abstract terms, either the promotion of legal harmonization or the protection of difference between legal cultures. Seeking similarity and appreciating difference make sense as aims only in relation to specific, differentiated categories of social relationships and purposes of regulation. It follows that comparative law can solve its general epistemological and ontological problems only by confronting the social armed with appropriate theoretical resources.

In a globalizing world, it is necessary to distinguish carefully the components of law's social environment. Identifying different bases of community life is a step towards this. It allows us to begin to conceptualize the complexity of law's tasks in regulating social relations and groups, and to give proper attention theoretically to social relations that are other or more than instrumental. This is particularly necessary today when the importance of instrumental economic relations is so strongly emphasized politically, and legal analysis seems impelled towards a similar emphasis.

I have focused here on aspects of comparative law's concerns that might bring comparatists and legal sociologists closer together in their research objectives. By elaborating a legal concept of community, legal sociology can serve comparative law. In turn, comparative law can address practical issues of regulating community life. Comparative lawyers may be better fitted to achieve success in this than other legal interpreters because they are well used to legal analysis not confined by the limits of state legal authority. They should be able to appreciate ways in which types of community are expressed in social relationships that are often located within state boundaries, but increasingly extend beyond them. So, techniques of unifying and harmonizing law that comparatists have long worked with can be used to solve transnational regulatory problems of community in these contexts.

But the slow liberation of legal analysis from its imprisonment within the boundaries of nation state jurisdiction,[5] a liberation comparatists have usually welcomed and promoted, should also lead to a radical rethinking of possibilities for legal localization. The nation state will surely remain for the foreseeable future the single focus of much legal regulation. But comparatists and legal sociologists should be able to combine to explore needs for regulatory localization *within* the state, or *irrespective* of it (in special jurisdictions not confined within states). Again, I suggest that the guiding concept in this enterprise should be that of community. Its fourfold typology is an aid towards understanding, for regulatory purposes, contemporary patterns of social relations in their fluidity and variety.

It is time to escape the limits of the familiar but now largely empty rhetoric of 'law and society' or even 'law in society', a rhetoric that obscures the sheer complexity and frequent indeterminacy of what society means today as the environment of legal regulation.

---

5 Cf. Lawson 1977: 73, noting that, for the lawyer, comparative legal study is 'like escaping from prison into the open air'.

Conclusion

Frontiers of Community

'Law seems to bespeak an absence of community, and law grows ever more prominent as the dissolution of community proceeds'. With these words the legal sociologist Donald Black (1971: 1108) expresses a widely held view. But I think this statement, setting law against community, is wrong in every important respect. The studies in this book have attempted to show why this is so. They have done this, first, by developing a view of the nature of law (and legal theory) that implies the need for sociolegal studies of community. Secondly, they have explored a distinctive, flexible, sociologically informed concept of community that is intended to be useful for the study of law.

Far from law's existence implying the absence of community, law is rooted in and expressive of types of community. Far from community dissolving as law becomes more prominent, the growing complexity and bulk of law reflects the increasing complexity, intricacy and richness of communal social relations in their various networks. To see law as opposed to community (see also, for example, Horne 2000), presumes too narrow a conception of community – one that is rooted ultimately in images of pre-modern, close-knit, relatively static communities based on kin and neighbourhood. It contrasts the warmth of this kind of *Gemeinschaft* communality (Tönnies 1955) with the cold impersonality and 'moral minimalism' that sociologists recognize in privatized contemporary lifestyles of the city and the suburb (see Baumgartner 1988). But, as earlier chapters have tried to show, a useful idea of community embraces the diverse, contrasting kinds of moral bonds and legal challenges that arise from many kinds of instrumental, traditional, affective and belief-based social relations. As law thrives, there is no 'absolute erosion of community' but a 'fragmentation and change in patterns of community' and 'a variety of conflicting, perhaps overlapping and intersecting, communities' (Norrie 2005: 96). But this complexity can be understood only by radically rethinking the idea of community and identifying its distinct types, as this book has tried to do.

The idea that law and community are necessarily opposed often presupposes not only a narrow view of community but also a narrow view of *law*, associating it almost entirely with the law of the nation state as a relatively centralized form of regulation. But a pluralist view of law, as defended in this book, does not see the nation state as the source of all law or all legal authority. Law's sources are varied. They may be found in religious communities or organizations (for example, canon law; Islamic law), localities within the nation state (local authority regulation; the law of autonomous regions; provincial or state law in federal systems), minority ethnic groups (traditional law and custom) shared or collective projects (the internal regulation of corporations; professional self-regulation; contracts), the interaction of states (international law; European Union law), etc. Once the variety of types of law, the fluidity of the idea of law itself and the range of law's sources or constituencies are recognized, the utility of linking these to various types and networks of community becomes apparent.

Community and Responsibility

A legal-theoretical concern with community cannot assume that the existence of any particular community is a good thing. But the social phenomenon of community – the existence of social relations based on mutual interpersonal trust – is valuable in itself, because social life in any stable and rewarding sense is impossible without it. To facilitate social relations of community in general is to enrich social life in its various forms. Hence, empirical studies of community may help in deciding how the social *should* be organized and regulated legally. Sociological inquiries may indicate parameters within which legal strategies are feasible (see Chapter 3, above, and Cotterrell 1999: 15–17), or conditions that give meaning to moral or legal debates. Trust, on which community depends, is also a general resource essential to social life – though its focus may differ with different types of community. So, legal scholars and social theorists surely have some interest in the general promotion of trust in social life.

But matters are more complex than this. What are the rights and wrongs of participation in community? If law is a regulation of networks of community, rather than a regulation directly of individuals, what bearing does this have on the concept of individual responsibility which is at the heart of modern Western law? Two contrasting problem situations may illustrate some of the issues.

Consider first the general problem of corporate liability: for example, the possible liability of a company for deaths and injuries caused in a train crash resulting from the company's failure to carry out its responsibility to maintain railway tracks properly. Who should be liable? Does responsibility lie inside the web of (primarily) instrumental social relations of community that make up the company, here treated in law as a corporate person? Is it a responsibility of particular individuals who took, or failed to take decisions; or who carried out or failed to carry out the track repairs? While law can make the corporate entity (seen in a law-and-community perspective as a network of social relations) liable, the attaching of legal responsibility may not seem adequate unless it directly recognizes and addresses the moral failings of individuals. Can one be allowed to hide within community to escape personal liability? If not, to whom should liability attach? What should have to be proved of an individual to show that he or she is responsible for a chain of consequences arising from the existence of a particular network of community?

Consider now a different matter: the 'banality of evil' which Hannah Arendt discussed in connection with Adolf Eichmann's participation in the Nazi Holocaust.[1] What is to be said, in terms of responsibility, of a man like Eichmann who sees himself as a mere functionary with no personal guilt as regards the morally disastrous outcome of a network of (primarily) instrumental social relations in which he participates? Arendt wrote of Eichmann's trial, which she attended:

> We heard the protestations of the defence that Eichmann was after all only a 'tiny cog' in the machinery of the Final Solution, and of the prosecution, which believed it had discovered in Eichmann the actual motor. I myself attributed no more importance to both theories than did the Jerusalem court, since the whole cog theory is legally pointless and therefore it does not matter at all what order of magnitude is assigned to the 'cog' named Eichmann. In its judgment the court naturally conceded that such a crime could be committed only by a giant bureaucracy using the resources of government. But in so far as it remains a crime – and that, of course, is the premise for a trial – all the cogs in the machinery, no matter how insignificant, are in court transformed back into perpetrators, that is to say, into human beings (Arendt 1965: 289).

Surely, it is right that individual human beings are responsible; they should not be able to hide inside a 'giant bureaucracy'. Yet the question remains of how to deal with 'the utter disproportion between the crimes Eichmann had participated in and his own consciousness of what he was doing'; between 'such enormous crimes and such a pygmy criminal' (Canovan 1974: 46). The genocidal organization, in which Eichmann took part, was, in my terms, a massive network of primarily instrumental community. Obviously, then, networks of community are not necessarily 'good'. They may be murderous and barbarous, as judged by the standards of *other* networks. Even for those involved in it, a network of community may not be optimal. Social relations of community are often unequal. Mutual interpersonal trust can exist between a general and his troops, an employer and employee, even a master and slave. People find themselves trapped in social relations on which they depend but which they might not freely choose. Others may be blind to the larger context of their acts – the overall shape and significance of networks of community in which they participate. What responsibility, in general, attaches to individuals in social relations of community?

In contemporary law and morality, responsibility usually attaches to individuals. The virtue of imposing liability on a state (such as to make reparation for mass murder done in its name) or a corporation (for example, to compensate for the injuries resulting from its maintenance failures) is that, in both cases, this expresses corporate but not collective responsibility. It creates responsibility without attaching guilt or fault to all potentially implicated individuals. But in ordinary moral understandings, it is *people*, not the abstractions of 'state' or 'corporation', that can have intentions, motives and consciences and so may harbour guilt, attract blame or be at fault.

---

1   I am indebted to Alan Norrie for drawing the significance of Arendt's work on responsibility in this context to my attention.

Social relations of community are moral relations (varying with the types of community involved) between the individuals related. Hence moral responsibility, and legal responsibility built on this, is a responsibility of individuals, but always in the context of their community memberships. Recently Alan Norrie has argued for a 'relational' concept of responsibility that captures much of what is being suggested here. Community, as such, does not *create* responsibility since community is not a moral agent but only a social relationship. Neither do individuals *inherently* possess responsibility since they acquire it only in relations with other individuals in community. So, as Norrie (2005: 109) suggests, responsibility is created dialectically, *between* individual and community.

This has complex ramifications. If individuals have responsibility only in relation to some community in which they participate, no judgment of responsibility is possible outside this community. But, as has been seen throughout this book, individuals are usually involved simultaneously in many different networks of community. Hence the judgment of their actions in the context of one such network may be very different from the judgment of the same action seen in the context of a different network of community in which they find themselves participating. Thus, the moral and legal supports of Nazism's networks of community are judged as immoral and criminal in a different context of post-war international networks of community. And, to return to our other example, the responsibility of business executives informed by the ethos of a corporation as a network of community may be judged (perhaps as *irresponsibility*) against criteria formed in wider networks of community. These wider networks link the corporation's members and officers to the larger society that is the corporation's environment of operations.

Responsibility, seen in a law-and-community perspective, is the individual's obligation to maintain mutual interpersonal trust in the form necessary for the particular social relationships of community in which that individual is involved. Betrayal of this trust is what can give rise to liability, to some kind of sanctioning of the individual within the community. Trust can be of different kinds for different types of communal bonds. Business communities no doubt need honesty, fair dealing and good faith to some degree among their members to be secure; local communities thrive on the courtesy and mutual consideration of neighbours; religious communities rely on their members' integrity, sincerity of belief and mutual identification. Families and friendship groups flourish where there is empathy, and mutual care and concern. Liability should surely normally depend (as it often does in modern law) on both actual or constructive knowledge – on an understanding of the nature of the networks of community in which one is involved, but also on what, as a reasonable member, one should be expected to know. And reasonableness is a matter to be judged in sociological perspective, because it will vary with the nature of the specific types and networks of community involved.

Clearly, many conflicting judgments of responsibility could be made, depending on what context of social relations of community is being considered. If this plurality seems bewildering, it is surely consistent with everyday experience. In practice, where no other means of reconciliation are possible, the most powerful regulation

– often the law of the state – puts an end to disagreement about where responsibility lies and what it entails (see Cover 1983: 40). State law adjudicates between the claims and perspectives of different communities, and purports to rule conclusively about liability. Like the cavalry in an old Western film, the state often arrives 'in the nick of time' (before limited conflict can turn into serious civil unrest) to restore order and end moral confusion arising from the coexistence of many forms of communal life with competing moralities, ideas of trust, allocations of responsibility, and judgments of liability.

Even now the picture is not quite complete. In a legal pluralist perspective, the 'cavalry' does not necessarily win the day. At least, the battle may not be conclusive. Questions about responsibility and the ultimate authority by which it is to be judged might still remain open. At least, they might still be subject to dispute. Or there might be 'stragglers' that the cavalry have not noticed and who have escaped to fight again – I mean networks of community that have somehow escaped the gaze of the law of the nation state and so continue their existence unregulated by it. Alternatively, they may relate to state law in ways that are consistent with their communal requirements but inconsistent with the legal outlook of state authorities. Thus, although all responsibility in the fullest sense is the responsibility of individual human beings, it is formed and judged in the context of communities, which are heterogeneous and potentially conflicting. The state attempts to impose sufficient uniformity on the attribution of responsibility and the imposition of liability, but from a legal pluralist point of view there should not be an assumption that it invariably succeeds in doing so.

National Community?

Where, in a law-and-community perspective, does state law – the law of the nation state – get authority to adjudicate between different attributions of responsibility in different networks of community? If all law is the law of communities, this should be true of nation state law. But how does this law relate to community? The answer depends on the relation of nation and community, a matter discussed briefly earlier in Chapters 4 and 9.

Nationalism, as a political doctrine, 'holds that humanity can be divided into separate, discrete units – nations – and that each nation should constitute a separate political unit – a state' (Spencer 1996: 391). The idea of nation links a distinct population to distinct political representation, or to an aspiration towards this, or perhaps to a memory of it. What identifies the population? As noted earlier, the nation is often, in Benedict Anderson's (1991) term, an *imagined community*. It is imagined in ways that portray it as one or more of the pure types of community: as instrumental community (for example, marked by collective economic performance; gross national product); community of belief or values (for example, enshrined in a constitution or bill of rights, or in the tenets of a civil religion); affective community (often symbolized in flags, emblems and national songs, or expressed in patriotic myths and ideas of national spirit); or traditional community (focused on territory, or common history, traditions or language).

None of these types of community fully encompasses the idea of nation, but the search for national identity often makes appeals to each of them in various ways. The nation is a network of social relations of community, not a type of community as such. It is a mere contingent amalgam of communal relations of many different kinds. But the national need for unity and identity will often lead to serious efforts to associate one or more of the ideal types of community, and probably all of them, with the nation as a whole. This is ultimately the work of ideology – transforming the nation mythically into a community. While each pure type of community finds integrity in its *raison d'être* (for example, common or convergent projects, shared values or beliefs, common environment or traditions, or mutual affection), the nation as a vast, complex network has no such natural integrity and unity. Any unity is constructed in a national imagination.

Thus, nation state law, in its primary aspect, is a purported, overall, coordinating regulation of this diverse, huge and sprawling national network of community. The complexity of contemporary law mirrors the complexity of this network. Insofar as nation state law achieves a kind of unity it is through the pursuit of reason and principle (*ratio*) on the one hand, and reliance on political authority (*voluntas*) and coercive force on the other (Cotterrell 1995: 317–25).

One way to understand *ratio* in a law-and-community perspective is to see it as the result of (inevitably unsuccessful) efforts to make the law of the nation state express the idea of the nation as a community. For example, the rationalization of law addressing social relations of instrumental community (such as contract, corporate or commercial law) implies a *national community* of instrumental relations to be unified, integrated and harmonized. By contrast, the effort to trace broad values (for example, human rights) in law or declare fundamental liberties or duties in legal form implies a *national community* of values, or aspires to help build one. The rationalization of other law implies the idea of the nation as a shared environment – this is law concerned with safety, security, health, risk, peaceful coexistence in general, the enjoyment of national heritage, environment protection and natural resources. The image on the legal horizon here is (in law-and-community terms) that of national traditional community, of coexistence in an inherited shared environment. Perhaps some similar legal rationalization relates to affective community. The image here might be of law organized to serve a national community of mutual support and collective care, perhaps exemplified in a welfare state.

What accounts for the special coercive power of state law and its authority (*voluntas*) element, which can put an end to disputes about *ratio*, forcing the acceptance of a decision that ends legal disagreements? We have seen that communal relations are often unequal social relations; some participants have more power than others. In the complex network of community that is the nation, elites will inevitably emerge from the social relations of community that make up this network. The existence of structures of power in communities may be enough to explain how power becomes concentrated in the nation state and eventually available to ensure state law's coercive force. The interest of elites in dominating and controlling the social may be enough to explain why the state initially intervenes in the regulation of communal relations. And, eventually, formal democratic structures surely play a key role in creating legitimacy; transforming social power into authority to clothe legal force. It would take us too far beyond the legal concerns of this book to explore this matter further. But it might be very important to emphasize the creation or development of the major Western nation states through conquest, territorial acquisition, colonialism and the expropriation or subjugation of established populations – in other words, in situations that have little to do with mutual interpersonal trust and community, and much to do with war and terror. The legacy of the vast concentrations of power – the state's monopoly of force – achieved or reinforced by such means surely remains in the structures of military and police power that support the at least formal dominance of the law of the contemporary state.

Global Community?

What authority can law claim as it expresses the regulatory requirements of networks of community that extend beyond the nation state, networks that are no longer the responsibility of particular national legal systems? This question was left open at the end of Chapter 1 although its urgency was noted there. A provisional view might be that the criteria of legal authority here are much the same as for the authority of nation state law. First, since these varied and numerous transnational networks of community have their particular regulatory needs and aspirations they inspire new legal forms to meet these needs. Law emerges to express social relations of transnational community. Second, the disordered mass of regulation, which reflects the vast, continually evolving constellation of transnational networks of community, is subjected to efforts at rationalization, efforts to develop the *ratio* of various kinds of transnational law on a broader scale. The rhetoric of, for example, international human rights, a new *lex mercatoria*, international criminal justice, European constitutionalism and citizenship, a European common law, and a worldwide international legal order in general, comes into play. To call it rhetoric is not to demean or belittle it, but only to note that juristic portrayals of these various legal regimes often go beyond what experience of them in practice will fully justify. Legal ideology – the creation of absolute legal world views that actually reflect only partial and limited practical legal experience – thrives in this climate. Third, behind everything stands military and economic power and the threat or use of international violence and war. Ultimately, while the *ratio* of transnational regulation may be developed out of the collective experience of transnational community and the desire for a coherent legal world view based on this, the guarantee of transnational legal authority – the *voluntas* that ultimately puts an end to legal argument – depends on power-politics, the unequal military and economic relations between nation states.

If the *voluntas* of transnational law is ultimately of this nature, this shows how fragile any emerging structures of an integrated transnational legal order are.

While there is now much transnational regulation in many fields, its unification or organization into a stable transnational legal order depends on the balance of international power. But such a balance is by its nature unstable and ever-changing. The relative power of various nation states will not stay constant. This era's superpower will cede its position to another or to others. The centre of gravity of world economic and military power will shift. How can some stability be achieved in the vitally important emerging structures of transnational regulation? How can there be some equivalent to the slowly consolidated power of successful states over their own territory, which gives stability to their national law?

If the only reliable legitimation of nation state legal authority today is, as many argue, representative democracy, there seems little prospect of achieving legitimacy (that is, unqualified acceptance as authoritative) for international or transnational legal systems that entirely lack this foundation. Instead, the governments of some nations ultimately control the *voluntas* element of transnational law and so impose their will on the citizens of others without any democratic mandate to do so. Often the moral distance between transnational law-makers and regulated populations is very great, although concepts such as 'subsidiarity', 'regionalism' and 'delegation of authority' may help. Yet, arguably, the most stable contemporary nation states have achieved their enviable situation not just by appeals to democracy, but by a degree of success in presenting themselves as national communities of belief or values focused on individualism in Emile Durkheim's (1975a) particular sense – that is, on the idea that the autonomy and dignity of every individual are inherently valuable and worthy of absolute legal protection. As Durkheim implied, such a value system, which emphasizes fundamental human equality in conditions of ever-increasing social diversity and complexity, may be the only form of community of values that is relevant to the overall unification and integration of modern nation states (Cotterrell 1999: 195–6, 201–3).

Does this value system of moral individualism have any relevance for transnational networks of community and for a potential transnational legal order to integrate them? I suspect it does, but we quickly run into familiar cultural relativism issues (see, for example, Steiner and Alston 2000: 366–402) when it becomes associated, as it inevitably must be, with international human rights. Individualism, for Durkheim, has nothing in common with egoism or selfishness because it demands, above all, respect for the dignity and autonomy of *others* (Cotterrell 1999: 112–15). But Durkheim's sociology strongly suggests that moral individualism may not be a *universally* appropriate value system, at least in the way Western traditions understand it. Its adoption is sociologically appropriate in complex, extremely diversified societies, with a highly developed division of labour (that is, a high degree of specialization of occupations and social or economic functions). In such societies it facilitates rapid, extensive, diverse and often short-term social and economic interactions by ensuring that strangers (and social groups that are strangers to each other) can rely on being treated respectfully in their mutual dealings. So, this value system encourages (indeed, in a Durkheimian view, makes possible) the high degree of ongoing social interaction on which complex contemporary societies depend. But the nature of individual autonomy and dignity and who is to define these remain important questions.

I think that Durkheimian individualism is the only possible realistic basis for viewing large, complex and diverse contemporary nations as – in one aspect – communities of belief or values. But this moral individualism may be only partly accepted in popular opinion and is sometimes significantly undermined by legal and political developments in nations that trumpet it. Thus, it has all the characteristics of ideology when proclaimed as the nation's unifying value system. Nevertheless, with all its limitations and practical contradictions it remains significant. Equally, it may be the only basis on which a global community of values could be envisaged. A comparable idea of global *traditional* community would be one that sees the world as a single shared environment of coexistence. And global *instrumental* community as an aspiration would emphasize, for example, worldwide economic and technological cooperation and mutual benefit.

Yet, to aspire to achieve a secure, pervasive legal unity of transnational networks of community is, at present, entirely utopian. It involves nothing less than the end of wars and the creation of a transnational rule of law that serves all the peoples of the world. Only when the most powerful nation states see the merit of this aspiration (and the huge long-term risks of belittling it through their actions) will there be the genuine possibility of moving a little way towards its realization.

Bibliography

Abel, R.L. (1978), 'Comparative Law and Social Theory', **26** *American Journal of Comparative Law* 219–26.

Abel, R.L. (1982a), 'The Contradictions of Informal Justice', in R.L. Abel (ed.) *The Politics of Informal Justice* vol. 1 pp. 267–320 (New York: Academic Press).

Abel, R.L. (1982b), 'Law as Lag: Inertia as a Social Theory of Law', **80** *Michigan Law Review* 785–809.

Abrams, P. (1985), 'The Uses of British Sociology 1831–1981', in M. Bulmer (ed.) *Essays on the History of British Sociological Research* pp. 181–205 (Cambridge: Cambridge University Press).

Ajani, G. (1995), 'By Chance and Prestige: Legal Transplants in Russia and Eastern Europe', **43** *American Journal of Comparative Law* 93–117.

Alford, W.P. (1986), 'On the Limits of "Grand Theory" in Comparative Law', **61** *Washington Law Review* 945–56.

Amin, S.H. (1985), *Islamic Law in the Contemporary World* (Glasgow: Royston).

Anderson, B. (1991), *Imagined Communities: Reflections on the Origin and Spread of Nationalism* revised edn (London: Verso).

Anderson, P. (1994), *The Invention of the Region 1945-1990*, EUI Working Paper EUF 94/2 (Florence: European University Institute).

Arendt, H. (1965), *Eichmann in Jerusalem: A Report on the Banality of Evil*, revised edn (London: Penguin reprint, 1994).

Arnaud, A.-J. (1995), 'Legal Pluralism and the Building of Europe', in H. Petersen and H. Zahle (eds) *Legal Polycentricity: Consequences of Pluralism in Law* pp. 149–69 (Aldershot: Dartmouth).

Arnold, T.W. (1935), *The Symbols of Government* (New York: Harcourt, Brace & World edn, 1962).

Arthurs, H.W. (1985), *'Without the Law': Administrative Justice and Legal Pluralism in Nineteenth-Century England* (Toronto: University of Toronto Press).

Aubert, V. (1963), 'The Structure of Legal Thinking', in J. Andenaes et al., *Legal Essays: A Tribute to Frede Castberg* pp. 41–63 (Oslo: Universitetsforlaget).

Austin, J. (1832), *The Province of Jurisprudence Determined* (Cambridge: Cambridge University Press edn, 1995).

Axford, B. (1995), *The Global System: Economics, Politics and Culture* (Cambridge: Polity).

Bainham, A. (1995), 'Family Law in a Pluralistic Society', **22** *Journal of Law and Society* 234–47.

Baldwin, R. (1995), *Rules and Government* (Oxford: Clarendon Press).

Balkin, J.M. (1996), 'Interdisciplinarity as Colonization', **53** *Washington and Lee Law Review* 949–70.

Barber, B. (1983), *The Logic and Limits of Trust* (New Brunswick: Rutgers University Press).

Barrett, S. and Fudge, C. (eds) (1981), *Policy and Action: Essays on the Implementation of Public Policy* (London: Methuen).

Baudrillard, J. (1983), *In the Shadow of the Silent Majorities Or, The End of the Social and Other Essays*, transl. by P. Foss, J. Johnston and P. Patton (New York: Semiotext(e)).

Bauman, Z. (1987), *Legislators and Interpreters: On Modernity, Post-modernity and Intellectuals* (Cambridge: Polity).

Bauman, Z. (1989), *Modernity and the Holocaust* (Cambridge: Polity).

Bauman, Z. (1992), *Intimations of Postmodernity* (London: Routledge).

Bauman, Z. (1993), *Postmodern Ethics* (Oxford: Blackwell).

Baumgartner, M.P. (1988), *The Moral Order of a Suburb* (New York: Oxford University Press).

Beck, U. (1992), *Risk Society: Towards a New Modernity* (London: Sage).

Beck, U. (2000), *What is Globalization?*, transl. by P. Camiller (Cambridge: Polity).

Beck, U. and Beck-Gernsheim, E. (2002), *Individualization: Institutionalized Individualism and its Social and Political Consequences*, transl. by P. Camiller (London: Sage).

Beck, U., Giddens, A. and Lash, S. (1994), *Reflexive Modernization: Politics, Tradition and Aesthetics in the Modern Social Order* (Stanford CA: Stanford University Press).

Belgesay, M.R. (1957), 'Social, Economic and Technical Difficulties Experienced as a Result of the Reception of Foreign Law', **9** *International Social Science Bulletin* 49–51.

Belley, J.-G. (1986), 'Georges Gurvitch et les professionels de la pensée juridique', **4** *Droit et Société* 353–71.

Belley, J.-G. (1988), 'Deux journées dans la vie du droit: Georges Gurvitch et Ian R. Macneil', **3** *Canadian Journal of Law and Society* 27–52.

Bentham, J. (1970), *Of Laws in General* (London: University of London Athlone Press).

Black, D.J. (1971), 'The Social Organisation of Arrest', **23** *Stanford Law Review* 1087–111.

Black, D.J. (1976), *The Behavior of Law* (New York: Academic Press).

Black, D.J. (1989), *Sociological Justice* (New York: Oxford University Press).

Blankenberg, E. (1997), 'Civil Litigation Rates as Indicators for Legal Cultures', in D. Nelken (ed.) *Comparing Legal Cultures* pp. 41–68 (Aldershot: Dartmouth).

Bohannon, P. (1967), 'The Differing Realms of the Law', in P. Bohannan (ed.) *Law and Warfare: Studies in the Anthropology of Conflict* pp. 43–56 (Garden City NY: Natural History Press).

Bonell, M.J. (1995), 'The UNIDROIT Principles of International Commercial Contracts', in R. Cotterrell (ed.) *Process and Substance: Butterworth Lectures in Comparative Law 1994* pp. 45–107 (London: Butterworths).

Boyum, K.O. and Mather, L. (eds) (1983), *Empirical Theories About Courts* (New York: Longman).

Bradney, A. (1993), *Religions, Rights and Laws* (Leicester: Leicester University Press).

Brigham, J. (1996), *The Constitution of Interests: Beyond the Politics of Rights* (New York: New York University Press).

Broekman, J.M. (1989), 'Revolution and Moral Commitment to a Legal System', in N. MacCormick and Z. Bankowski (eds) *Enlightenment, Rights and Revolution: Essays in Legal and Social Philosophy* pp. 315–36 (Aberdeen: Aberdeen University Press).

Cain, M. and Hunt, A. (eds) (1979), *Marx and Engels on Law* (New York: Academic Press).

Campbell, C. M. (1974), 'Legal Thought and Juristic Values', 1 *British Journal of Law and Society* 13–30.

Canovan, M. (1974), *The Political Thought of Hannah Arendt* (London: Methuen).

Carbonnier, J. (1969), 'L'apport du droit comparé à la sociologie juridique' in *Livre du centenaire de la Société de Législation Comparé* pp. 75–87 (Paris: Librairie Générale de Droit et de Jurisprudence).

Carbonnier, J. (1994), *Sociologie juridique*, 2nd edn (Paris: Presses Universitaires de France).

Carter, J. (1907), *Law: Its Origin, Growth and Function* (New York: Da Capo reprint, 1974).

Cassirer, E. (1944), *An Essay on Man: An Introduction to a Philosophy of Human Culture* (New Haven CT: Yale University Press reprint, 1992).

Cohen, A.P. (1985), *The Symbolic Construction of Community* (London: Routledge).

Colvin, E. (1978), 'The Sociology of Secondary Rules', 28 *University of Toronto Law Journal* 195–214.

Cooper, D. (1996), 'Talmudic Territory? Space, Law and Modernist Discourse', 23 *Journal of Law and Society* 529–48.

Cooper, D. (1998), *Governing Out of Order: Space, Law and the Politics of Belonging* (London: Rivers Oram Press).

Cornell, D. (1992), *The Philosophy of the Limit* (New York: Routledge).

Cotterrell, R. (1992), 'Some Sociological Aspects of the Controversy Around the Legal Validity of Private Purpose Trusts', in S. Goldstein (ed.) *Equity and Contemporary Legal Developments* pp. 302–34 (Jerusalem: Hebrew University).

Cotterrell, R. (1993), 'Trusting in Law: Legal and Moral Concepts of Trust', 46 *Current Legal Problems* 75–95.

Cotterrell, R. (1995), *Law's Community: Legal Theory in Sociological Perspective* (Oxford: Clarendon Press).

Cotterrell, R. (1999), *Emile Durkheim: Law in a Moral Domain* (Stanford CA: Stanford University Press / Edinburgh: Edinburgh University Press).

Cotterrell, R. (2003), *The Politics of Jurisprudence: A Critical Introduction to Legal Philosophy*, 2nd edn (London: LexisNexis / Oxford University Press).

Cotterrell, R. (2005), 'Durkheim's Loyal Jurist? The Sociolegal Theory of Paul Huvelin', **18** *Ratio Juris* 504–18.

Cover, R. (1983), 'The Supreme Court 1982, Foreword: *Nomos* and Narrative', **97** *Harvard Law Review* 4–68.

Curran, V.G. (1998), 'Cultural Immersion, Difference and Categories in US Comparative Law', **46** *American Journal of Comparative Law* 43–92.

Damaska, M.R. (1986), *The Faces of Justice and State Authority: A Comparative Approach to the Legal Process* (New Haven CT: Yale University Press).

David, R. and Brierley, J.E.C. (1985), *Major Legal Systems in the World Today* 3rd edn (London: Stevens).

Davies, N. (1996), *Europe: A History* (London: Pimlico reprint, 1997).

Dezalay, Y. and Garth, B.G. (1996), *Dealing in Virtue: International Commercial Arbitration and the Construction of a Transnational Legal Order* (Chicago IL: University of Chicago Press).

Donzelot, J. (1980), *The Policing of Families: Welfare Versus the State*, transl. by R. Hurley (London: Hutchinson).

Douzinas, C. (1996), 'Justice and Human Rights in Postmodernity', in C. Gearty and A. Tomkins (eds) *Understanding Human Rights* pp. 115–37 (London: Pinter).

Douzinas, C. and Warrington, R. (1991), *Postmodern Jurisprudence: The Law of Texts in the Texts of Law* (London: Routledge).

Durkheim, E. (1961), *Moral Education*, transl. by E.K. Wilson and H. Schnurer (New York: Free Press).

Durkheim, E. (1975a), 'Individualism and the Intellectuals', in W.S.F. Pickering (ed.) *Durkheim on Religion: A Selection of Readings with Bibliographies* pp. 59–73 (London: Routledge & Kegan Paul).

Durkheim, E. (1975b), *Textes 1: Eléments d'une théorie sociale* (Paris: Les Editions de Minuit).

Durkheim, E. (1975c), *Textes 2: Religion, morale, anomie* (Paris: Les Editions de Minuit).

Durkheim, E. (1975d), *Textes 3: Fonctions sociales et institutions* (Paris: Les Editions de Minuit).

Durkheim, E. (1982), *The Rules of Sociological Method and Selected Texts on Sociology and Its Method*, transl. by W.D. Halls (London: Macmillan).

Durkheim, E. (1984), *The Division of Labour in Society*, transl. by W.D. Halls (London: Macmillan).

Dworkin, R. (1977), *Taking Rights Seriously*, revised edn (London: Duckworth).

Dworkin, R. (1985), *A Matter of Principle* (Cambridge MA: Harvard University Press).

Dworkin, R. (1986), *Law's Empire* (Oxford: Hart reprint, 1998).

Edwards, S.S.M. (1996), *Sex and Gender in the Legal Process* (London: Blackstone).

Ehrlich, E. (1936), *Fundamental Principles of the Sociology of Law*, transl. by W.L. Moll (New Brunswick: Transaction reprint, 2002).

Ellen, R., Gellner, E., Kubicka, G. and Mucha, J. (eds) (1988), *Malinowski Between Two Worlds: The Polish Roots of an Anthropological Tradition* (Cambridge: Cambridge University Press).

Ericson, R. and Haggerty, K. (1997), *Policing the Risk Society* (Toronto: University of Toronto Press).

Ewald, F. (1990), 'Norms, Discipline, and the Law', **30** *Representations* 138–61.

Ewald, W. (1995a), 'Comparative Jurisprudence (I): What Was It Like To Try a Rat?', **143** *University of Pennsylvania Law Review* 1889–2149.

Ewald, W. (1995b), 'Comparative Jurisprudence (II): The Logic of Legal Transplants', **43** *American Journal of Comparative Law* 489–510.

Ewick, P. and Silbey, S.S. (1998), *The Common Place of Law: Stories from Everyday Life* (Chicago IL: University of Chicago Press).

Figgis, J.N. (1914), *Churches in the Modern State* 2nd edn (Bristol: Thoemmes Press reprint, 1997).

Findikoglu, L.F. (1957), 'A Turkish Sociologist's View', **9** *International Social Science Bulletin* 13–20.

Finn, P.D. (1989), 'The Fiduciary Principle', in T.G. Youdan (ed.) *Equity, Fiduciaries and Trusts* pp. 1–56 (Toronto: Carswell).

Finnis, J. (1980), *Natural Law and Natural Rights* (Oxford: Clarendon Press).

Firth, R. (1988), 'Malinowski in the History of Social Anthropology', in R. Ellen, E. Gellner, G. Kubicka and J. Mucha (eds) *Malinowski Between Two Worlds: The Polish Roots of an Anthropological Tradition* pp. 12–42 (Cambridge: Cambridge University Press).

Fitzpatrick, P. (1984), 'Law and Societies', **22** *Osgoode Hall Law Journal* 115–38.

Fitzpatrick, P. (1992), *The Mythology of Modern Law* (London: Routledge).

Fitzpatrick, P. (1995), 'Being Social in Socio-Legal Studies', **22** *Journal of Law and Society* 105–12.

Fitzpatrick, P. (2001), *Modernism and the Grounds of Law* (Cambridge: Cambridge University Press).

Foucault, M. (1977), *Discipline and Punish: The Birth of the Prison*, transl. by A. Sheridan (London: Allen Lane).

Foucault, M. (1979), *The History of Sexuality, Volume 1: An Introduction*, transl. by R. Hurley (London: Allen Lane).

Foucault, M. (1991), 'Governmentality', in G. Burchell, C. Gordon and P. Miller (eds) *The Foucault Effect: Studies in Governmentality with Two Lectures by and an Interview with Michel Foucault* pp. 87–104 (London: Harvester Wheatsheaf).

Franklin, J. (1998), *The Politics of Risk Society* (Cambridge: Polity).

Freeman, M.D.A. (1995), 'The Morality of Cultural Pluralism', **3** *International Journal of Children's Rights* 1–17.

Friedman, L.M. (1975), *The Legal System: A Social Science Perspective* (New York: Russell Sage Foundation).

Friedman, L.M. (1977), *Law and Society: An Introduction* (Englewood Cliffs NJ: Prentice-Hall).

Friedman, L.M. (1979), 'Book Review', **6** *British Journal of Law and Society* 127–9.

Friedman, L.M. (1985a), *Total Justice* (Boston: Beacon Press).

Friedman, L.M. (1985b), *A History of American Law* 2nd edn (New York: Simon and Schuster).

Friedman, L.M. (1986), 'Legal Culture and the Welfare State', in G. Teubner (ed.) *Dilemmas of Law in the Welfare State* pp. 13–27 (Berlin: de Gruyter).

Friedman, L.M. (1990), *The Republic of Choice: Law, Authority, and Culture* (Cambridge MA: Harvard University Press).

Friedman, L.M. (1994), 'Is There a Modern Legal Culture?', **7** *Ratio Juris* 117–31.

Friedman, L.M. (1997), 'The Concept of Legal Culture: A Reply', in D. Nelken (ed.) *Comparing Legal Cultures* pp. 33–9 (Aldershot: Dartmouth).

Friedmann, W. (1967), *Legal Theory*, 5th edn (New York: Columbia University Press).

Frug, M.J. (1992), *Postmodern Legal Feminism* (New York: Routledge).

Fuller, L.L. (1946), 'Reason and Fiat in Case Law', **59** *Harvard Law Review* 376–95.

Fuller, L.L. (1969), 'Human Interaction and the Law', reprinted in L.L. Fuller, *The Principles of Social Order: Selected Essays* revised edn pp. 231–66 (Oxford: Hart, 2001).

Galanter, M. (1981), 'Justice in Many Rooms: Courts, Private Ordering and Indigenous Law', **19** *Journal of Legal Pluralism and Unofficial Law* 1–47.

Garapon, A. (1995), 'French Legal Culture and the Shock of "Globalization"', **4** *Social and Legal Studies* 493–506.

Geertz, C. (1973), *The Interpretation of Cultures: Selected Essays* (New York: Basic Books).

Geertz, C. (1983), *Local Knowledge: Further Essays in Interpretive Anthropology* (New York: Basic Books).

Gerth, H.H. and Mills, C.W. (eds) (1948), *From Max Weber: Essays in Sociology* (London: Routledge & Kegan Paul).

Gierke, O. (1900), *Political Theories of the Middle Age*, transl. by F.W. Maitland (Cambridge: Cambridge University Press).

Glenn, H.P. (2003), 'The Nationalist Heritage', in P. Legrand and R. Munday (eds) *Comparative Law: Traditions and Transitions* pp. 76–99 (Cambridge: Cambridge University Press).

Glenn, H.P. (2004), *Legal Traditions of the World: Sustainable Diversity in Law*, 2nd edn (Oxford: Oxford University Press).

Golding, M.P. (2002), 'The Cultural Defense', **4** *Ratio Juris* 146–58.

Goldstein, S. (1995), 'On Comparing and Unifying Civil Procedural Systems', in R. Cotterrell (ed.) *Process and Substance: Butterworth Lectures in Comparative Law 1994* pp. 1–43 (London: Butterworths).

Goodrich, P. (1990), *Languages of Law: From Logics of Memory to Nomadic Masks* (London: Weidenfeld & Nicolson).

Graveson, R.H. (1977), *One Law: On Jurisprudence and the Unification of Law: Selected Essays Volume II* (Amsterdam: North-Holland).

Greenhouse, C.J. (1986), *Praying for Justice: Faith, Order and Community in an American Town* (Ithaca NY: Cornell University Press).

Griffith, J.A.G. (1993), *Judicial Politics Since 1920: A Chronicle* (Oxford: Blackwell).

Griffiths, J. (1986), 'What is Legal Pluralism?', **24** *Journal of Legal Pluralism and Unofficial Law* 1–55.

Gurvitch, G. (1935), *L'expérience juridique et la philosophie pluraliste du droit* (Paris: Pedone).

Gurvitch, G. (1947), *Sociology of Law* (London: Routledge & Kegan Paul).

Gutteridge, H. (1949), *Comparative Law* 2nd edn (London: Wildy reprint, 1971).

Habermas, J. (1975), *Legitimation Crisis*, transl. by T. McCarthy (Boston MA: Beacon Press).

Habermas, J. (1987), *The Philosophical Discourse of Modernity: Twelve Lectures*, transl. by F.G. Lawrence (Cambridge: Polity).

Habermas, J. (1996), *Between Facts and Norms: Contributions to a Discourse Theory of Law and Democracy*, transl. by W. Rehg (Cambridge: Polity).

Hall, J. (1963), *Comparative Law and Social Theory* (Baton Rouge LA: Louisiana State University Press).

Hallis, F. (1930), *Corporate Personality* (Aalen: Scientia Verlag reprint, 1978).

Hamilton, P. (1985), 'Editor's Foreword', in A.P. Cohen *The Symbolic Construction of Community* pp. 7–9 (London: Routledge).

Harding, A. and Örücü, E. (eds) (2002), *Comparative Law in the 21st Century* (The Hague: Kluwer).

Harrington, C.B. (1985), *Shadow Justice: The Ideology and Institutionalization of Alternatives to Courts* (Westport CT: Greenwood).

Harris, P. (1997), *Black Rage Confronts the Law* (New York: New York University Press).

Hart, H.L.A. (1968), 'Kelsen's Doctrine of the Unity of Law', reprinted in H.L.A. Hart *Essays in Jurisprudence and Philosophy* pp. 309–42 (Oxford: Clarendon Press, 1983).

Hart, H.L.A. (1994), *The Concept of Law* 2nd edn (Oxford: Clarendon Press).

Hartney, M. (1995), 'Some Confusions Concerning Collective Rights', in W. Kymlicka (ed.) *The Rights of Minority Cultures* pp. 202–27 (Oxford: Oxford University Press).

Hazard, J.N. (1964), 'Book review', **39** *Indiana Law Journal* 411–16.

Henry, S. (1983), *Private Justice: Towards Integrated Theorising in the Sociology of Law* (London: Routledge & Kegan Paul).

Hirst, P.Q. (ed.) (1989), *The Pluralist Theory of the State: Selected Writings of G.D.H. Cole, J.N. Figgis and H.J. Laski* (London: Routledge).

Hobbes, T. (1971), *A Dialogue Between a Philosopher and a Student of the Common Laws of England* J. Cropsey edn (Chicago IL: University of Chicago Press).

Hogg, M.A. and Abrams, D. (1988), *Social Identifications: A Social Psychology of Intergroup Relations and Group Processes* (London: Routledge).

Honoré, T. (1987), *Making Law Bind: Essays Legal and Philosophical* (Oxford: Clarendon Press).

Horne, C. (2000), 'Community and the State: The Relationship between Normative and Legal Controls', **16** *European Sociological Review* 225–43.

Hunt, A. (1987), 'The Critique of Law: What is "Critical" about Critical Legal Theory', in P. Fitzpatrick and A. Hunt (eds) *Critical Legal Studies* pp. 5–19 (Oxford: Blackwell).

Hunt, A. (1993), *Explorations in Law and Society: Toward a Constitutive Theory of Law* (New York: Routledge).

Hunt, A. (1996), 'Law, Community, and Everyday Life: Yngvesson's Virtuous Citizens and Disruptive Subjects', **21** *Law and Social Inquiry* 173–84.

Hyde, A. (1983), 'The Concept of Legitimation in the Sociology of Law', [1983] *Wisconsin Law Review* 379–426.

Jamin, C. (2000), 'Le vieux rêve de Saleilles et Lambert revisité: A propos du centenaire du Congrès internationale de droit comparé de Paris', **52** *Revue internationale de droit comparé* 733–51.

Jessop, B. (1980), 'On Recent Marxist Theories of Law, the State, and Juridico-Political Ideology', **8** *International Journal of the Sociology of Law* 339–68.

Kahn-Freund, O. (1974), 'On Uses and Misuses of Comparative Law', **37** *Modern Law Review* 1–27.

Kantorowicz, E.H. (1957), *The King's Two Bodies: A Study in Medieval Political Theology* (Princeton NJ: Princeton University Press).

Keedy, E.R. (1951), 'A Remarkable Murder Trial: Rex v. Sinnisiak', **100** *University of Pennsylvania Law Review* 48–67.

Kelley, D.R. (1990), *The Human Measure: Social Thought in the Western Legal Tradition* (Cambridge MA: Harvard University Press).

Kelsen, H. (1941), 'The Pure Theory of Law and Analytical Jurisprudence', reprinted in H. Kelsen, *What is Justice? Justice, Law and Politics in the Mirror of Science* pp. 266–87 (Berkeley CA: University of California Press, 1957).

Kelsen, H. (1945), *General Theory of Law and State*, transl. by A. Wedberg (New York: Russell & Russell edn, 1961).

Kelsen, H. (1991), *General Theory of Norms*, transl. by M. Hartney (Oxford: Clarendon Press).

Kelsen, H. (1992), *Introduction to the Problems of Legal Theory*, transl. by B.L. Paulson and S.L. Paulson (Oxford: Clarendon Press).

Kettle, M. (2000), 'Dead Certainties', *The Guardian* (London), 29 May, p. 18.

King, M. (1997), 'Comparing Legal Cultures in the Quest for Law's Identity', in D. Nelken (ed.) *Comparing Legal Cultures* pp. 119–34 (Aldershot: Dartmouth).

King, M. and Piper, C. (1995), *How the Law Thinks About Children* 2nd edn (Aldershot: Gower).

Kronman, A.T. (1983), *Max Weber* (London: Edward Arnold).

Kubali, H.N. (1957), 'Modernization and Secularization as Determining Factors in Reception in Turkey', **9** *International Social Science Bulletin* 65–9.

Kymlicka, W. (1989), *Liberalism, Community and Culture* (Oxford: Clarendon Press).

Kymlicka, W. (1995), *Multicultural Citizenship: A Liberal Theory of Minority Rights* (Oxford: Clarendon Press).

Kymlicka, W. (ed.) (1995), *The Rights of Minority Cultures* (Oxford: Oxford University Press).

Lacey, N. (1998), *Unspeakable Subjects: Feminist Essays in Legal and Social Theory* (Oxford: Hart).

Lambert, E. (1903), *La fonction du droit civil comparé. I. Les conceptions étroites ou unilatérales* (Paris: Giard & Brière).

Lambert, E. (1926), 'Préface', in E. Lévy, *La vision socialiste du droit* pp. v–xvi (Paris: Giard).

Lambert, E. (1931), 'Comparative Law', **4** *Encyclopedia of the Social Sciences* 126–9 (New York: Macmillan).

Laski, H.J. (1921), 'The Problem of Administrative Areas', reprinted in P.Q. Hirst (ed.) *The Pluralist Theory of the State: Selected Writings of G.D.H. Cole, J.N. Figgis and H.J. Laski* pp. 131–63 (London: Routledge, 1989).

Lasswell, H.D. and McDougal, M.S. (1943), 'Legal Education and Public Policy: Professional Training in the Public Interest', **52** *Yale Law Journal* 203–95.

Lawson, F.H. (1977), *The Comparison: Selected Essays, Volume II* (Amsterdam: North-Holland).

Legrand, P. (1996), 'European Legal Systems are not Converging', **45** *International and Comparative Law Quarterly* 52–81.

Legrand, P. (1997), 'Against a European Civil Code', **60** *Modern Law Review* 44–63.

Legrand, P. (1999), *Fragments on Law-as-Culture* (Deventer: W. E. J. Tjeenk Willink).

Legrand, P. (2001), 'What "Legal Transplants"?', in D. Nelken and J. Feest (eds) *Adapting Legal Cultures* pp. 55–70 (Oxford: Hart).

Legrand, P. and Munday, R. (eds) (2003), *Comparative Law: Traditions and Transitions* (Cambridge: Cambridge University Press).

Lepaulle, P. (1922), 'The Function of Comparative Law, with a Critique of Sociological Jurisprudence', **35** *Harvard Law Review* 838–58.

Levy, E. (1950), 'The Reception of Highly Developed Legal Systems by Peoples of Different Cultures', **25** *Washington Law Review* 233–45.

Lewis, P. (1988), 'Notes for a Socio-Legal Jurisprudence', in A. Febbrajo, B.-M. Blegvad and D. Kalogeropoulos (eds) *European Yearbook in the Sociology of Law 1988* pp. 209–26 (Milano: Giuffrè).

Lipstein, K. (1957), 'Conclusions', **9** *International Social Science Bulletin* 70–81.

Llewellyn, K.N. (1940), 'The Normative, the Legal, and the Law-Jobs: The Problem of Juristic Method', **49** *Yale Law Journal* 1355–400.

López, I.F.H. (1996), *White by Law: The Legal Construction of Race* (New York: New York University Press).

Luhmann, N. (1979), 'Trust: A Mechanism for the Reduction of Social Complexity', in N. Luhmann, *Trust and Power: Two Works*, transl. by H. Davis, J. Raffan and K. Rooney pp. 4–103 (Chichester: John Wiley).

Luhmann, N. (1981), 'Communication about Law in Action Systems', in K. Knorr-Cetina and A. Cicourel (eds) *Advances in Social Theory and Methodology* pp. 234–56 (London: Routledge & Kegan Paul).

Luhmann, N. (1988), 'Closure and Openness: On Reality in the World of Law', in G. Teubner (ed.) *Autopoietic Law: A New Approach to Law and Society* pp. 335–48 (Berlin: de Gruyter).

Luhmann, N. (1989), *Ecological Communication*, transl. by J. Bednarz (Cambridge: Polity).

Luhmann, N. (1992a), 'Operational Closure and Structural Coupling: The Differentiation of the Legal System', **13** *Cardozo Law Review* 1419–41.

Luhmann, N. (1992b), 'The Coding of the Legal System', in G. Teubner and A. Febbrajo (eds) *State, Law and Economy as Autopoietic Systems: Regulation and Autonomy in a New Perspective* pp. 145–85 (Milano: Giuffrè).

Luhmann, N. (1995), *Social Systems*, transl. by J. Bednarz with D. Baecker (Stanford CA: Stanford University Press).

Luhmann, N. (1997), 'Globalisation ou société du monde: comment concevoir la société moderne?', in D. Kalogeropoulos (ed.) *Regards sur la complexité sociale et l'ordre légal à la fin du XXe siècle* pp. 7–31 (Brussels: Bruylant).

Lyotard, J.-F. (1984), *The Postmodern Condition: A Report on Knowledge*, transl. by G. Bennington and B. Massumi (Manchester: Manchester University Press).

MacCormick, D.N. (1981), *H.L.A. Hart* (London: Edward Arnold).

MacCormick, D.N. (1993), 'Beyond the Sovereign State', **56** *Modern Law Review* 1–18.

McEwan, C.A. and Maiman, R.J. (1986), 'In Search of Legitimacy: Toward an Empirical Analysis', **8** *Law and Policy* 257–73.

MacKinnon, C.A. (1989), *Toward a Feminist Theory of the State* (Cambridge MA: Harvard University Press).

McLennan, G. (1995), *Pluralism* (Buckingham: Open University Press).

Malinowski, B. (1926), *Crime and Custom in Savage Society* (London: Routledge & Kegan Paul).

Malinowski, B. (1944), *A Scientific Theory of Culture and Other Essays* (Chapel Hill NC: University of North Carolina Press).

Markesinis, B. (1990), 'Comparative Law – A Subject in Search of an Audience', **53** *Modern Law Review* 1–21.

Massell, G.J. (1968), 'Law as an Instrument of Revolutionary Change in a Traditional Milieu: The Case of Soviet Central Asia', **2** *Law and Society Review* 179–228.

Mathiesen, T. (1980), *Law, Society and Political Action: Towards a Strategy under Late Capitalism* (London: Academic Press).

Mauss, M. (1990), *The Gift: The Form and Reason for Exchange in Archaic Societies*, transl. by W.D. Halls (London: Routledge).

Menski, W.F. (2006), *Comparative Law in a Global Context: The Legal Systems of Asia and Africa*, 2nd edn (Cambridge: Cambridge University Press).

Merry, S.E. (1988), 'Legal Pluralism', **22** *Law and Society Review* 869–96.

Merry, S.E. (1990), *Getting Justice and Getting Even: Legal Consciousness Among Working-Class Americans* (Chicago IL: University of Chicago Press).

Merryman, J.H. (1977), 'Comparative Law and Social Change: On the Origins, Style, Decline and Revival of the Law and Development Movement', **25** *American Journal of Comparative Law* 457–91.

Misztal, B.A. (1996), *Trust in Modern Societies: The Search for the Bases of Social Order* (Cambridge: Polity).

Munro, V. (2001), 'Legal Feminism and Foucault: A Critique of the Expulsion of Law', **28** *Journal of Law and Society* 546–67.

Murphy, W.T. (1991), 'The Oldest Social Science? The Epistemic Properties of the Common Law Tradition', **54** *Modern Law Review* 182–215.

Neill, S. and Wright, T. (1988), *The Interpretation of the New Testament 1861–1986* (Oxford: Oxford University Press).

Nelken, D. (1986), 'Beyond the Study of "Law and Society"? Henry's *Private Justice* and O'Hagan's *The End of Law*', [1986] *American Bar Foundation Research Journal* 323–38.

Nelken, D. (1994), 'The Truth about Law's Truth', in A. Febbrajo and D. Nelken (eds) *European Yearbook in the Sociology of Law 1993* pp. 87–160 (Milano: Giuffrè).

Nelken, D. (1995), 'Disclosing/Invoking Legal Culture: An Introduction', **4** *Social and Legal Studies* 435–52.

Nelken, D. (1996), 'Can there be a Sociology of Legal Meaning?', in D. Nelken (ed.) *Law as Communication* pp. 107–28 (Aldershot: Dartmouth).

Nelken, D. (1998), 'Blinding Insights? The Limits of a Reflexive Sociology of Law', **25** *Journal of Law and Society* 407–26.

Nelken, D. (ed.) (1997), *Comparing Legal Cultures* (Aldershot: Dartmouth).

Nelken, D. and Feest, J. (eds) (2001), *Adapting Legal Cultures* (Oxford: Hart).

Neumann, F.L. (1949), 'Editor's Introduction: Montesquieu', in C. de Montesquieu, *The Spirit of the Laws* pp. ix–lxiv (New York: Hafner Press).

Neumann, F.L. (1986), *The Rule of Law: Political Theory and the Legal System in Modern Society* (Leamington Spa: Berg).

Neumann, F.L. (1996), 'The Change in the Function of Law in Modern Society', in W.E. Scheuerman (ed.) *The Rule of Law under Siege: Selected Essays of Franz L. Neumann and Otto Kirchheimer* pp. 101–41 (Berkeley CA: University of California Press).

Neumann, I.B. (1995), *Collective Identity Formation: Self and Other in International Relations*, EUI Working Paper RSC 95/36 (Florence: European University Institute).

Nicholls, D. (1994), *The Pluralist State: The Political Ideas of J.N. Figgis and his Contemporaries*, 2nd edn (Basingstoke: Macmillan).

Norrie, A. (2005), *Law and the Beautiful Soul* (London: GlassHouse Press).

Ogus, A.I. (2002), 'The Economic Basis of Legal Culture: Networks and Monopolization', **22** *Oxford Journal of Legal Studies* 419–34.

Paluch, A.K. (1988), 'Malinowski's Theory of Culture', in R. Ellen et al. (eds) *Malinowski Between Two Worlds: The Polish Roots of an Anthropological Tradition* pp. 65–87 (Cambridge: Cambridge University Press).

Parsons, T. (1964), 'Evolutionary Universals in Society', **29** *American Sociological Review* 339–57.

Parsons, T. (1977), *The Evolution of Societies* (Englewood Cliffs NJ: Prentice-Hall).

Pearl, D. (1997), 'The Application of Islamic Law in the English Courts', **12** *Arab Law Quarterly* 211–19.

Pennisi, C. (1997), 'Sociological Uses of the Concept of Legal Culture', in D. Nelken (ed.) *Comparing Legal Cultures* pp. 105–18 (Aldershot: Dartmouth).

Péteri, Z. (1970), 'Some Aspects of the Sociological Approach in Comparative Law', in Z. Péteri (ed.) *Hungarian Law – Comparative Law: Essays for the 8th International Congress of Comparative Law* pp. 75–94 (Budapest: Académiai Kiadó).

Petersen, H. and Zahle, H. (eds) (1995), *Legal Polycentricity: Consequences of Pluralism in Law* (Aldershot: Dartmouth).

Petrazycki, L. (1955), *Law and Morality*, transl. by H.W. Babb (Cambridge MA: Harvard University Press).

Posner, R.A. (1987), 'The Decline of Law as an Autonomous Discipline 1962–1987', **100** *Harvard Law Review* 761–80.

Postema, G.J. (1986), *Bentham and the Common Law Tradition* (Oxford: Clarendon Press).

Poulantzas, N. (1978), *State, Power, Socialism* (London: New Left Books).

Poulter, S.M. (1986), *English Law and Ethnic Minority Customs* (London: Butterworths).

Poulter, S.M. (1987), 'African Customs in an English Setting: Legal and Policy Aspects of Recognition', **31** *Journal of African Law* 207–25.

Poulter, S.M. (1989), 'Divorce Reform in a Multicultural Society', **19** *Family Law* 99–101.

Poulter, S.M. (1991), 'Towards Legislative Reform of the Blasphemy and Racial Hatred Laws', [1991] *Public Law* 371–85.

Poulter, S.M. (1997), 'Muslim Headscarves in School: Contrasting Legal Approaches in England and France', **17** *Oxford Journal of Legal Studies* 43–74.

Přibáň, J. and Nelken, D. (eds) (2001), *Law's New Boundaries: The Consequences of Legal Autopoiesis* (Aldershot: Ashgate).

Rawls, J. (1999), *A Theory of Justice* revised edn (Oxford: Oxford University Press).

Raz, J. (1979), *The Authority of Law: Essays on Law and Morality* (Oxford: Clarendon Press).

Raz, J. (1980), *The Concept of a Legal System: An Introduction to the Theory of Legal System* 2nd edn (Oxford: Clarendon Press).

Raz, J. (1994), *Ethics in the Public Domain: Essays in the Morality of Law and Politics* (Oxford: Clarendon Press).

Raz, J. (1998), 'Multiculturalism', **11** *Ratio Juris* 193–205.

Renner, K. (1949), *The Institutions of Private Law and Their Social Functions*, transl. by A. Schwarzschild (London: Routledge & Kegan Paul).

Rheinstein, M. (1938), 'Teaching Comparative Law', reprinted in M. Rheinstein *Collected Works Volume 1: Jurisprudence and Sociology, Comparative Law and Common Law (USA)* pp. 294–303 (Tübingen: J.C.B. Mohr, 1979).

Rheinstein, M. (1979), *Collected Works Volume 1: Jurisprudence and Sociology, Comparative Law and Common Law (USA)* (Tübingen: J.C.B. Mohr).

Richardson, G. with Ogus, A. and Burrows, P. (1983), *Policing Pollution: A Study of Regulation and Enforcement* (Oxford: Clarendon Press).

Riles, A. (ed.) (2001), *Rethinking the Masters of Comparative Law* (Oxford: Hart).

Rose, N. (1996), 'The Death of the Social? Re-figuring the Territory of Government', **25** *Economy and Society* 327–56.

Rose, N. and Valverde, M. (1998), 'Governed by Law?', **7** *Social and Legal Studies* 541–51.

Rosenberg, A. (1979), 'Can Economic Theory Explain Everything?', **9** *Philosophy of the Social Sciences* 509–29.

Rosenberg, G.N. (1991), *The Hollow Hope: Can Courts Bring About Social Change?* (Chicago IL: University of Chicago Press).

Rottleuthner, H. (1989), 'Sociology of Law and Legal Practice', in A.-J. Arnaud (ed.) *Legal Culture and Everyday Life* pp. 77–84 (Oñati: International Institute for the Sociology of Law).

Sacco, R. (1991), 'Legal Formants: A Dynamic Approach to Comparative Law', **39** *American Journal of Comparative Law* 1–34, 343–401.

Samek, R.A. (1974), *The Legal Point of View* (New York: Philosophical Library).

Santos, B. de S. (2002), *Toward a New Legal Common Sense: Law, Globalization and Emancipation* 2nd edn (London: Butterworths / Cambridge University Press).

Sarat, A. (1990a), '"The Law is All Over": Power, Resistance and the Legal Consciousness of the Welfare Poor', **2** *Yale Journal of Law and the Humanities* 343–79.

Sarat, A. (1990b), 'Off to Meet the Wizard: Beyond Validity and Reliability in the Search for a Post-empiricist Sociology of Law', **15** *Law and Social Inquiry* 155–70.

Sarat, A. and Felstiner, W.L.F. (1995), *Divorce Lawyers and Their Clients: Power and Meaning in the Legal Process* (New York: Oxford University Press).

Savigny, F.C. von (1831), *Of the Vocation of Our Age for Legislation and Jurisprudence*, transl. by A. Hayward (New York: Arno reprint, 1975).

Schlesinger, R.B. (1965), 'Book review', **50** *Cornell Law Quarterly* 570–1.

Schmitt, C. (1976), *The Concept of the Political*, transl. by G. Schwab (New Brunswick: Rutgers University Press).

Schutz, A. (1957), 'Equality and the Meaning Structure of the Social World', reprinted in A. Schutz (1964), *Collected Papers Vol. 2: Studies in Social Theory* pp. 226–73 (The Hague: Martinus Nijhoff).

Schwartz, R.D. (1965), 'Book review', **30** *American Sociological Review* 290–1.

Seidman, R.B. (1965), 'Witch Murder and *Mens Rea*: A Problem of Society under Radical Social Change', **28** *Modern Law Review* 46–61.

Seidman, R.B. (1975), 'Book review', **55** *Boston University Law Review* 682–7.

Selznick, P. (1992), *The Moral Commonwealth: Social Theory and the Promise of Community* (Berkeley CA: University of California Press).

Shah, P. (2005), *Legal Pluralism in Conflict: Coping with Cultural Diversity in Law* (London: GlassHouse Press).

Shapiro, M. (1981), *Courts: A Comparative and Political Analysis* (Chicago IL: University of Chicago Press).

Sheffield, G.K. (1997), *The Arbitrary Indian: The Indian Arts and Crafts Act of 1990* (Norman OK: University of Oklahoma Press).

Silbey, J.M. (2002), 'What We Do When We Do Law and Popular Culture', **27** *Law and Social Inquiry* 139–68.

Simmel, G. (1971), *On Individuality and Social Forms: Selected Writings* (Chicago IL: University of Chicago Press).

Simon, J. (1999), 'Law after Society', **24** *Law and Social Inquiry* 143–94.

Smart, B. (1993), *Postmodernity* (London: Routledge).

Smart, C. (1989), *Feminism and the Power of Law* (London: Routledge).

Snyder, F.G. (1981), 'Anthropology, Dispute Processes and Law: A Critical Introduction', **8** *British Journal of Law and Society* 141–80.

Sommerville, J.P. (1999), *Royalists and Patriots: Politics and Ideology in England 1603–1640* 2nd edn (London: Longman).

Spencer, J. (1996), 'Nationalism', in A. Barnard and J. Spencer (eds) *Encyclopedia of Social and Cultural Anthropology* pp. 391–3 (London: Routledge).

Spink, P. (1997), 'Direct Effect: The Boundaries of the State', **113** *Law Quarterly Review* 524–9.

Starr, J. (1992), *Law as Metaphor: From Islamic Courts to the Palace of Justice* (Albany NY: State University of New York Press).

Starr, J. and Pool, J. (1974), 'The Impact of a Legal Revolution in Rural Turkey', **8** *Law and Society Review* 533–60.

Steiner, H.J. and Alston, P. (2000), *International Human Rights in Context: Law, Politics, Morals* 2nd edn (Oxford: Oxford University Press).

Stoljar, S.J. (1973), *Groups and Entities: An Inquiry into Corporate Theory* (Canberra: Australian National University Press).

Strange, S. (1996), *The Retreat of the State: The Diffusion of Power in the World Economy* (Cambridge: Cambridge University Press).

Tamanaha, B.Z. (1993), 'The Folly of the "Social Scientific" Concept of Legal Pluralism', **20** *Journal of Law and Society* 192–217.

Tamanaha, B.Z. (1997), *Realistic Socio-Legal Theory: Pragmatism and a Social Theory of Law* (Oxford: Clarendon Press).

Teubner, G. (1989), 'How the Law Thinks: Toward a Constructivist Epistemology of Law', **22** *Law and Society Review* 727–57.

Teubner, G. (1992), 'The Two Faces of Janus: Rethinking Legal Pluralism', **5** *Cardozo Law Review* 1443–62.

Teubner, G. (1993), *Law as an Autopoietic System*, transl. by A. Bankowska and R. Adler (Oxford: Blackwell).

Teubner, G. (1997), '"Global Bukowina": Legal Pluralism in the World Society', in G. Teubner (ed.) *Global Law Without a State* pp. 3–28 (Aldershot: Dartmouth).

Teubner, G. (1998), 'Legal Irritants: Good Faith in British Law or How Unifying Law Ends Up in New Divergences', **61** *Modern Law Review* 11–32.

Teubner, G. (ed.) (1987), *Juridification of Social Spheres: A Comparative Analysis in the Areas of Labour, Corporate, Antitrust and Social Welfare Law* (Berlin: de Gruyter).

Teubner, G. (ed.) (1997), *Global Law Without a State* (Aldershot: Dartmouth).

Timasheff, N.S. (1939), *An Introduction to the Sociology of Law* (Westport CT: Greenwood Press reprint, 1974).

Timur, H. (1957), 'Civil Marriage in Turkey: Difficulties, Causes and Remedies', **9** *International Social Science Bulletin* 34–6.

Tönnies, F. (1955), *Community and Association*, transl. by C.P. Loomis (London: Routledge & Kegan Paul).

Torres, G. and Milun, K. (1995), 'Stories and Standing: The Legal Meaning of Identity', in D. Danielsen and K. Engle (eds) *After Identity* pp. 129–42 (New York: Routledge).

Travers, M. (1993), 'Putting Sociology Back into the Sociology of Law', **20** *Journal of Law and Society* 438–51.

Tribe, L.H. (1992), *Abortion: The Clash of Absolutes* 2nd edn (New York: W.W. Norton).

Turner, S.P. and Factor, R.A. (1994), *Max Weber: The Lawyer as Social Thinker* (London: Routledge).

Twining, W. (1974), 'Law and Social Science: the Method of Detail', *New Society*, 27 June, pp. 758–61.

Twining, W. (1997), 'Other People's Power: The Bad Man and English Positivism, 1897–1997', **63** *Brooklyn Law Review* 189–223.

Tyler, T.R. (1990), *Why People Obey the Law: Procedural Justice, Legitimacy, and Compliance* (New Haven CT: Yale University Press).

Tyler, T.R., Boeckmann, J., Smith, H.J. and Huo, Y.J. (1997), *Social Justice in a Diverse Society* (Boulder CO: Westview Press).

Van Gerven, W. (1996), 'Bridging the Unbridgeable: Community and National Tort Laws after *Francovich* and *Brasserie*', **45** *International and Comparative Law Quarterly* 507–44.

Van Hoecke, M. and Ost, F. (1997), 'Legal Doctrine in Crisis: Towards a European Legal Science', in A. Aarnio, R. Alexy and G. Bergholtz (eds) *Justice, Morality and Society: A Tribute to Aleksander Peczenik* pp. 189–209 (Lund: Juristförlaget).

Von Mehren, A.T. (1965), 'Book review', **16** *University of Toronto Law Journal* 187–8.

Waelde, T.W. and Gunderson, J.L. (1994), 'Legislative Reform in Transitional Economies: Western Transplants – A Short-cut to Social Market Economy Status?', **43** *International and Comparative Law Quarterly* 347–78.

Wagner, W.J. (1964), 'Book review', **64** *Columbia Law Review* 985–93.

Walzer, M. (1995), 'Pluralism: A Political Perspective', in W. Kymlicka (ed.) *The Rights of Minority Cultures* pp. 139–54 (Oxford: Oxford University Press).

Ward, I. (1996), '(Pre)conceptions in European Law', **23** *Journal of Law and Society* 198–212.

Wasserstrom, R. (1964), 'Book review', **17** *Journal of Legal Education* 105–9.

Watson, A. (1977), *Society and Legal Change* (Edinburgh: Scottish Academic Press).

Watson, A. (1981), *The Making of the Civil Law* (Cambridge MA: Harvard University Press).

Watson, A. (1985a), *Sources of Law, Legal Change and Ambiguity* (Edinburgh: T. & T. Clark).

Watson, A. (1985b), *The Evolution of Law* (Oxford: Blackwell).

Watson, A. (1988), *Failures of the Legal Imagination* (Edinburgh: Scottish Academic Press).

Watson, A. (1991), *Legal Origins and Legal Change* (London: Hambledon Press).

Watson, A. (1993), *Legal Transplants* 2nd edn (Athens GA: University of Georgia Press).

Watson, A. (1995), 'From Legal Transplants to Legal Formants', **43** *American Journal of Comparative Law* 469–76.

Watson, A. (1996), 'Aspects of Reception of Law', **44** *American Journal of Comparative Law* 335–51.

Webb, L.C. (ed.) (1958), *Legal Personality and Political Pluralism* (Melbourne: Melbourne University Press).

Weber, M. (1968), *Economy and Society: An Outline of Interpretive Sociology*, transl. by E. Fischoff et al. (Berkeley CA: University of California Press reprint, 1978).

Welsh, J.M. (1993), *A Peoples' Europe? European Citizenship and European Identity*, EUI Working Paper ECS 93/2 (Florence: European University Institute).

Wiener, J. (1999), *Globalization and the Harmonization of Law* (London: Pinter).

Wise, E.M. (1990), 'The Transplant of Legal Patterns', **38** *American Journal of Comparative Law*, supplement 1–22.

Woolf, S. (1991), *Europe and the Nation-State*, EUI Working Paper HEC 91/11 (Florence: European University Institute).

Yngvesson, B. (1993), *Virtuous Citizens, Disruptive Subjects: Order and Complaint in a New England Town* (New York: Routledge).

Young, I.M. (1995), 'Together in Difference: Transforming the Logic of Group Political Conflict', in W. Kymlicka (ed.) *The Rights of Minority Cultures* pp. 155–76 (Oxford: Oxford University Press).

Zekoll, J. (1996), 'Kant and Comparative Law – Some Reflections on a Reform Effort', **70** *Tulane Law Review* 2719–49.

Ziegert, K.A. (1979), 'The Sociology behind Eugen Ehrlich's Sociology of Law', **7** *International Journal of the Sociology of Law* 225–73.

Zweigert, K. (1975), 'Quelques réflexions sur les relations entre la sociologie juridique et le droit comparé', in R. Cassin et al., *Aspects nouveau de la pensée juridique: Recueil d'études en hommage à Marc Ancel* pp. 81–93 (Paris: Pedone).

Zweigert, K. and Kötz, H. (1998), *An Introduction to Comparative Law* 3rd edn, transl. by T. Weir (Oxford: Clarendon Press).

Index

About the Author

Roger Cotterrell FBA is Anniversary Professor of Legal Theory at Queen Mary and Westfield College, University of London. He studied law and sociology at London University and, before joining the Queen Mary faculty, taught at the University of Leicester. A former trustee of the Law and Society Association, he has held visiting positions at universities in Belgium, Italy, Spain, Sweden, Hong Kong and the United States. His other books include *The Sociology of Law: An Introduction* (2nd edn, 1992), *Law's Community: Legal Theory in Sociological Perspective* (1995), *Emile Durkheim: Law in a Moral Domain* (1999), *The Politics of Jurisprudence: A Critical Introduction to Legal Philosophy* (2nd edn, 2003) and three edited works published by Ashgate: *Law and Society* (1994), *Sociological Perspectives on Law* (two volumes, 2001) and *Law in Social Theory* (2006).